Lecture Notes in Artificial Intelligence   11986

Subseries of Lecture Notes in Computer Science

More information about this series at http://www.springer.com/series/1244

Vincent Lemaire · Simon Malinowski ·
Anthony Bagnall · Alexis Bondu ·
Thomas Guyet · Romain Tavenard (Eds.)

Advanced Analytics and Learning on Temporal Data

4th ECML PKDD Workshop, AALTD 2019
Würzburg, Germany, September 20, 2019
Revised Selected Papers

 Springer

Editors
Vincent Lemaire (iD)
Orange Labs
Lannion, France

Anthony Bagnall (iD)
University of East Anglia
Norwich, UK

Thomas Guyet (iD)
Irisa
Agrocampus Ouest
Rennes, France

Simon Malinowski
Inria
University of Rennes
Rennes, France

Alexis Bondu
Orange Labs
Châtillon, France

Romain Tavenard
University of Rennes 2
Rennes, France

ISSN 0302-9743   ISSN 1611-3349 (electronic)
Lecture Notes in Artificial Intelligence
ISBN 978-3-030-39097-6   ISBN 978-3-030-39098-3 (eBook)
https://doi.org/10.1007/978-3-030-39098-3

LNCS Sublibrary: SL7 – Artificial Intelligence

This Springer imprint is published by the registered company Springer Nature Switzerland AG
The registered company address is: Gewerbestrasse 11, 6330 Cham, Switzerland

Preface

Workshop Description

The European Conference on Machine Learning and Principles and Practice of Knowledge Discovery in Databases (ECML PKDD) is the premier European machine learning and data mining conference and builds upon over 17 years of successful events and conferences held across Europe. This year, ECML PKDD 2019, was held in Würzburg, Germany, during September 16–20. It was complemented by a workshop program, where each workshop was dedicated to specialized topics, to cross-cutting issues, and to upcoming trends. This stand-alone LNAI volume includes the selected papers of the Advanced Analytics and Learning on Temporal Data (AALTD 2019) Workshop.

Motivation - Temporal data are frequently encountered in a wide range of domains such as bio-informatics, medicine, finance, and engineering, among many others. They are naturally present in applications motion and vision analysis, or more emerging ones such as energy efficient building, smart cities, dynamic social media, or sensor networks. Contrary to static data, temporal data are of complex nature, they are generally noisy, of high dimensionality, they may be non stationary (i.e. first order statistics vary with time) and irregular (involving several time granularities), and they may have several invariant domain-dependent factors such as time delay, translation, scale, or tendency effects. These temporal peculiarities limit the majority of standard statistical models and machine learning approaches, that mainly assume i.i.d data, homoscedasticity, normality of residuals, etc. To tackle such challenging temporal data, one appeals for new advanced approaches at the bridge of statistics, time series analysis, signal processing, and machine learning. Defining new approaches that transcend boundaries between several domains to extract valuable information from temporal data is undeniably a hot topic in the for near future, that has been the subject of active research this last decade.

Workshop Topics - The aim of this fourth edition of the workshop, AALTD 2019[1], held in conjunction with ECML PKDD 2019, was to bring together researchers and experts in machine learning, data mining, pattern analysis, and statistics to share their challenging issues and advances in temporal data analysis. Analysis and learning from temporal data covers a wide scope of tasks including learning metrics, learning representations, unsupervised feature extraction, clustering, and classification.

The proposed workshop received papers that cover one or several of the following topics:

- Temporal Data Clustering
- Classification of Univariate and Multivariate Time Series
- Early Classification of Temporal Data

---

[1] https://project.inria.fr/aaltd19/.

- Deep Learning and Learning Representations for Temporal Data
- Modeling Temporal Dependencies
- Advanced Forecasting and Prediction Models
- Space-Temporal Statistical Analysis
- Functional Data Analysis Methods
- Temporal Data Streams
- Interpretable Time-Series Analysis Methods
- Dimensionality Reduction, Sparsity, Algorithmic Complexity, and Big Data Challenges
- Bio-Informatics, Medical, Energy Consumption, and Temporal Data

Outcomes - AALTD 2019 was structured as a full-day workshop. We encouraged submissions of regular papers that were up to 16 pages of unpublished work. All submitted papers were peer reviewed (double-blind) by two or three reviewers from the Program Committee, and selected on the basis of these reviews. AALTD 2019 received 31 submissions, among which 16 papers were accepted for inclusion in the proceedings. The papers with higher review ratings were selected for an oral presentation, and the others were given the opportunity to present a poster through a spotlight session and a discussion session. The workshop started with an invited talk "Time Series Classification at Scale"[2] given by Francois Petitjean from the Monash University, Australia.

We thank all organizers and reviewers for the time and effort invested. We would also like to express our gratitude to the members of the Program Committee. We also thank the ECML, the Organizing Committee (particularly Peggy and Kurt, the workshop and tutorial chairs), and the local staff who helped us. Sincere thanks are due to Springer for their help in publishing the proceedings. Lastly, we thank all participants and invited speaker of the ECML PKDD 2019 workshops for their contributions that made the workshop really interesting.

November 2019

Vincent Lemaire
Simon Malinowski
Anthony Bagnall
Alexis Bondu
Thomas Guyet
Romain Tavenard

---

[2] https://www.francois-petitjean.com/Research/Petitjean-AALTD2019.pdf.

Organization

Program Committee Chairs

Anthony Bagnall	University of East Anglia, UK
Alexis Bondu	Orange Labs, France
Thomas Guyet	IRISA, France
Vincent Lemaire	Orange Labs, France
Simon Malinowski	Université de Rennes, Inria, CNRS, IRISA, France
Romain Tavenard	Université de Rennes 2, COSTEL, France

Program Committee

Amaia Abanda	Basque Center for Applied Mathematics (BCAM), Spain
Mustafa Baydoğan	Boğaziçi University, Turkey
Albert Bifet	LTCI, Télécom ParisTech, France
Andreas Brandmaier	Max Planck Institute for Human Development, Germany
Clément Christophe	ERIC, Université Lyon 2, France
Hoang Anh Dau	University of California, Riverside, USA
Germain Forestier	Université de Haute-Alsace, France
Dominique Gay	Université de La Réunion, France
David Guijo-Rubio	Universidad de Córdoba, Spain
Paul Honeine	Université de Rouen, France
Hassan Ismail Fawaz	Universite de Haute-Alsace, France
Isak Karlsson	Stockholm University, Sweden
Nikos Katzouris	NCSR Demokritos, Greece
James Large	University of East Anglia, UK
Jason Lines	University of East Anglia, UK
Usue Mori	University of the Basque Country, Spain
Pierre Nodet	Orange Labs, France
Charlotte Pelletier	Université de Bretagne-Sud, IRISA, France
Francois Petitjean	Monash University, Australia
Patrick Schäfer	Humboldt Universität zu Berlin, Germany
Pavel Senin	Los Alamos National Laboratory, USA
Chang Wei	Monash University, Australia
Julien Velcin	ERIC, Université Lyon 2, France

Contents

Oral Presentation

Robust Functional Regression for Outlier Detection

Harjit Hullait[1]([✉]), David S. Leslie[1]([✉]), Nicos G. Pavlidis[1]([✉]),
and Steve King[2]([✉])

[1] Lancaster University, Lancaster, UK
{h.hullait,d.leslie,n.pavlidis}@lancaster.ac.uk
[2] Rolls Royce PLC, Derby, UK
DrStephen.King@Rolls-Royce.com

Abstract. In this paper we propose an outlier detection algorithm for
temperature sensor data from jet engine tests. Effective identification
of outliers would enable engine problems to be examined and resolved
efficiently. Outlier detection in this data is challenging because a human
controller determines the speed of the engine during each manoeuvre.
This introduces variability which can mask abnormal behaviour in the
engine response. We therefore suggest modelling the dependency between
speed and temperature in the process of identifying abnormalities. The
engine temperature has a delayed response with respect to the engine
speed, which we will model using robust functional regression. We then
apply functional depth with respect to the residuals to rank the samples
and identify the outliers. The effectiveness of the outlier detection algorithm is shown in a simulation study. The algorithm is also applied to real
engine data, and identifies samples that warrant further investigation.

Keywords: Robust functional data analysis · Robust model
selection · Outlier detection

Before a jet engine is delivered it must complete a Pass-Off test. In a Pass-Off
test a controller performs manoeuvres, which can be defined as various engine
accelerations and decelerations starting and ending at a set idle speed. The purpose of this test is to ensure the engine complies with set standards. During the
test, data is captured by sensors measuring engine speed, pressure, temperature
and vibration in different parts of the engine. This high-frequency measurement
data offers the ability to automate the detection of engine problems. By building statistical models for the Pass-Off test data we can aid the engineers in
identifying engine issues efficiently.

One of the key manoeuvres in a Pass-Off test is the Vibration Survey (VS).
In this manoeuvre the engine is accelerated slowly to a certain speed then slowly
decelerated. We have 199 VS datasets, which include the turbine pressure ratio
(TPR) that measures the engine speed, and the turbine gas temperature (TGT)
which is a key temperature feature. In Fig. 1 we have plots of the TPR and TGT

© Springer Nature Switzerland AG 2020
V. Lemaire et al. (Eds.): AALTD 2019, LNAI 11986, pp. 3–13, 2020.
https://doi.org/10.1007/978-3-030-39098-3_1

for the 30 VS manoeuvres. We have transformed the time index to the interval $[0, 1]$ and the range of sensor measurements to $[0, 100]$.

Automated detection of abnormal engine behaviour has been studied before [9,14]. Both approaches require a training set of "normal" samples to build a normality model. They then apply novelty detection using an appropriate distance measure and threshold. We will instead use Functional Data Analysis (FDA) methods to identify VS manoeuvres that display unusual temperature behaviour in response to the variable (human-controlled) TPR time series. We will robustly build a normality model without requiring a set of "normal" samples. FDA techniques have been used effectively to model sensor data [13], as they combine information across samples and exploit the underlying behavioural structure. However this is to the best of our knowledge the first time these techniques are being used for modelling jet engine data.

We will use robust Functional Linear Regression (FLR) to build a model of "normal" behaviour. We shall then use the residuals from this model to identify outlying behaviour. The residuals are time series therefore using metrics such as the mean-square error means we lose a lot of information. Instead we will apply functional depth [6], which is capable of identifying various types of outlier behaviour.

There are a number of functional outlier detection methods, including the threshold approach [8], the Functional Boxplot [22] and the Outliergram [2], which use functional depth [15] to rank the curves. Alternative approaches use Directional Outlyingness measures, such as MS-plots [7] and Functional Outlier Maps [19]. There are also approaches for multivariate functional data [10]. These methods do not model the dependency between the functional response and functional input, and may therefore miss important outliers. Robust FLR can model this dependency structure, which can improve the detection of outliers.

This paper is organised as follows. In Sect. 1 we summarise the FDA methods, which will be used in the outlier detection algorithm. In Sect. 2, we will develop robust FDA techniques to obtain a robust regression model. In Sect. 3, we show how the robust regression model can be used to identify outliers. In Sect. 4 we give simulation results comparing the robust model with a classical model.

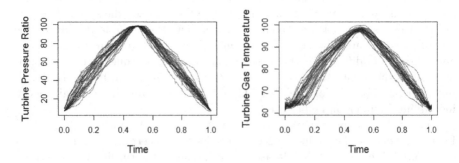

Fig. 1. Plots of 30 TPR and TGT time series.

Finally in Sect. 5 we apply the robust model on the engine data and highlight the outliers identified.

1 Classical Functional Data Analysis

In this section we give a brief summary of the FDA tools that we will later apply in our model. In the following sections we will use the vector space $L^2(I)$ which is the Hilbert space of square integrable functions on the compact interval I with the inner product $\langle f, g \rangle = \int_I f(t)g(t)dt$ for functions $f, g \in L^2(I)$.

We will define $X(t), Y(t)$ to be univariate stochastic processes defined on I, with mean functions $\mu^X(t)$ and $\mu^Y(t)$, and covariance functions $C_X(s,t) = cov\{X(s), X(t)\}$ and $C_Y(s,t) = cov\{Y(s), Y(t)\}$ for all $s, t \in I$. We shall define $x(t) = [x_1(t), ..., x_n(t)]$ and $y(t) = [y_1(t), ..., y_n(t)]$ be n samples from $X(t)$ and $Y(t)$ respectively.

In practice we observe $x_i(t)$ and $y_i(t)$ at discrete time points. We shall assume for simplicity of exposition that observations are made at equally spaced time points $t_1, ..., t_N$. We will outline Functional Linear Regression and Functional Principal Component Analysis with respect to the underlying functions. In Sect. 1.3 we need to use the discretely observed data to define a suitable model selection criterion.

1.1 Functional Linear Regression

In this section we will introduce the FLR model [16], which we will use to model the relationship between TGT and TPR for the VS manoeuvre. In FLR we model the relationship between predictor $x_i(t)$ and response $y_i(t)$ as:

$$y_i(t) = \alpha(t) + \int_I x_i(s)\beta(s,t)ds + \epsilon_i(t), \qquad (1)$$

where $\alpha(t)$ is the intercept function, $\beta(s,t)$ is the regression function and $\epsilon_i(t)$ is the error process. For a fixed t, we can think of $\beta(s,t)$ as the relative weight placed on $x_i(s)$ to predict $y_i(t)$. For simplicity we will assume the mean functions $\mu^X(t) = 0$ and $\mu^Y(t) = 0$ which thereby means $\alpha(t) = 0$. This is a reasonable assumption as in practice we can calculate the mean functions $\mu^X(t)$ and $\mu^Y(t)$ efficiently for dense data and then pre-process the data by subtracting $\mu^X(t)$ and $\mu^Y(t)$ from the observed curves.

FLR in the function-on-function case is a well studied model. There are typically two approaches taken: basis methods [5,23] and grid based methods [11,20]. The basis approach will be used as it is computationally efficient.

We will represent $x_i(t)$ and $y_i(t)$ in terms of M pre-chosen basis functions $\phi_j^X(t), \phi_j^Y(t)$ respectively:

$$x_i(t) = \sum_{j=1}^{M} z_{ij}\phi_j^X(t) \text{ and } y_i(t) = \sum_{j=1}^{M} w_{ij}\phi_j^Y(t).$$

For notational simplicity we have assumed that $x_i(t)$ and $y_i(t)$ can be represented by the same number of functions M, however this assumption can be easily relaxed.

We define $\phi^X(t) = [\phi_1^X(t), ..., \phi_M^X(t)]$, $\phi^Y(s) = [\phi_1^Y(s), ..., \phi_M^Y(s)]$, $z_i = [z_{i1}, ..., z_{iM}]$ and $w_i = [w_{i1}, ..., w_{iM}]$. We will then model the regression surface using a double basis expansion [17]:

$$\beta(s,t) = \sum_{l=1}^{M} \sum_{m=1}^{M} b_{ml} \phi_m^X(s) \phi_l^Y(t) = \phi^X(s)^T B \phi^Y(t), \tag{2}$$

for an $M \times M$ regression matrix B. We can then write:

$$y_i(t) = z_i B \phi^Y(t) + \epsilon_i(t). \tag{3}$$

Letting $\epsilon_i(t) = q_i \phi^Y(t)$ [5] we can reduce Eq. (3) to:

$$w_i = z_i B + q_i. \tag{4}$$

This simplification enables us to estimate B using standard multivariate regression methods.

1.2 Functional Principal Component Analysis

In this section we describe Functional Principal Component Analysis (FPCA), which we will use to build data-driven basis functions $\phi^X(t)$ and $\phi^Y(t)$ for $x_i(t)$ and $y_i(t)$, respectively. These basis functions give effective, low-dimensional representations and will be used in the Functional Linear Regression model described in Sect. 1.1.

Functional Principal Component Analysis (FPCA) is a method of finding dominant modes of variance for functional data. These dominant modes of variance are called the Functional Principal Components (FPCs). FPCA is also used as a dimensionality reduction tool, as a set of observed curves can be effectively approximated by a linear combination of a small set of FPCs. These FPCs form an orthonormal basis over $L^2(I)$ [21].

The FPCs, $\phi_k^X(t)$ for $k = 1, 2, ...$, are the eigenfunctions of the covariance function $C_X(s,t)$ with eigenvalues λ_k^X. Note that the eigenfunctions are ordered by the respective eigenvalues. The Karhunen-Loéve theorem shows that $x_i(t)$ can be decomposed as $x_i(t) = \sum_{k=1}^{\infty} z_{ik} \phi_k^X(t)$ where the principal component score $z_{ik} = \int_I x_i(t) \phi_k^X(t) dt$.

We can define the M-truncation as:

$$\hat{x}_i(t) = \sum_{k=1}^{M} z_{ik} \phi_k^X(t), \tag{5}$$

which gives the minimal residual error:

$$\frac{1}{n} \sum_{i=1}^{n} ||x_i - \hat{x}_i||^2 = \frac{1}{n} \sum_{i=1}^{n} \int_I [x_i(t) - \hat{x}_i(t)]^2 dt, \tag{6}$$

over all possible M functions. To choose M we will use an information criterion outlined in Sect. 1.3.

1.3 Bayesian Information Criterion for FLR

In this section we formulate a Bayesian Information Criterion (BIC) to determine the basis size M, similarly to Matsui [12]. A component of the BIC is the log likelihood, often expressed as a squared error term. It is tempting to use the squared error resulting from Eq. (4). However the objective is to fit the data y_i so we must use a likelihood of this data instead of a squared error term of basis coefficients.

Letting $y = [y_1, ..., y_n]$, where $y_i = [y_i(t_1), ..., y_i(t_N)]$, and $\phi^Y = [\phi^Y(t_1), ..., \phi^Y(t_N)]$ we obtain the discrete version of Eq. (3):

$$y_i = z_i B \phi^Y + \epsilon_i, \tag{7}$$

where the error $\epsilon_i = [\epsilon_i(t_1), ..., \epsilon_i(t_N)]$ is assumed for simplicity to be sampled from $N(0, v^2 I_N)$, where I_N is the identity matrix of size N.

Using Eq. (7) we can define the likelihood for sample i under parameters $\theta = (B, v^2, M)$ as:

$$f(y_i|\theta) = \frac{1}{(2\pi)^{\frac{N}{2}} v} \exp \left\{ -\frac{1}{2v^2} ||y_i - z_i B \phi^Y||_2^2 \right\}. \tag{8}$$

Then the log-likelihood is $l(\theta) = \sum_{i=1}^{n} \log(f(y_i|\theta))$. We can then write:

$$BIC(M) = -l(\theta) + \frac{1}{2}[M^2 + 1] \log(n). \tag{9}$$

where the number of free parameters is equal to $M^2 + 1$ [12], where M^2 comes from the regression terms and the 1 comes from the estimation of v^2 in the covariance matrix of the residuals.

To summarise, we estimate the FPCs for X and Y and solve the FLR model for multiple M values. We then choose the value of M that minimises the BIC criterion. The robust equivalent of this procedure is given in Algorithm 1.

2 Robust FLR Model

In Sect. 1 we have defined the FLR model and have outlined the use of FPCA bases to estimate parameters of the model. In this section we will introduce robust versions of the FDA techniques outlined in Sect. 1. This will allow us to fit a normality model even in the presence of outliers. We shall also propose a robust BIC procedure for model selection.

We will replace classical FPCA, which can be shown to be heavily affected by outliers [3], with robust FPCA estimates by Boente and Salibian-Barrera [4]. Analogous to Eq. (5), the robust FPCs $\tilde{\phi}_k^X(t)$, $\tilde{\phi}_k^Y(t)$, $k = 1, ..., M$ are orthonormal functions such that:

$$x_i(t) \approx \sum_{k=1}^{M} \tilde{z}_{ik} \tilde{\phi}_k^X(t) \quad y_i(t) \approx \sum_{k=1}^{M} \tilde{w}_{ik} \tilde{\phi}_k^Y(t).$$

are good approximations for $x_i(t)$ and $y_i(t)$.

We define $\tilde{y}_i(t) = \tilde{w}_i \tilde{\phi}^Y(t)$ and assume as in Eq. (4) that $\epsilon_i = \tilde{q}_i \tilde{\phi}^Y(s)$. We can now write the robust counterpart of Eq. (4) as:

$$\tilde{w}_i = \tilde{z}_i \tilde{B} + \tilde{q}_i. \tag{10}$$

To obtain a robust estimate of the regression matrix $\tilde{B}$, we will use the Multivariate Least Trimmed Squares (MLTS) [1] estimator. The objective of MLTS is to find a subset of our data of some pre-chosen size k, which gives minimal L^2 error over all possible subsets of size k. This is robust as outliers will not be in the subset by definition so shall not affect the model estimation. We will choose a subset of size $k = \lceil 0.8n \rceil$.

In Sect. 1.3 we defined a BIC procedure to choose the number of basis functions M. In our case we wish to estimate M in the presence of outliers, we therefore propose a robust BIC (RBIC) procedure. As in the BIC procedure in Sect. 1.3 we shall use the observed data y_i. We can then define the Mahalanobis distance for sample i under model M as:

$$\Delta_i(M) = \frac{1}{v^2}(y_i - \tilde{z}_i \tilde{B} \tilde{\phi}^Y)^T (y_i - \tilde{z}_i \tilde{B} \tilde{\phi}^Y). \tag{11}$$

To make the information criteria robust, we shall take a subset S of size k with the smallest Mahalanobis distances analogous to MLTS. We obtain the log-likelihood $\tilde{l}(\theta) = \sum_{i \in S} \log(f(y_i|\theta))$, which we use to obtain:

$$RBIC(M) = -\tilde{l}(\theta) + \frac{1}{2}(M^2 + 1)\log(k). \tag{12}$$

In Algorithm 1 we outline the calculation of the robust FLR model. In the algorithm we estimate the model for different values of M and choose the model with the minimum RBIC value. We consider $M = 1, \ldots, P$ where P is chosen to ensure that 99.99% of the variance in the raw data is captured by the first P FPCs.

3   Outlier Detection

In this section we will describe an outlier detection procedure using the robust FLR model estimated in Algorithm 1. We will use the robust FLR model to obtain estimates $\tilde{y}_i = \tilde{z}_i \tilde{B} \tilde{\phi}^Y$ for $i = 1, \ldots, n$.

For an outlier we expect the residual $r_i = y_i - \tilde{y}_i$ to deviate in behaviour from the other residuals. Traditionally, we would use the L^2 error to identify outliers. However we have found using a functional depth approach [8] is more effective in identifying outliers. The approach assigns a depth value to samples r_i. Samples with small depth values lie far away from the other samples.

Data: Let (x_i, y_i) be time series of length N for $i = 1, ..., n$, and P be the number of models.

1. Estimate mean functions $\tilde{\mu}_X(t)$ and $\tilde{\mu}_Y(t)$ [18]
2. Centre the time series (x_i, y_i)
3. Estimate $\{\tilde{\phi}_1^X(t), ..., \tilde{\phi}_P^X(t)\}$, $\{\tilde{\phi}_1^Y(t), ..., \tilde{\phi}_P^Y(t)\}$ [4].

for $M = 1$ to P **do**

    Estimate the regression matrix B using MLTS [1].

    Obtain the RBIC value using Eq. (12)

end for

4. Select model M^* with smallest RBIC value

return Regression matrix $\tilde{B}$ from model M^* and $\{\tilde{\phi}_1^X(t), ..., \tilde{\phi}_{M^*}^X(t)\}$, $\{\tilde{\phi}_1^Y(t), ..., \tilde{\phi}_{M^*}^Y(t)\}$

Algorithm 1: Robust FLR procedure

We will use the h-modal depth [6] to rank samples r_i. For a given kernel K (typically Gaussian with bandwidth h), the h-modal depth of r_i with respect to $r = \{r_1, ..., r_n\}$ is given by:

$$D(r_i|r, h) = \frac{1}{n} \sum_{l=1}^{n} K\left(\frac{||r_i - r_l||_2}{h}\right). \tag{13}$$

with the bandwidth h taken to be the 15th percentile of the empirical distribution of $\{||r_i - r_j||_2^2, i, j = 1, ..., n\}$ [8].

In the algorithm we need a threshold to identify outliers, which is chosen such that $P(D(r_i|r, h) \leq C) = \delta$, where δ is a pre-chosen percentile. We take a sample of size m from the set of samples excluding the $\alpha\%$ of samples with the smallest depth. Then we bootstrap to obtain an estimate of the threshold C. We describe the outlier detection algorithm in Algorithm 2.

Data: Centred time series (x_i, y_i) for $i = 1, ..., n$ and percentile δ.

1. Use Algorithm 1 to obtain $\tilde{\phi}_k^Y(t)$, $\tilde{z}_k$ and $\tilde{B}$.
2. Take $\tilde{\phi}^Y = (\tilde{\phi}^Y(t_1), ..., \tilde{\phi}^Y(t_N))$
3. Estimate residual vectors r_i as follows:

for $i = 1$ to n **do**

    Estimate $\tilde{y}_i = \tilde{z}_i \tilde{B} \tilde{\phi}^Y$

    Obtain residual vectors $r_i = y_i - \tilde{y}_i$

end for

4. Estimate bandwidth h [8]
5. For each r_i calculate $D(r_i|r, h)$.
6. Estimate C [8] for given percentile δ
7. If $D(r_i|r, h) < C$ sample i is an outlier.

Algorithm 2: Outlier Detection

4   Simulations

In this section we will outline simulation results comparing the effectiveness of
BIC and RBIC in identifying the true model. Using the true model we shall also
compare our robust FLR model to the classical FLR approach in terms of outlier
detection.

4.1   Scenario

We will generate samples $x(t)$ using a FPCA based model with mean function
$\mu_X(t) = -10(t - 0.5)^2 + 2$ for $t \in [0, 1]$ and eigenfunctions:

$$\phi_1^X = \sqrt{2}\sin(\pi t), \ \ \phi_2^X = \sqrt{2}\sin(7\pi t), \ \ \phi_3^X = \sqrt{2}\cos(7\pi t).$$

The principal scores are sampled from Gaussian distributions with mean 0 and
variances 20, 10 and 5 for the eigenfunctions respectively. We generate 100 samples, $x_1(t), ..., x_{100}(t)$. Note that we do not create any outliers in the predictors.

The samples $y(t)$ will have eigenfunctions:

$$\phi_1^Y = \sqrt{2}\sin(12\pi t), \ \ \phi_2^Y = \sqrt{2}\sin(5\pi t), \ \ \phi_3^Y = \sqrt{2}\cos(2\pi t).$$

Using these eigenfunctions we will generate $\beta(s, t) = \phi^X(s)^T B \phi^Y(t)$ where B
will have random entries between $[-1, 1]$. Outliers will be generated by replacing
B with $B' = B + R$ where R has random entries sampled from $N(0, 0.5)$. We will
then add a mean function $\mu^Y(t) = 80\exp(-(t-1)^2)$. The residual function $\epsilon_i(t)$
will be a linear combination of $\phi^Y(t)$ with coefficients sampled from $N(0, 0.1)$.
We will consider three cases when the number of outliers are $a = 1, 5$ and 10.

4.2   Results

We have used $M = 3$ principal components to generate $x(t)$ and $y(t)$ and $\beta(s, t)$.
To test BIC and RBIC we will make 200 repetitions and calculate the proportion
of times the true model is chosen. The results are given in Table 1. BIC and RBIC
have similar levels of accuracy for small number of outliers. However for large
number of outliers $a = 10$ RBIC outperforms BIC considerably.

Next we will compare the outlier detection capabilities of the Robust FLR
(RFLR) model and the classical FLR (CFLR) model. To compare the models
we will use the sensitivity (sens) defined as the the proportion of actual outliers
detected and specificity (spec) defined as the proportion of non-outlying samples
correctly identified as non-outliers. We want a model that has high sensitivity
and specificity. The outlier detection algorithm relies on choosing a suitable
percentile δ. In our simulated data we choose δ equal to the true proportion of
outliers in the simulated data.

In Table 2 we have the sensitivity and specificity for the robust and non-
robust model. We can see the robust model and non-robust model have the
same level of sensitivity however the robust model has higher specificity. This
shows the robust model is more effective in differentiating between non-outliers
and outliers.

Table 1. Proportion of times true model chosen using BIC and RBIC over 200 replications.

	a = 0	a = 1	a = 5	a = 10
BIC	1	0.995	0.99	0.965
RBIC	1	0.995	0.995	0.995

Table 2. Sensitivity and specificity over 200 replications.

	a = 1		a = 5		a = 10	
	sens	spec	sens	spec	sens	spec
Classical FLR	1	0.956	0.999	0.959	1	0.957
Robust FLR	1	0.964	1	0.970	1	0.964

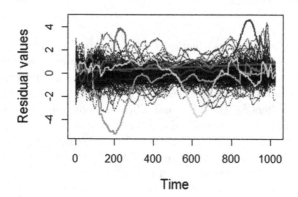

Fig. 2. Residuals using robust FLR model on TGT response and TPR predictor functions. The four outliers identified using Algorithm 2 are coloured.

5   Engine Data

In Fig. 1 we have a plot of 30 VS TPR and TGT time series. The TPR is controlled during the test, and therefore the variability comes from the controller performing the manoeuvre. This causes variability in the TGT time series. We therefore want to model the TGT and TPR relationship to account for this controller induced variability.

Applying Algorithm 1 we select model $M = 9$, which we use in Algorithm 2 to obtain the residual curves in Fig. 2. Using a percentile $\delta = 0.01$ we obtain four outliers, which seem plausible from a visual inspection. We know that the test with the smallest depth value corresponds to an engine with damaged hardware. The other three outliers obtained for this value of δ are currently being investigated. Instead of using a fixed value for δ, the user can apply the proposed algorithm to sort the residual time series in increasing order of depth and thus obtain a priority list of tests to be investigated by engineers.

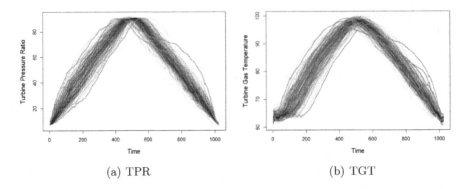

(a) TPR   (b) TGT

Fig. 3. Plots of the TPR and TGT time series with outliers using RFLR in red and those using a standard outlier detection approach [8] on the TPR and TGT curves directly in green. (Color figure online)

Standard outlier detection methods for functional data do not model the dependency between the predictor and response functions, and may therefore miss outliers. To show this explicitly we applied the outlier detection algorithm [8] on the TPR and TGT time series. The outlier detection algorithm outputs the same three outliers for the TPR and TGT, as shown in green in Fig. 3. This supports our argument that abnormal speed profiles cause abnormal temperature profiles, which in turn can mask real outliers. In comparison our approach models the relationship between the TPR and TGT time series and is therefore able to identify four different outliers shown in red in Fig. 3.

6   Conclusion

We have proposed a new outlier detection method to identify anomalous samples with respect to the engine temperature. We have built a robust functional regression model to capture the temporal relationship between speed and temperature and have used this model to identify outliers. In our experimental results we have shown that this model is capable of detecting outliers effectively, and identified samples of interest in the jet engine data.

In future work we aim to investigation the connection between the outliers identified and possible engine issues. We shall also develop theoretical results for the robust FLR model and BIC procedure.

References

1. Agulló, J., Croux, C., Van Aelst, S.: The multivariate least-trimmed squares estimator. J. Multivar. Anal. **99**(3), 311–338 (2008)
2. Arribas-Gil, A., Romo, J.: Shape outlier detection and visualization for functional data: the outliergram. Biostatistics **15**(4), 603–619 (2014)

3. Bali, J.L., Boente, G., Tyler, D.E., Wang, J.L.: Robust functional principal components: a projection-pursuit approach. Ann. Stat. **39**(6), 2852–2882 (2011)
4. Boente, G., Salibian-Barrera, M.: S-estimators for functional principal component analysis. J. Am. Stat. Assoc. **110**(511), 1100–1111 (2015)
5. Chiou, J.M., Yang, Y.F., Chen, Y.T.: Multivariate functional linear regression and prediction. J. Multivar. Anal. **146**, 301–312 (2016). Special Issue on Statistical Models and Methods for High or Infinite Dimensional Spaces
6. Cuevas, A., Febrero, M., Fraiman, R.: Robust estimation and classification for functional data via projection-based depth notions. Comput. Stat. **22**(3), 481–496 (2007)
7. Dai, W., Genton, M.G.: Multivariate functional data visualization and outlier detection. J. Comput. Graph. Stat. **27**(4), 923–934 (2018)
8. Febrero-Bande, M., Galeano, P., González-Manteiga, W.: Outlier detection in functional data by depth measures, with application to identify abnormal NOX levels. Environmetrics **19**, 331–345 (2008)
9. Hayton, P.M., Schölkopf, B., Tarassenko, L., Anuzis, P.: Support vector novelty detection applied to jet engine vibration spectra, pp. 946–952 (2001)
10. Hubert, M., Rousseeuw, P.J., Segaert, P.: Multivariate functional outlier detection. Stat. Methods Appl. **24**(2), 177–202 (2015)
11. Ivanescu, A.E., Staicu, A.M., Scheipl, F., Greven, S.: Penalized function-on-function regression. Comput. Stat. **30**(2), 539–568 (2015)
12. Matsui, H.: Quadratic regression for functional response models. arXiv e-prints (2017)
13. Morris, J.S.: Functional regression. Annual Rev. Stat. Appl. **2**, 321–359 (2015)
14. Nairac, A., Townsend, N.W., Carr, R., King, S., Cowley, P., Tarassenko, L.: A system for the analysis of jet engine vibration data. Integr. Comput. Aided Eng. **6**, 53–66 (1999)
15. Nieto-Reyes, A., Battey, H.: A topologically valid definition of depth for functional data. Stat. Sci. **31**(1), 61–79 (2016)
16. Ramsay, J.O., Dalzell, C.J.: Some tools for functional data analysis. J. Roy. Stat. Soc. Ser. B (Methodol.) **53**(3), 539–572 (1991)
17. Ramsay, J.O., Silverman, B.W.: Functional Data Analysis. Springer Series in Statistics. Springer, New York (2005). https://doi.org/10.1007/b98888
18. Rousseeuw, P.J., Driessen, K.V.: A fast algorithm for the minimum covariance determinant estimator. Technometrics **41**(3), 212–223 (1999)
19. Rousseeuw, P.J., Raymaekers, J., Hubert, M.: A measure of directional outlyingness with applications to image data and video. J. Comput. Graph. Stat. **27**(2), 345–359 (2018)
20. Scheipl, F., Staicu, A.M., Greven, S.: Functional additive mixed models. J. Comput. Graph. Stat. **24**(2), 477–501 (2015)
21. Shang, H.L.: A survey of functional principal component analysis. AStA Adv. Stat. Anal. **98**(2), 121–142 (2014)
22. Sun, Y., Genton, M.G.: Functional boxplots. J. Comput. Graph. Stat. **20**(2), 316–334 (2011)
23. Yao, F., Müller, H.G., Wang, J.L., et al.: Functional linear regression analysis for longitudinal data. Ann. Stat. **33**(6), 2873–2903 (2005)

Transform Learning Based Function Approximation for Regression and Forecasting

Kriti Kumar[1]([⊠]), Angshul Majumdar[2], M. Girish Chandra[1], and A. Anil Kumar[1]

[1] TCS Research and Innovation, Bangalore, India
{kriti.kumar,m.gchandra,achannaanil.kumar}@tcs.com
[2] IIIT Delhi, New Delhi, India
angshul@iiitd.ac.in

Abstract. Regression and forecasting can be viewed as learning the functions with the appropriate input and output variables from the data. To capture the complex relationship among the variables, different techniques like, kernelized dictionary learning are being explored in the existing literature. In this paper, the transform learning based function approximation is presented which has computational and performance advantages over dictionary based techniques. Apart from providing the formulation and derivation of the necessary update steps, the performance results obtained with both synthetic and real data are presented in the paper. The initial results obtained with both the basic and kernelized versions demonstrate the usefulness of the proposed technique for regression and forecasting tasks.

Keywords: Transform learning · Dictionary learning · Kernel methods · Regression

1 Introduction

We are living in the era of massive data generation from different entities around us; for instance, the huge amount of data being emanated from the Internet of Things (IoT). The major applications of which lie in the consumer, commercial, industrial and infrastructure sectors. Major challenges faced by any IoT application is to clean, process and make requisite inferences from the vast amount of data acquired by the sensors. Classification and regression are two important facets of inference. Both of these can be viewed as function approximation problem with appropriate input and output variables. For instance, in classification, the input variable is a data vector and the output corresponds to the class label. In regression, the output variable is continuous in nature and the function captures the relationship of the output with the input variables. With the abundance of data at our disposal, the trend is to derive the said function approximation from the data (data-driven).

© Springer Nature Switzerland AG 2020
V. Lemaire et al. (Eds.): AALTD 2019, LNAI 11986, pp. 14–25, 2020.
https://doi.org/10.1007/978-3-030-39098-3_2

It is well known that regression plays an important role in a lot of applications like, finding causal relationship between variables in biological systems, weather data analysis, market research studies, customer survey results, fine-tuning manufacturing and delivery processes etc. Regression models are functions depicting the regression which can range from simple to complex models. This function approximation interpretation also enables the time series forecasting to be viewed as a regression problem. In all these applications, getting an accurate model which can represent the data well is of prime importance. For this purpose, various signal processing based data representation models using dictionaries and transforms have been explored in literature [2,5,13,15,18–20,22].

Dictionaries learnt from the data are actively researched in the last decade in the signal processing community for both synthesis and analysis problems [3,7,23,24]. The synthesis dictionary based models especially those involving sparsity are more popular having many successful applications like, denoising, inpainting, image super resolution, compressed sensing (MRI, CT), classification, etc. The basic formulation of synthesis dictionary learning is given as [15]:

$$X = DZ \tag{1}$$

where, $X \in \mathbb{R}^{L \times N}$ is the data that is represented by the learnt dictionary $D \in \mathbb{R}^{L \times K}$ containing K atoms as its columns and the learnt coefficients $Z \in \mathbb{R}^{K \times N}$.

Recently, the traditional and the kernelized dictionary versions [14] have also been used for learning data representations to facilitate regression problems [6,11]. There are two different ways in which they are utilized for machine learning tasks: (i) as a two stage approach where, the dictionary coefficients are learnt in the first stage and then fed as features for machine learning based classifiers/regressors in the second stage [16]; (ii) as a single stage approach where, the features and classification/regression weights are learnt together in a joint optimization framework [6,10,11]. The single stage approach has a better performance compared to two stage approach since, the output label/variable is utilized effectively while learning the dictionary and the associated coefficients. Although being successful, the sparse coding solved repeatedly for dictionary learning is NP-hard and the approximate synthesis sparse coding algorithms can be computationally expensive. Moreover, the dictionary learning problem is highly non-convex, and there is a high chance of algorithms getting stuck in bad local minima. To address these problems, transform learning based techniques have gained more importance.

Transform learning is an analysis approach, where the data is analyzed by learning a transform to produce the associated coefficients. Unlike dictionary which is an inverse learning problem, transform is a forward learning problem. In signal processing literature, it is well known that transform learning has an advantage over dictionaries in terms of application scenarios, accuracy and complexity [18,19,21,22]. Especially in the image domain, transform learning methods produces state-of-the-art results [12,17,22].

Motivated by the low complexity and performance advantages of transform learning, in this paper, an attempt has been made to formulate the regression problem using transform learning framework. A joint optimization is carried out to learn the transform, associated coefficients and regression weights together. Formulations for both, the basic (Transform Learning for Regression (TLR)) and the kernelized versions (Kernel Transform Learning for Regression (KTLR)) of the transform are proposed here. To the best of our knowledge, these techniques have not been explored so far in the literature. Viewing regression as function approximation problem, the scope of the proposed techniques have been extended to the important problem of time-series forecasting. Extensive study on different datasets are presented along with comparisons with both (basic and kernel) dictionary versions (Dictionary Learning for Regression (DLR), Kernel Dictionary Learning for Regression (KDLR), Kernel Regression (KR) and Linear Regression (LR). The results demonstrate the potential of the proposed techniques for regression.

Towards providing the necessary details of the proposed techniques, the rest of the paper is organized as follows. Section 2 presents in brief, the formulation of basic and kernel transform learning techniques. This is followed by Sect. 3 which gives the details of the proposed methodology for regression using both basic and kernel transform learning methods. Section 4 provides the experimental results obtained with synthetic and real data along with the performance comparisons with other methods. Finally, Sect. 5 concludes the work.

2   Introductory Aspects Related to Transform Learning

This section presents a brief background on both the basic and kernel versions of transform learning to set the stage for the proposed formulation for regression.

2.1   Basic Transform Learning

Transform learning is an analysis approach for data representation whose basic formulation is given as [18]:

$$TX = Z \tag{2}$$

where, $X \in \mathbb{R}^{L \times N}$ is the data matrix, $T \in \mathbb{R}^{K \times L}$ is the transform and $Z \in \mathbb{R}^{K \times N}$ are the coefficients.

Ravishankar and Bresler [19], formulated the transform learning problem as:

$$\min_{T,Z} \|TX - Z\|_F^2 + \lambda(\|T\|_F^2 - \log \det T) + \mu\|Z\|_0 \tag{3}$$

where, a transform T is learnt such that the computed coefficients Z are sparse. The second term in (3) is a regularizer where, the factor $-\log \det T$ imposes a full rank on the learned transform and $\|T\|_F^2$ balances the scale. This term is added to prevent trivial solutions and control the condition number of T. Solving the optimization problem in (3) using alternate minimization technique results in the following closed form updates for T and Z [12]:

$$Z \leftarrow \min_{Z} \|TX - Z\|_F^2 + \mu\|Z\|_0 \tag{4}$$

$$Z = (abs(TX) \geq \mu). \, TX \tag{5}$$

where, the term in the bracket is hard thresholded against the value μ and '.' denotes the element-wise product.

$$T \leftarrow \min_{T} \|TX - Z\|_F^2 + \lambda(\|T\|_F^2 - \log \det T). \tag{6}$$

Using Cholesky decomposition followed by singular value decomposition we get:

$$XX^T + \lambda I = LL^T \tag{7}$$

$$L^{-1}XZ^T = USV^T \tag{8}$$

$$\hat{T} = 0.5V(S + (S^2 + 2\lambda I)^{1/2})U^T L^{-1}. \tag{9}$$

This is guaranteed to be a global optimum compared to iterative optimization methods such as conjugate gradients and it allows for both cheap and exact computation of the transform [22]. This framework can be used to learn the data representation and carry out classification or regression tasks depending whether the output variable is discrete or continuous.

2.2   Kernel Transform Learning

To capture the non-linearities in the data, the kernel transform learning problem is formulated as [12]:

$$B\mathcal{K}(X, X) = Z \tag{10}$$

where B is the transform and $\mathcal{K}(X, X)$ is the kernel matrix which can be defined upfront unlike in dictionary based methods and is expressed as:

$$\mathcal{K}(X, X) = \varphi(X)^T \varphi(X) \tag{11}$$

$$B\varphi(X)^T \varphi(X) = Z. \tag{12}$$

The overall formulation of kernel transform learning involving sparsity is given as:

$$\min_{B,Z} \|B\mathcal{K}(X, X) - Z\|_F^2 + \lambda(\|B\|_F^2 - \log \det B) + \mu\|Z\|_0. \tag{13}$$

The closed form solution of transform and coefficients in the kernel transform learning remain the same as in the case of basic transform learning with the difference that in the former case, the kernelized version of input data is utilized instead of raw input data.

3 Proposed Transform Learning Methodology for Regression

With the brief introduction to transform learning in the previous section, the proposed formulation for regression considering both the basic and kernel versions of transforms is presented in the following.

3.1 Transform Learning for Regression (TLR)

Given a multi-variate data of N samples, let $\boldsymbol{X} \in \mathbb{R}^{L \times N}$ denote the feature vector of length L (i.e. independent variables of the regressor) and $\boldsymbol{y} \in \mathbb{R}^{1 \times N}$ represent the output of the regressor (i.e. dependent variable(s)). The transform learning framework can be utilized for regression tasks by adding a ridge regression penalty term and carrying out a joint optimization to learn the transform, coefficients and regression weights together. The said joint optimization problem is given as:

$$\min_{T,Z,w} \|\boldsymbol{TX} - \boldsymbol{Z}\|_F^2 + \lambda(\|\boldsymbol{T}\|_F^2 - \log \det \boldsymbol{T}) + \gamma\|\boldsymbol{y} - \boldsymbol{wZ}\|_2^2 \tag{14}$$

where, $\boldsymbol{w} \in \mathbb{R}^{1 \times K}$ are the regression weights with K being the number of atoms in the transform $\boldsymbol{T}$. Here, sparsity constraint on $\boldsymbol{Z}$ is not considered because the transform learnt to model the data is not overcomplete.

The transform, coefficients and the regression weights are learnt in the **training phase** and later utilized in the test phase for regression tasks. Alternate minimization technique is used to compute the closed form updates for all the variables. The sub-problems to solve in the training phase are:

$$\boldsymbol{Z} \leftarrow \min_{\boldsymbol{Z}} \underbrace{\|\boldsymbol{TX} - \boldsymbol{Z}\|_F^2 + \gamma\|\boldsymbol{y} - \boldsymbol{wZ}\|_2^2}_{M} \tag{15}$$

$$\boldsymbol{w} \leftarrow \min_{\boldsymbol{w}} \gamma\|\boldsymbol{y} - \boldsymbol{wZ}\|_2^2. \tag{16}$$

For the transform update $\boldsymbol{T}$, the problem remains the same as in (6) and hence the closed form solution is similar to (9). The closed form update for $\boldsymbol{w}$ is direct and computed as $\boldsymbol{w} = \boldsymbol{yZ}^\dagger$, where '†' denotes pseudo inverse. Solving for $\boldsymbol{Z}$, for any matrix $\boldsymbol{A}$, using the identity $\|\boldsymbol{A}\|_F^2 = \text{tr}\,(\boldsymbol{A}^T\boldsymbol{A})$ and using the first order derivative condition $\frac{\partial M}{\partial Z} = 0$, we get the following closed form update:

$$\boldsymbol{Z} = (1 + \gamma\boldsymbol{w}^T\boldsymbol{w})^\dagger(\boldsymbol{TX} + \gamma\boldsymbol{w}^T\boldsymbol{y}). \tag{17}$$

In the **test phase**, given new test samples $\boldsymbol{x}_{test} \in \mathbb{R}^{L \times n}$, the dependent variable $\hat{\boldsymbol{y}}_{test}$ is computed using the model learnt in terms of the $\boldsymbol{T}$ and $\boldsymbol{w}$ in the training phase. The coefficients $\boldsymbol{z}_{test}$ and output $\hat{\boldsymbol{y}}_{test}$ are computed as:

$$\boldsymbol{z}_{test} = \boldsymbol{Tx}_{test} \tag{18}$$

$$\hat{\boldsymbol{y}}_{test} = \boldsymbol{wz}_{test}. \tag{19}$$

This formulation can be extended to kernel transform learning based methods, which effectively capture the complex non-linear relationship in the data and is described in the next section.

3.2   Kernel Transform Learning for Regression (KTLR)

Similar to transform learning based method, kernel transform learning method can also be formulated to cater for regression problems by inserting an additional ridge regression penalty term. The regression formulation is given as:

$$\min_{B,Z,w} \|B\mathcal{K}(X,X) - Z\|_F^2 + \lambda(\|B\|_F^2 - \log \det B)$$
$$+\gamma\|y - wZ\|_2^2. \tag{20}$$

In the **training phase**, since the update of transform B is not affected by the added ridge regression penalty term, it remains the same as given for T (*i.e.* from (7) to (9)) with the only difference that the input data X in (7) is replaced by the kernelized version of the data $\mathcal{K}(X,X)$.

To solve for Z, the following sub-problem is required to be solved:

$$Z \leftarrow \min_Z \|B\mathcal{K}(X,X) - Z\|_F^2 + \gamma\|y - wZ\|_2^2. \tag{21}$$

The closed form update for Z is similar to (17) and can be expressed as:

$$Z = (1 + \gamma w^T w)^\dagger (B\mathcal{K}(X,X) + \gamma w^T y). \tag{22}$$

The update of w is identical to the previous case.

In the **test phase**, the coefficient z_{test} is computed utilizing the transform B learnt in the training phase and is given by:

$$B\varphi(x_{test})^T \varphi(X) = z_{test}. \tag{23}$$

The output $\hat{y}_{test}$ is computed in the same way as in (19).

The pseudo code of TLR and KTLR algorithm is summarized in Algorithm 1.

4   Experimental Results and Discussion

In this section, we demonstrate the functionality of the proposed framework of transform learning for regression tasks. Apart from synthetic data, two real-life datasets are considered for performance evaluation. For comparative study, the estimation results of the proposed TLR and KTLR algorithms are presented along with those obtained from Kernel Regression (KR) [4], Linear Regression (LR), Dictionary counterparts for regression (Kernel Dictionary Learning for Regression (KDLR), Dictionary Learning for Regression (DLR)). The dictionary (DLR and KDLR) methods consider similar joint optimization mentioned in (14, 20) for learning the dictionary and regression weights together [11]. For all the

---

Algorithm 1. Transform and Kernel Transform Learning for Regression (TLR or KTLR)

Input: Set of training data, $X = X_{train}$, $y = y_{train}$, K (size of transform (atoms)), parameters (λ, γ) and kernel function κ to compute kernel matrix $\mathcal{K}(X, X)$, $\mathcal{K}(x_{test}, X)$ and test data x_{test}

Output: Learnt transform T or B, weight vector w, estimated output $\hat{y}_{test}$

Initialization: Set Z_0 to random matrix with real numbers between 0 and 1 drawn from a uniform distribution, $w_0 = yZ^{\dagger}$ and T_0 or $B_0 = O$, iteration $i = 1$

1: **procedure**
2:    *loop*: Repeat until convergence (or fixed number of iterations *Maxitr*)
3:       T_i or $B_i \leftarrow 0.5V_i(S_i + (S_i^2 + 2\lambda I)^{1/2})U_i^T L_i^{-1}$
4:       $Z_i \leftarrow$ update using T_i or B_i & w_{i-1} using (17 or 22)
5:       $w_i \leftarrow yZ_i^{\dagger}$
6:       $i \leftarrow i + 1$
7:       **if** $\|T_i(orB_i) - T_{i-1}(orB_{i-1})\|_F < Tol$ or $i == Maxitr$ **then**
8:          $z_{test} \leftarrow$ update using (18 or 23)
9:          $\hat{y}_{test} \leftarrow wz_{test}$
10:         **close;**
11:      **else go to** *loop*

---

datasets, the data is normalized (using min-max normalization) before subjecting it to different regression methods and the estimation results are appropriately scaled back. The kernel based methods make use of the 'radial basis function' kernel for fair comparison with the scaling factor $\sigma = 0.8$. Three metrics namely, Mean Squared Error (MSE), Mean Absolute Error (MAE) and Pearson's Correlation Coefficient (PCC) are used for performance evaluation of the algorithms.

A. Synthetic Dataset: The simulated non-linear data considered in [8,9] is used for evaluation by taking 3 predictors and 1 response variable of the data of length 500 samples. Randomly 90% of the data ($N = 450$) is used for training and the remaining for testing. The estimation results of the response variable with different methods are presented in Fig. 1. Table 1 summarizes the performance metrics obtained with all the methods using 5-fold cross-validation. It can be seen, for the linear case, TLR, DLR and LR all have similar performance. For the kernel case, KTLR has the least MSE and performs slightly better than KR.

Table 1. Results with synthetic dataset

Algorithm	MSE	MAE	PCC
KTLR	**0.0017 ± 0.0003**	**0.0374 ± 0.0022**	**0.963**
TLR	0.0088 ± 0.0017	0.0755 ± 0.0079	0.836
KDLR	0.0047 ± 0.0016	0.0510 ± 0.0088	0.924
DLR	0.0087 ± 0.0015	0.0750 ± 0.0062	0.837
KR	0.0024 ± 0.0005	0.0413 ± 0.0043	0.963
LR	0.0087 ± 0.0015	0.0750 ± 0.0062	0.837

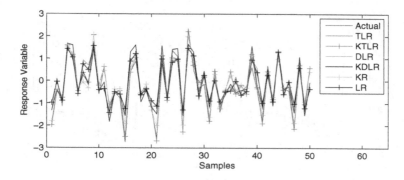

Fig. 1. Response variable estimation

B. Public Dataset: One of the UCI datasets, *Energy Efficiency* is considered for regression analysis. This dataset is used to assess the heating and cooling load requirements of buildings as a function of 8 building parameters (Relative compactness, Surface area, Wall area, Roof area, Overall height, Orientation, Glazing area, Glazing area distribution) [1]. The dataset comprises of 768 samples from 12 different building shapes. Here again, randomly 90% of the data ($N = 691$) is considered for training and the remaining for testing. It is worth noting that, although the proposed formulation considers single output variables, the dictionary and transform based techniques discussed here can be extended to handle multiple output variables in the same way. Here, a joint set of weights are computed for the dual outputs (i.e. heating and cooling loads). The estimation results of the heating load with different methods are presented in Fig. 2. Tables 2 and 3 give the summary of the results obtained for heating and cooling load estimation respectively using 5-fold cross-validation. Similar to the previous case, KTLR performs better than other kernel methods. It can be seen, for heating load estimation, KTLR has the least MSE and highest PCC and for the cooling load estimation, its performance is similar to KR.

Table 2. Results for heating load estimation

Algorithm	MSE	MAE	PCC
KTLR	**0.0045 ± 0.0011**	**0.0497 ± 0.0080**	**0.974**
TLR	0.0077 ± 0.0016	0.0693 ± 0.0068	0.953
KDLR	0.0065 ± 0.0034	0.0601 ± 0.0118	0.961
DLR	0.0095 ± 0.0012	0.0778 ± 0.0050	0.942
KR	0.0053 ± 0.0009	0.0521 ± 0.0056	0.973
LR	0.0076 ± 0.0016	0.0645 ± 0.0061	0.955

C. Building Power Consumption Data: Power consumption data from office building is considered for electrical load forecasting. Load forecasting is

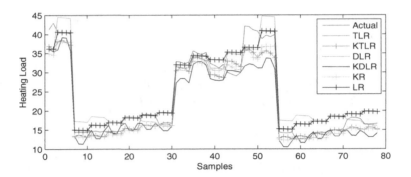

Fig. 2. Heating load estimation for building

Table 3. Results for cooling load estimation

Algorithm	MSE	MAE	PCC
KTLR	**0.0070 ± 0.0009**	**0.0585 ± 0.0047**	**0.958**
TLR	0.0098 ± 0.0027	0.0690 ± 0.0123	0.938
KDLR	0.0085 ± 0.0045	0.0610 ± 0.0108	0.940
DLR	0.0100 ± 0.0080	0.0705 ± 0.0201	0.923
KR	**0.0070 ± 0.0022**	**0.0578 ± 0.0087**	**0.961**
LR	0.0098 ± 0.0039	0.0692 ± 0.0126	0.938

framed as a function approximation problem where, temperature, previous day power consumption, previous week same day power consumption data and contextual information like weekdays and weekends are considered as potential inputs for producing a day ahead power consumption forecast. Office building data comprises of aggregate power consumption data for 6 months, sampled every 15 min. To keep track of seasonal changes, one month data ($N = 2880$) is used for training to produce day ahead forecast ($n = 96$). Although it could be extended to produce week ahead forecast in the same way, results with day ahead forecast alone is presented to demonstrate the applicability of the proposed method for time-series forecasting. The day ahead forecast results with KTLR, TLR and KR are presented in Fig. 3. Table 4 gives the estimation results obtained with different methods for day ahead forecast averaged over 7 days. As is evident from the plot, KTLR is able to track the actual load much better than KR and TLR. Figure 4 presents the boxplot of the MAE which demonstrate the superior performance of KTLR compared to other methods.

It is worth noting that the performance of dictionary and transform-based regression depends on the number of atoms and how well the hyperparameters of the optimization function are tuned. In this work, the hyperparameters for these methods are obtained through extensive search and tuned appropriately for each dataset. The results presented here made use of the best configurations (in terms of atoms size K) of the respective dictionaries and transforms for making fair comparisons.

Table 4. Results with building power consumption data

Algorithm	MSE	MAE	PCC
KTLR	**0.0016 ± 0.0022**	**0.0218 ± 0.0082**	**0.976**
TLR	0.0046 ± 0.0029	0.0529 ± 0.0148	0.946
KR	0.0018 ± 0.0021	0.0252 ± 0.0078	0.971

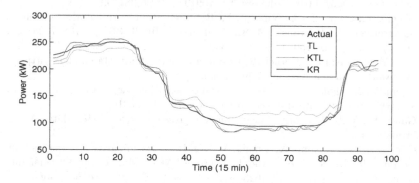

Fig. 3. Day ahead load forecast for building

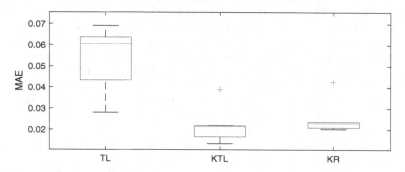

Fig. 4. Box plot of MAE for day ahead load forecast

5   Conclusion

The paper systematically presented the transform learning based approach for regression using a joint optimization of the transform, associated coefficients and the regression weights. The results obtained with different datasets are presented which demonstrate the potential and utility of the proposed function approximation technique for modeling and forecasting of the time series (signals).

References

1. Tsanas, A., Xifara, A.: Accurate quantitative estimation of energy performance of residential buildings using statistical machine learning tools. Energy Build. **49**, 560–567 (2012)
2. Aharon, M., Elad, M., Bruckstein, A.: K-SVD: an algorithm for designing overcomplete dictionaries for sparse representation. IEEE Trans. Signal Process. **54**(11), 4311–4322 (2006). https://doi.org/10.1109/TSP.2006.881199
3. Bengio, Y., Courville, A., Vincent, P.: Representation learning: a review and new perspectives. IEEE Trans. Pattern Anal. Mach. Intell. **35**(8), 1798–1828 (2013). https://doi.org/10.1109/TPAMI.2013.50
4. Cao, Y.: Multivariant Kernel Regression and Smoothing, March 2008. https://in.mathworks.com/matlabcentral/fileexchange/19279
5. Chen, G., Needell, D.: Compressed sensing and dictionary learning. Finite Frame Theory: Complet. Introd. Overcompleteness **73**, 201 (2016)
6. Ganti, R., Willett, R.M.: Sparse Linear regression with missing data. ArXiv e-prints (2015)
7. Guo, J., Guo, Y., Kong, X., Zhang, M., He, R.: Discriminative analysis dictionary learning. In: Proceedings of the Thirtieth AAAI Conference on Artificial Intelligence, AAAI 2016, pp. 1617–1623. AAAI Press (2016), http://dl.acm.org/citation.cfm?id=3016100.3016125
8. Hsieh, W.W.: Nonlinear canonical correlation analysis by neural networks. Neural Netw. **13**(10), 1095–1105 (2000). https://doi.org/10.1016/S0893-6080(00)00067-8
9. Hsieh, W.W.: Machine Learning Methods in the Environmental Sciences: Neural Networks and Kernels, 1st edn. Cambridge University Press, New York (2009)
10. Jiang, Z., Lin, Z., Davis, L.S.: Label consistent K-SVD: learning a discriminative dictionary for recognition. IEEE Trans. Pattern Anal. Mach. Intell. **35**(11), 2651–2664 (2013). https://doi.org/10.1109/TPAMI.2013.88
11. Kumar, K., Majumdar, A., Chandra, M.G., Kumar, A.A.: Regressing kernel dictionary learning. In: 2018 IEEE International Conference on Acoustics, Speech and Signal Processing (ICASSP), April 2018
12. Maggu, J., Majumdar, A.: Kernel transform learning. Pattern Recognit. Lett. **98**, 117–122 (2017). https://doi.org/10.1016/j.patrec.2017.09.002
13. Mairal, J., Ponce, J., Sapiro, G., Zisserman, A., Bach, F.R.: Supervised dictionary learning. In: Koller, D., Schuurmans, D., Bengio, Y., Bottou, L. (eds.) Advances in Neural Information Processing Systems, vol. 21, pp. 1033–1040. Curran Associates, Inc. (2009). http://papers.nips.cc/paper/3448-supervised-dictionary-learning.pdf
14. Nguyen, H.V., Patel, V.M., Nasrabadi, N.M., Chellappa, R.: Kernel dictionary learning. In: 2012 IEEE International Conference on Acoustics, Speech and Signal Processing (ICASSP), pp. 2021–2024, March 2012. https://doi.org/10.1109/ICASSP.2012.6288305
15. Olshausen, B.A., Field, D.J.: Sparse coding with an overcomplete basis set: a strategy employed by v1? Vis. Res. **37**(23), 3311–3325 (1997). https://doi.org/10.1016/S0042-6989(97)00169-7, http://www.sciencedirect.com/science/article/pii/S0042698997001697
16. Peng, C., Cheng, H., Ko, M.: An efficient two-stage sparse representation method. Int. J. Pattern Recognit. Artif Intell. **30**(01), 1651001 (2016)
17. Ravishankar, S., Bresler, Y.: Learning doubly sparse transforms for images. IEEE Trans. Image Process. **22**(12), 4598–4612 (2013). https://doi.org/10.1109/TIP.2013.2274384

18. Ravishankar, S., Bresler, Y.: Learning overcomplete sparsifying transforms for signal processing. In: 2013 IEEE International Conference on Acoustics, Speech and Signal Processing, pp. 3088–3092, May 2013. https://doi.org/10.1109/ICASSP.2013.6638226

19. Ravishankar, S., Bresler, Y.: Learning sparsifying transforms. IEEE Trans. Signal Process. **61**(5), 1072–1086 (2013). https://doi.org/10.1109/TSP.2012.2226449

20. Ravishankar, S., Bresler, Y.: Efficient blind compressed sensing using sparsifying transforms with convergence guarantees and application to magnetic resonance imaging. SIAM J. Imaging Sci. **8**(4), 2519–2557 (2015). https://doi.org/10.1137/141002293

21. Ravishankar, S., Bresler, Y.: Online sparsifying transform learning part II: convergence analysis. IEEE J. Sel. Top. Signal Process. **9**(4), 637–646 (2015). https://doi.org/10.1109/JSTSP.2015.2407860

22. Ravishankar, S., Wen, B., Bresler, Y.: Online sparsifying transform learning part I: algorithms. IEEE J. Sel. Top. Signal Process. **9**(4), 625–636 (2015). https://doi.org/10.1109/JSTSP.2015.2417131

23. Tang, W., Otero, I.R., Krim, H., Dai, L.: Analysis dictionary learning for scene classification. In: 2016 IEEE Statistical Signal Processing Workshop (SSP), pp. 1–5, June 2016. https://doi.org/10.1109/SSP.2016.7551849

24. Tosic, I., Frossard, P.: Dictionary learning: what is the right representation for my signal? IEEE Signal Process. Mag. **28**(2), 27–38 (2011)

Proactive Fiber Break Detection Based on Quaternion Time Series and Automatic Variable Selection from Relational Data

Vincent Lemaire[1]([✉]), Fabien Boitier[2], Jelena Pesic[2], Alexis Bondu[1], Stéphane Ragot[1], and Fabrice Clérot[1]

[1] Orange Labs, 2 Avenue Pierre Marzin, 22307 Lannion Cedex, France
vincent.lemaire@orange.com
[2] Nokia Bell Labs, Route de Villejust, 91620 Nozay, France

Abstract. We address the problem of event classification for proactive fiber break detection in high-speed optical communication systems. The proposed approach is based on monitoring the State of Polarization (SOP) via digital signal processing in a coherent receiver. We describe in details the design of a classifier providing interpretable decision rules and enabling low-complexity real-time detection embedded in network elements. The proposed method operates on SOP time series, which define trajectories on the 3D sphere; SOP time series are low-pass filtered (to reduce measurement noise), pre-rotated (to provide invariance to the starting point of trajectories) and converted to quaternion domain. Then quaternion sequences are recoded to relational data for automatic variable construction and selection. We show that a naïve Bayes classifier using a limited subset of variables can achieve an event classification accuracy of more than 99% for the tested conditions.

1 Introduction

The requirements for future 5G networks bring new challenges to ensure the reliability of communication infrastructure at affordable cost. While the overall network management is becoming more dynamic and elastic in the metropolitan area thanks to the use of Software Defined Network (SDN) [32], the hardware resource allocation to ensure its resilience is becoming more complex and costly. This is especially true at the optical physical layer where the usual resilience mechanism – called dedicated 1+1 optical protection leads to 50% idle network capacity and duplicates a large part of deployed resources to enable path separation [36]. A solution to avoid this constraint while maintaining a high level of availability is to rely on a proactive restoration mechanism where monitoring triggers, before the failure occurs, the configuration of a new route [38].

During the last forty years, several technologies have been developed to use the optical fiber as a sensor, gathered under the Distributed Acoustic Sensing (DAS) field of research [35]. While most of these technologies have a great

© Springer Nature Switzerland AG 2020
V. Lemaire et al. (Eds.): AALTD 2019, LNAI 11986, pp. 26–42, 2020.
https://doi.org/10.1007/978-3-030-39098-3_3

sensitivity and demonstrated their potential in pre-warning of infrastructure damage [1], the limited maximum distance reach, the compatibility with an optical network in operation and cost still prevent large scale deployment. At the optical network level, the most probable failure root causes, especially in the metropolitan area, are fiber cuts due to digging activities during civil engineering works [39], [24]. In this context, the sensors that trigger a proactive restoration do not require the sensitivity reached by DAS systems but their outputs have to accurately discriminate the cause. It was shown in [37] that the measurement of the State of Polarization (SOP) of an unmodulated laser light traveling through the optical fiber with a commercial polarimeter could provide an adequate sensor that enables the classification of mechanical events. This was recently confirmed in [44], where a low-cost implementation was proposed with only two simple photodiodes and a polarizer with a shorter reach – limited to a single span of fiber between optical amplifiers.

In this paper, we present the results of a joint study conducted by two companies in the framework of a Celtic+ project [40]. The objective was to design a proactive fiber break detection system based on machine learning with a very strong integration into deployed equipment and the following capabilities: (i) detecting and classifying different kinds of mechanical events; (ii) assuming low cost implementation in networks elements without any additional hardware; (iii) providing interpretable decision results; (iv) allowing real-time hitless restoration mechanisms. In this paper we demonstrate a proactive fiber break detection system based on machine learning implementable as an extension of a high-speed optical receiver. The proposed method operates on SOP time series, which define spherical trajectories; SOP time series are low-pass filtered (to reduce measurement noise), pre-rotated (to provide invariance to the starting point of trajectories) and converted to quaternion domain. After this pre-processing, quaternion sequences are recoded to relational data for automatic variable construction and selection.

The present paper brings several new contributions on top of [5,6] where this work has been partly published. First, a quaternion representation is proposed to exploit the spherical nature of SOP data, avoid overtraining and improve interpretability of decision rules. Second, recoding to relational data with naïve Bayes classification is used to get low-complexity decision rules adapted to real-time implementation as in [5,6]; we provide here a comprehensive description and evaluation of a 'data science' solution implemented in a real-time prototype. Third, the SOP database and quaternion pre-processing are made publicly available and a free access to the machine learning software used in this work is provided for the sake of reproducibility (see details at the end of this paper). From a research point of view, we note that the present paper has some limitations (e.g. lack of benchmarking with a reference classification method) which will be addressed in future work.

The paper is organized as follows. Section 2 gives a concise review on related work for time series classification to explain that we are interested in method which provide simple rules and which can be embedded in network elements.

Sect. 3 describes the fiber break proactive detection principle and the nature of the data used in this work. The real fiber cuts or fiber damages are not rare events but to our knowledge there is no existing process for the on-field data collection with the required accuracy. Therefore, Sect. 4 describes (i) how we collect "emulated" data in order to learn on it and (ii) how these data have been pre-processed. Then since our data are represented as time series Sect. 5 describes the method we used as "classification approach" to discover concise rules if any. Finally, Sect. 6 presents experimental results and Sect. 7 describes a proof of concept on a network scenario, before a brief discussion of current limitations and perspectives.

2   Brief Review of Time Series Classification

The field of time series classification represents an extensive literature, and progress has mainly focused on improving the accuracy of classifiers. One interesting point consists in selecting an appropriate representation [20] of time series and extracting a table of descriptors in order to train a classifier. Time series classification approaches can be categorized into two classes: *distance-based* and *feature-based* ones. *Distance-based* approaches make a point-wise comparison of entire time series by using similarity measures. As mentioned in [42], these techniques are successful when applied on smooth and short time series, but fail for noisy or long time series. In contrast, *feature-based* approaches use features generated from sub-structures of time series in order to make their predictions. For instance, a shapelet is defined as a time series sub-sequences that is maximally representative of a particular class value. The Shapelet Transform approach [25] uses the distance to the shapelets as input features for an ensemble of classifier. Generally speaking, ensemble methods are very accurate for time series classification. The key idea of these approaches is to combine different core classifiers and aggregate their predictions using techniques like bagging or majority voting. Diversity in all combined classifiers must be ensured to properly design an ensemble approach. To do this, classifiers of a very diverse nature can be combined. Some approaches ensure diversity by handling multiple representations (derivative, integral ...) of time series (e.g. Elastic Ensemble [34], COTE ensemble [2]).

Numerous data transformation methods for time series have been suggested in the literature such as polynomial, symbolic, spectral or wavelet transformations [41, 46]. The underlying idea of using data transformation is to look for a new representation space [3] where class-characteristic patterns could be easily detected, compared to the original time domain.

The TwoPatterns dataset [15] is an interesting illustrative example (see Fig. 1). The objective is to learn a binary classifier from a set of labeled time series. In the original time domain, the class values seem difficult to distinguish (see Fig. 1a). However, the learning task appears easier in the alternative representation obtained by using a cumulative integral transformation (see Fig. 1b). From this representation we count the number of values below -10 for

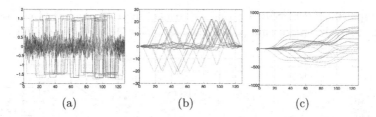

(a)   (b)   (c)

Fig. 1. TwoPattern dataset in time, cumulative and double cumulative integral representations.

$t \in [20, 100]$ the classification could be solved (the resulting rule in this case could be formed as $R_1 = $ 'Count(Signals(t) ≤ -10) where t in [20,100]'). At last, using a cumulative double integral transformation makes the classification problem trivial: all curves with value greater than 100 at the last timestamp belong to the blue class, while all other curves belong to the red class (see Fig. 1c). The rule R_1 described above is exactly the one which is automatically discovered by the method describes in Sect. 5 for the TwoPatterns dataset when using the cumulative integral representation.

This simple example shows that transforming the original time series into an alternative representation space can drastically improve the learned classifier. Moreover this example shows that the use of a adapted representation could help to find simple rules to solve the classification problem. In this paper we will explain in Sect. 4 how and why the data have been processed to have a adapted representation and Sect. 5 presents a method coming from the multitable data mining community that discovers simple rules to solve the classification problem.

3   Proactive Fiber Break Detection Based on SOP Data

Modern high speed optical communication systems are based on coherent technologies where the light is frequency and polarization multiplexed, and modulated using advanced modulation format where the information is carried not only by the light amplitude but also by its phase [26]. To recover such a signal from physical impairments occurring during propagation in the fiber and retrieve the sent data, many Digital Signal Processing (DSP) algorithms have been developed and are now commonly used in commercial products.

In this work, we propose to use a coherent receiver which is used in operation to decode data. An extension algorithm is embedded in this receiver to track the SOP, thus avoiding additional dedicated hardware or dedicated optical channel. To limit the required computing power, the proactive detection is based on two key ingredients: (i) rotation speed of SOP and (ii) event classification, which have sufficiently low complexity to be embedded in the coherent receiver.

Figure 2 describes the principle of the proposed approach to collect and classify events at the receiver. In step #1, we take advantage of the DSP block which is required to demultiplex signal polarizations and compensate –among others impairments–for SOP fluctuations occurring over time. For this purpose, Constant Modulus Algorithm (CMA) [26] is a widespread method implemented today.

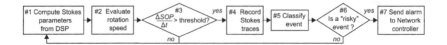

Fig. 2. Flow-chart of the proactive fiber break detection.

The digitized received signal is the projection of the received complex electrical field with an arbitrary polarization on the receiver polarization basis. In order to express the electrical field in the transmitter polarization basis and above all to track this required transformation over time, the CMA algorithm uses four filters (vector) in a butterfly configuration to ensure that the received intensity on each polarization remains constant (a property of the used modulation format where the information is coded in phase only and the intensity is the electrical field modulus). The two input signal components over time are convoluted with the vector of the filter respective to the output basis. The values of the vector are then updated by taking into account the error between the obtained intensity and the expected constant value. This equalizer H can be seen as the inverse of the fiber propagation matrix and allows to compute the SOP expressed in the Stokes coordinates S_1, S_2, S_3 [23]. For the "y" component, the SOP and the SOP rotation speed can be written:

$$S_0 \propto |H_{xx}|^2 + |H_{yx}|^2 \tag{1a}$$

$$S_1 = \frac{|H_{xx}|^2 - |H_{yx}|^2}{s_0} \tag{1b}$$

$$S_2 = -2\frac{\Re\left(H_{yx}^* H_{xx}\right)}{s_0} \tag{1c}$$

$$S_3 = 2\frac{\Im\left(H_{yx}^* H_{xx}\right)}{s_0} \tag{1d}$$

$$\frac{\Delta SOP}{\Delta t} = \frac{2}{\Delta t}\sin^{-1}\left(\frac{1}{2}\sqrt{\sum_i (\Delta S_i)^2}\right) \tag{1e}$$

where H_{ij} is the sum of respective filter coefficients from the i-th input polarization to j-th output polarization. In step #2, the SOP rotation speed is tracked using Eq. 1e, where Δt is the time interval between consecutive computed SOP values and ΔS_i the associated Stokes parameter differences with $i = 1, 2, 3$. In step #3, the SOP rotation speed is compared to a threshold-value which can generate a trigger to move to step #4, i.e. the recording of an event during few seconds made of pre-trigger and post-trigger samples. In step #5, this saved event is then sent to the classifier which processes the data and identifies the class of event. Finally, in step #6, if the event is classified as "risky", the receiver raises an alarm through signal messaging to the control plane in step #7. The network controller decides the appropriate action (see Sect. 7).

4   SOP Data Collection and Pre-processing

4.1   Data Collection

Depending on the operator network size, fiber cuts or damages are likely to happen on a daily to weekly basis. Over the years many studies have been conducted on the occurrence of fiber cut incidents to determine the root causes for the cut frequency, the impacts on the network quality of service delivery and many other aspects [24].

Nevertheless, to the best of our knowledge, a database containing SOP variations just before or during the fiber cut does not exist yet. Therefore we provoked in our lab non-destructive mechanical perturbation in order to create a database of emulated events. These emulated events were used for learning and performing the prediction mechanism. In this section we describe the experimental setup we used to emulate the signature of a fiber cut and collect the related SOP events; since the data representation for time series classification is crucial [20], we describe method and reasons for coding the SOP time series as quaternions.

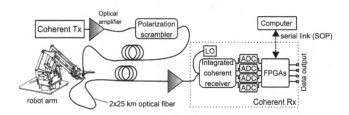

Fig. 3. Experimental setup scheme with programmable mechanical events driven by a robot arm.

Figure 3 shows the experimental setup. A signal carrying pseudo-random data is emitted by coherent transmitter at 28 Gb/s then amplified. After passing through a polarization scrambler which sets a new random polarization state between events, the signal propagates over 2×25 km of optical fiber. The claw of a robot arm controlled by an Arduino, provokes different mechanical events on the fiber in the middle. The fiber output is connected to a last optical amplifier to compensate propagation loss. The receiver board, which is presented in details in [16], consists in an integrated coherent receiver followed by four 5-bit Analog-to-Digital Converters (ADCs) operating at a frequency of two samples per symbol followed by FPGAs. All DSP occurs in one FPGA. The CMA aiming at demultiplexing tributaries of each polarization is implemented as the main adaptive 5-tap FIR filter operating on 128 samples in parallel.

The three Stokes parameters are computed accordingly to Eq. 1, rounded to 8-bit signed integers and sent to a computer via a serial interface (see details in [5]). The computer collects new Stokes parameters at a sampling rate $f_{col} = 1920$ Hz and the rotation speed threshold in step #3 is set to 0.7 rad/s. The saved event consists of 256 pre-triggered and 7872 post-triggered samples. At the end of the experimental phase we collected 16548 events. Each event consisted of a multivariate time series (MTS) of 3-dimensional data points $(S_1(t), S_2(t), S_3(t))$ coordinates on the polarization sphere (see Fig. 4), with a length of 8128 samples (256 pre-triggered and 7872 post-triggered samples). The robot arm was designed to create four types of events: "bending", "shaking", "small hit" and "up & down" represented respectively by 2873, 1921, 6562, 5195 MTS. Figure 4 shows an example of the evolution of the Stokes parameters as a function of time during one event and its representation on the Poincaré sphere. From this point the problem of proactive fiber break detection is thus turned into a classification problem of multivariate time series.

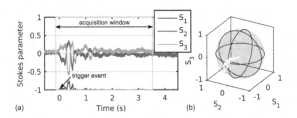

Fig. 4. (a) Example of Stokes parameters $(S1, S2, S3)$ vs time for a "shaking" event. Green rectangle shows the acquisition window. Green dashed line indicates the trigger signal raised in step #3 of Fig. 2. (b) The stokes parameters $(S1, S2, S3)$ represented (yellow points) as a 3D trajectory. (Color figure online)

4.2　Pre-processing: Low-Pass Filtering, Pre-rotation and Conversion to Quaternion Representation

As a preliminary step, the SOP data is passed through an exponential moving average (with forgetting factor $\alpha = 0.1$) applied independently to each Cartesian coordinate $(S1, S2, S3)$. This is equivalent to low-pass filtering of the input data and smoothing spherical trajectories; this step is commonly used to reduce measurement noise.

In this work we tried to take advantage of the spherical nature of SOP data. Indeed, a SOP time series can be seen as a trajectory on the 3D sphere as shown in Fig. 4. In exploratory steps of this work, which are not reported here by lack of space, it was found out that the classification method described in Sect. 5 resulted in decision rules and variables that could depend on for example the starting point of SOP trajectories[1]. This issue was due to the fact that SOP trajectories collected for learning and testing were produced with a costly

---

[1] Invariance to the starting point is quite different from invariance to time scale that could be addressed using dynamic time warping (DTW). Here DTW would not solve the problem of invariance to the starting point.

and time-consuming process, and the number of trajectories was too limited to prevent the starting point position (or derived statistics such as the average over the MTS) from being informative. These decision rules were not useful, interpretable by experts and could generate over-training which will give bad results on new MTS. Therefore, after several experiments, we considered using quaternions, which are a well-known representation in the fields of computer graphics [43] and physics (aerospace, robotics, etc.) [22]. We used this representation to provide invariance to the starting point of SOP trajectories and to convert XYZ coordinates in a domain which represents incremental rotational movements along spherical trajectories; the conversion to quaternion domain proved empirically to be efficient in getting variables and decision rules that are more useful and interpretable.

Quaternions (also called hypercomplex numbers or hamiltonians) were introduced in 1843 by Hamilton [21] to define a vectorial system generalizing complex numbers. A quaternion q is defined as $q = a + b\mathbf{i} + c\mathbf{j} + d\mathbf{k}$, where $(a, b, c, d) \in \mathbb{R}^4$, with the following rules for $\mathbf{i}, \mathbf{j}, \mathbf{k}$: $\mathbf{i}^2 = \mathbf{j}^2 = \mathbf{k}^2 = \mathbf{ijk} = -1$. One may also write q as $q = a + \mathbf{q}$, where a is the *scalar* (or real) part of q and $\mathbf{q} = b\mathbf{i} + c\mathbf{j} + d\mathbf{k}$ is the *vector* (or imaginary) part of q. Note that $\mathbf{q}$ may be interpreted as a 3D vector by identifying $\mathbf{i}, \mathbf{j}$ and $\mathbf{k}$ with three orthogonal Cartesian unit vectors. We do not review basic operations on quaternions the interested reader is referred to [14, 21, 22] for more details. We recall that the norm $|\mathbf{q}|$ of a quaternion is: $|q| = \sqrt{a^2 + b^2 + c^2 + d^2}$. When $|q| = 1$, q is said to be a *unit-norm quaternion*.

We used two important properties of quaternions. First, the set of 3D rotations can be mapped to the unit sphere in $\mathbb{R}^4$ under a one-to-two mapping [14, 22, 43], namely each 3D rotation matrix maps to two antipodal unit-norm quaternions: q and $-q$, therefore this mapping is not unique. Second, a 3D rotation of angle θ and normalized axis $\mathbf{n}$ (with $|\mathbf{n}| = 1$) is represented by the unit quaternion $q = \cos(\theta/2) + \sin(\theta/2)\mathbf{n}$ or its opposite $-q$. The 3D rotation matrix associated to a unit-norm quaternion $q = a + b\mathbf{i} + c\mathbf{j} + d\mathbf{k}$ is given by:

$$\mathbf{R}(q) = \begin{pmatrix} 1 - 2(c^2 + d^2) & 2(bc - ad) & 2(ac + bd) \\ 2(ad + bc) & 1 - 2(b^2 + d^2) & 2(cd - ab) \\ 2(bd - ac) & 2(ab + cd) & 1 - 2(b^2 + c^2) \end{pmatrix} \quad (2)$$

Quaternions were applied in this work for two purposes:

- Each SOP trajectory was pre-rotated such that the starting point was brought to the North pole of the 3D sphere. The time series $\mathbf{S}(t) = (S_1(t), S_2(t), S_3(t))^T$, with $t = 0, \ldots, L - 1$, defines a trajectory of points lying on the unit polarization sphere. A rotation matrix $\mathbf{R}(q)$ (from Eq. 2) allowing to bring the starting point $\mathbf{S}(0)$ of this trajectory to the North pole $\mathbf{p} = (0, 0, 1)^T$ was computed based on $q = cos(\theta/2) + sin(\theta/2)\mathbf{n}$, where the rotation angle θ is the angle between $\mathbf{S}(0)$ and $\mathbf{p}$, and the rotation axis $\mathbf{n}$ is the (normalized) cross product of $\mathbf{S}(0)$ and $\mathbf{p}$. This pre-rotation by $\mathbf{R}(q)$ was applied to the whole SOP time series $\mathbf{S}(t)$ to obtain $\mathbf{S}'(t) = \mathbf{R}(q)\mathbf{S}(t)$.

– Each (pre-rotated) SOP trajectory was converted to a quaternion time series representing successive rotations from one point to the next one. A straightforward approach would compute for each time instant a quaternion $q(t)$, $t = 1, \cdots, L - 1$, representing the incremental rotation from $\mathbf{S}'(t - 1)$ to $\mathbf{S}'(t)$, i.e. $q(t) = cos(\Omega(t)/2) + sin(\Omega(t)/2)\mathbf{r}(t)$, where $\Omega(t)$ is the angle between $\mathbf{S}'(t - 1)$ and $\mathbf{S}'(t)$ and $\mathbf{r}(t)$ is the (normalized) rotation axis given by their cross product. Due to the non-unique representation of rotations by antipodal unit-norm quaternions, we selected, among the two possible choices $\pm q(t)$, the *canonical* form of unit-norm quaternions having by convention a positive scalar part: $q_C(t) = q(t)$ if $cos(\Omega(t)/2) \geq 0$ and $-q(t)$ otherwise. Moreover, to ensure that the quaternion trajectory followed the shortest path on the 4D sphere [43], the relative angle between successive unit-norm quaternions was used to further select antipodal quaternions as follows: starting with $q_{SP}(1) = q_C(1)$, we set for $t = 2, \cdots, L-1$ $q_{SP}(t) = q_C(t)$ if $q_C(t) \cdot q_{SP}(t-1) \geq 0$ and $-q_C(t)$ otherwise, where $q_1 \cdot q_2$ is the dot product of q_1 and q_2 seen as two 4D vectors.

5 Time Series Classification Approach

Having an adapted representation of the input multivariate time series (MTS), we may use a method from the literature to build a classifier among the extensive literature (see Sect. 2 and [4]). Remind that our requirements are (i) low cost implementation in networks elements without any additional hardware; (ii) providing interpretable decision results if possible using a limited number of concise rules. The scalability is also an issue. Here we decided[2] to turn our time series problem into a relational problem, then apply an existing approach (able to discover rules) to deal with relational data and classification problems. Thus we essentially bring ideas from relational data mining to time series classification.

The time series classification used in this work follows three successive steps: (i) multivariate time series are recoded to relational data (i.e. several linked tables); (ii) a propositionalization approach [13] is then used to extract informative aggregate variables from relational data; (iii) a classifier is trained based on the extracted aggregate variables. Once the structure of the relational data is specified, the number of extracted aggregate variables is the only parameter (P below in the paper). This section presents in details this time series classification approach.

This kind of approach, described in [10,12,20], is fully automatic, scalable and highly robust, with test performance mainly equivalent to train performance. Furthermore, this approach obtained good ranking in classifying trajectories in the FedCSIS challenges in 2015, 2016 and the second place of the AALTD Challenge in 2016 [45].

---

[2] Up to now this is an adhoc decision discussed in the last section of this paper.

5.1   Encoding Multivariate Time Series as Relational Data

The first step of the used classification approach consists in gathering the previously computed quaternion sequences $q_{SP}(t) = (a(t), b(t), c(t), d(t))$ within a relational dataset. The "schema" of a relational dataset defines the structure of the included tables, their types (i.e. root or secondary tables) and their links. A large variety of possible schemes exist, and the choice of a particular schema may have a significant impact on quality of the learned classifier. As shown in Fig. 5 we consider two possible relational schemas: (i) the *"one-each"* schema includes a root table and four secondary tables (see Fig. 5a) and (ii) the *"all-in-one"* schema that contains a root table and a single secondary table (see Fig. 5b).

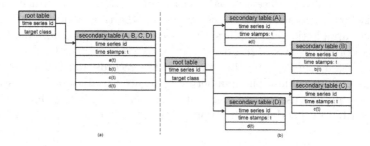

Fig. 5. Relational schemas for encoding multivariate time series as relational data. (a) *all-in-one* schema and (b) *one-each* schema.

These two kinds of schemas correspond to different ways of generating aggregate variables: (i) the *"all-in-one"* schema promotes the generation of "cross-quaternion" variables (i.e. jointly based on the four dimensions of our quaternion representation) (ii) the *"one-each"* schema prioritizes the mining of complex aggregates independently on each dimension of the quaternion representation. During the study we tested the two possibilities but in this paper we only present the result obtained with the *"all-in-one"* schema which gives the best results.

5.2   Automatic Variable Construction from Relational Data

The propositionalization approaches consist in learning a model from relational data by flattening the original relational data, which are stored in several linked tables (similarly to databases) [29]. These approaches come from the field of Relational Data Mining [17] and are not usually applied to time series. More precisely, relational data contains at least one root table where each row represents a statistical individual (e.g. 'id'of the time series) and another secondary table containing detail records (eg. the data points of the time series are represented by each row of the secondary table). The specificity of relational data is to involve one-to-many relationships between the tables (eg. a time series contains many data points). The propositionalization problem consists in transforming the relational data into a single attribute-value dataset in order to use regular machine learning methods.

Two kinds of propositionalization approaches can be distinguished (i) *logic-based* methods, such as RSD [31], SINUS [18], tackle the propositionalization task by constructing first-order logic attributes; (ii) the *database-inspired* methods such as RELAGGS [28] apply aggregation functions, such as Min, Max, and Mean in order to generate attributes. The interested reader can find a complete state-of-the-art and a comparative evaluation in [27].

In our study, we used a Minimal Description Length (MDL) based propositionalization approach recently presented in [13]. This approach exploits a Bayesian formalism to generate informative aggregate variables in a supervised way. To the best of our knowledge, this approach is the only one that avoids overfitting problems by regularizing the complexity of the generated variables.

Our relational data (see Fig. 5a) consists of the root table which contains 16548 instances, characterized by two variables: the time series identifiers and the target variable (i.e. class values). The secondary table contains 134 502 144 detailed records (16548×8128), described by six variables: the time series identifiers used as a join key, the timestamps of the records and the 4 dimensions of the quaternions values. The number of aggregate variables to be constructed (P) is the only one user parameter. Our relational data is transformed into a regular attribute-value dataset by applying the MDL based propositionalization approach.

5.3   Variable Selection and Learned Classifier

The used MDL approach is able to select the most informative aggregate variables in two ways: (i) by filtering uninformative aggregate variables; (ii) by finding the most informative and independent subset of variables.

Filtering Uninformative Variables: The filtering of the aggregate variables is based on previously developed supervised discretization [8] and grouping [7] methods. This Bayesian approach turns the learning task into a model selection problem. A prior distribution is defined on the model space that exploits the hierarchy of their parameters. In practice, this approach reaches a good trade-off between robust and accurate models. The prior favors simple models with few intervals, and the likelihood favors models that fit the data regardless of their complexity. The aggregate variables are evaluated, one by one, using a specifically designed MDL optimization criterion [13]. The complexity of the aggregate variables is taken into account by adding a construction cost in the prior. This criterion can be interpreted as a coding length according to information theory. Compression Gain (CG) compares the coding length of the learned model with the empty model that includes a single interval. CG measures the ability of the learned models to compress the training data, despite the additional construction cost. Only the Q variables with a positive CG are retained ($Q \leq P$).

Finding the Most Informative Subset of Variables: All the Q informative variables coming from the previous step (after discretization or grouping values) are gathered together and used to learn a Selective Naive Bayes classifier (a Naive Bayes which uses a subset of the Q variables defined by a selective process). The Selective Naive Bayes (SNB) aims to select the most informative and independent subset of variables by using a specifically designed MDL optimization criterion [9]. The used optimization algorithm consists in a sequence of feed-forward and feed-backward selection steps. These two selection steps are repeated as long as the optimization criterion reaches a better value. This heuristic is embedded into a multi-start (MS) algorithm, by repeating the feed-forward and feed-backward steps from several random orderings of the variables. At the end, we keep the most probable subset of variables compliant with the naive Bayes assumption, i.e. both informative and independent. This subset contains R aggregate variables, with $R \leq Q \leq P$.

Learning Classifier: Finally, the used classifier is a naive Bayes which takes the R selected aggregate variables as an input. As shown in Eq. 3, the naive Bayes classifier [30] estimates the distribution of a particular class value C_z conditionally to the input variables x_k.

$$P(C_z|x_k) = \frac{P(C_z) \prod_{j=1}^{J} P(V_j = x_{jk}|C_z)}{\sum_{t=1}^{C} \left[P(C_t) \prod_{j=1}^{R} P(V_j = x_{jk}|C_t) \right]} \tag{3}$$

C is the number of class values to be predicted (in this paper $C = 4$, see Sect. 4.1). This simple and efficient classifier makes the assumption that the distributions $P(V_j = x_{jk}|C_z)$ are independent. In practice, these conditional distributions are estimated in a frequentist way, by using the previously learned univariate discretization [8] and grouping [7] models. The denominator of Eq. 3 normalizes the estimated probability by making a sum of the numerator term over all the class values. At the end, the predicted class value given a particular x_k is the one that maximizes the conditional probabilities $P(C_z|x_k)$.

6   Results and Discussion

We trained the naïve Bayes classifier, with the aim to find a function f such as $Y = f(X)$ where Y represents the class, and X is vector of explanatory variables which contains a representation of the time-series $(S_1(t), S_2(t), S_3(t))$ as quaternion time values $q_{SP}(t) = (a(t), b(t), c(t), d(t))$. After the training phase, we can classify new events, i.e. 'unknown events', in order to predict their class. In the experiments, we divided the 16548 events into training and test parts according to the 10-fold cross validation process whatever their class (stratified random sampling).

The vector X is obtained following the steps method described in Sect. 5 above where: (i) P explanatory variables are constructed (ii) then Q variables (a subset of the P variables) are judged as informative, i.e. they bring information to predict Y, (iii) finally R explanatory variables (a subset of the Q variables) are kept using a forward backward selection mechanism.

The classifier uses a naïve Bayes classifier [30] relying on the R variables. Table 1 gives the values of P, Q and R and the classifier performance using two

Table 1. Number of constructed (P), informative (Q), used variables (R) and classification results obtained (mean ± standard deviation) over the 10 test-folds.

P	Q	R	Train AUC (x100)	Test AUC (x100)	Train ACC	Test ACC
10	7 ± 1.2	6 ± 1	92.36 ± 0.06	88.37 ± 6.61	73.35 ± 0.17	72.65 ± 0.92
100	82 ± 1.8	6.5 ± 0.67	99.96 ± 0.01	99.95 ± 0.03	99.05 ± 0.17	98.96 ± 0.27
1000	882 ± 4.2	4.2 ± 0.40	99.98 ± 0.01	99.96 ± 0.03	99.51 ± 0.07	99.50 ± 0.22
10000	9132 ± 4.7	4.7 ± 0.45	99.99 ± 0.01	99.97 ± 0.04	99.66 ± 0.10	99.62 ± 0.17

criteria: the Area Under the receiver operating characteristic Curve (AUC) [19] and the Accuracy (ACC, the rate of good classification) for the test.

The performance of the classifier increases with P until a stable level where constructing more variables does not bring real improvement. For $P = 1000$ ($R = 4.2 \pm 0.4$) the classifier exhibits excellent results (AUC and ACC close to 1 which is for both cases close to the upper bound) and excellent robustness (ratio train/test results close to 1). This last point ensures to have similar performances with unknown events.

Another interesting result is the low number of variables really needed in the classifier (R). This is key to enable a real-time implementation in a commercial transceiver, for which the R variables will be computed online. Moreover, most of them are easy to preprocess online to enable incremental learning [33] for fast predictions. We present here four typical examples of found variables (aggregates) of interest: (i) 'Sum(b(t)) where $t > 1.9835$'; (ii) 'Sum(d(t)) where $t \in]0.9252, 1.9835]$' (iii) 'Min(d(t)) where $t > 1.9835$'; (iv) 'Mean(c(t)) where $t \in]0.9252, 1.9835]$'.

These variables are easy to interpret. For example the second one based on d indicates the quantity of movement on the d component of the quaternion (the movement on initial $S_3(t)$) for a given period of time of the time series. From this point, we have a classifier with a very good accuracy and a low complexity that can be embedded in coherent receiver for a negligible cost.

These good results and the small number of variables used for classification are due to the proposed global processing chain: (i) a data transformation based on quaternions visibly well suited to the problem, (ii) a representation in multitable form coupled with an efficient search for informative aggregates, and (iii) the use of an interpretable classifier. For future works on SOP signals, the quaternion representation seems to be a very good recommendation

7   Proof of Concept

A proactive mechanism is expected to detect not only fiber breaks but also cases where the cut does not occur – e.g. an excavator near the fiber. In [38], it was suggested that a new data route should be established on an upper network layer (the IP layer) to avoid outages due to optical hardware reconfiguration. In [6] a new elastic transceiver architecture embedding a classifier similar to the one presented in the previous section was proposed, to enable a seamless optical restoration directly at the optical layer. A key enabler is the ability of this proto-type transceiver to emit on two distinct channels and to switch very quickly the decoding channel. This networking proof of concept was demonstrated in [6] and within the concerned companies. This prototype system has been upgraded with the classifier presented in the present paper, to take advantage of the improved performance.

8 Conclusion and Perspectives

From an 'applied data science' point of view, we proposed in this work to use a real-time coherent receiver coupled with machine learning to monitor mechanical events on an optical fiber, to proactively detect fiber breaks. We experimentally validated that multivariate time series (trajectories of SOP of light propagating through an optical fiber) could be represented efficiently using quaternions. Our system exhibits an accurate event classification with more than 99%. We developed a proof of concept which shows that it is possible to detect and classify different kinds of events in real time to have real-time seamless optical restoration mechanisms. Furthermore the small number of rules found by the classifier are concise, clearly interpretable. Nokia Bell Labs is currently studying the implementation of the method in the field.

From a research point of view some work remains to be done. We need to (i) see if building a multivariate time series classifier directly (without the multitable data mining approach) could give concise and interpretable rules, (ii) do a thorough comparison against a wide range of time series representations (e.g. variants of quaternion representations or other ways to represent spherical data).

Note on reproducibility: The following files can be downloaded at https://bit.ly/2WXu19V: (i) the SOP dataset (multitable representation, 700 MB zipped in split files, 10 GB unzipped). This dataset is released for the sake of verification and investigations of alternative methods; (ii) the Python module to convert the initial data to quaternions. A provisional license of the Khiops software implementing all the elements of Sects. 5.2 and 5.3 can be obtained for free from [11].

References

1. Adewuyi, A.P., Wu, Z., Serker, N.K.: Assessment of vibration-based damage identification methods using displacement and distributed strain measurements. Struct. Health Monit. **8**(6), 443–461 (2009)
2. Bagnall, A., Lines, J., Hills, J., Bostrom, A.: Time-series classification with COTE: the collective of transformation-based ensembles. IEEE Trans. Knowl. Data Eng. **27**(9), 2522–2535 (2015)
3. Bagnall, A., Davis, L., Hills, J., Lines, J.: Transformation based ensembles for time series classification. In: Proceedings of the 12th SDM, April 2012

4. Bagnall, A., Lines, J., Bostrom, A., Large, J., Keogh, E.: The great time series classification bake off: a review and experimental evaluation of recent algorithmic advances. Data Min. Knowl. Disc. **31**(3), 606–660 (2017)
5. Boitier, F., et al.: Proactive fiber damage detection in real-time coherent receiver. In: Proceedings of the ECOC (2017)
6. Boitier, F., et al.: Seamless optical path restoration with just-in-time resource allocation leveraging machine learning. In: Proceeding of the ECOC, Demo Session (2018)
7. Boullé, M.: A grouping method for categorical attributes having very large number of values. In: Perner, P., Imiya, A. (eds.) MLDM 2005. LNCS (LNAI), vol. 3587, pp. 228–242. Springer, Heidelberg (2005). https://doi.org/10.1007/11510888_23
8. Boullé, M.: MODL: a Bayes optimal discretization method for continuous attributes. Mach. Learn. **65**(1), 131–165 (2006)
9. Boullé, M.: Compression-based averaging of selective naive Bayes classifiers. J. Mach. Learn. Res. **8**, 1659–1685 (2007)
10. Boullé, M.: Tagging fireworkers activities from body sensors under distribution drift. In: Proceedings of Federated Conference on Computer Science and Information System, pp. 389–396 (2015)
11. Boullé, M.: Khiops: outil d'apprentissage supervisé automatique pour la fouille de grandes bases de données multi-tables. In: Extraction et Gestion des Connaissances, pp. 505–510 (2016). http://www.khiops.com
12. Boullé, M.: Predicting dangerous seismic events in coal mines under distribution drift. In: Ganzha, M., Maciaszek, L., Paprzycki, M. (eds.) Proceedings of Federated Conference on Computer Science and Information System, pp. 221–224 (2016)
13. Boullé, M., Charnay, C., Lachiche, N.: A scalable robust and automatic propositionalization approach for Bayesian classification of large mixed numerical and categorical data. Mach. Learn. **108**, 229–266 (2018)
14. Casteljau, P.D.: Les quaternions. Dunod, Paris (1987)
15. Chen, Y., et al.: The UCR time series classification archive, July 2015. www.cs.ucr.edu/~eamonn/time_series_data/
16. Dutisseuil, E., et al.: 34 Gb/s PDM-QPSK coherent receiver using SiGe ADCs and a single FPGA for digital signal processing. In: Proceedings of the OFC, p. OM3H.7 (2012)
17. Džeroski, S.: Relational data mining. In: Maimon, O., Rokach, L. (eds.) Data Mining and Knowledge Discovery Handbook, pp. 887–911. Springer, Boston (2009). https://doi.org/10.1007/978-0-387-09823-4_46
18. Dzeroski, S., Lavrac, N.: Inductive Logic Programming: Techniques and Applications. Prentice Hall, New York (1994)
19. Fawcett, T.: ROC graphs: notes and practical considerations for researchers. Technical Report HPL-2003-4, HP Laboratories (2004)
20. Gay, D., Guigourés, R., Boullé, M., Clérot, F.: Feature extraction over multiple representations for time series classification. In: International Workshop NFMCP held at ECML/PKDD, pp. 18–34 (2013)
21. Hamilton, W.R.: On a new species of imaginary quantities connected with a theory of quaternions. Proc. R. Ir. Acad. **2**, 424–434 (1843)
22. Hanson, A.J.: Visualizing Quaternions. Morgan Kaufmann Publishers, Burlington (2006)
23. Hauske, F.N., Kuschnerov, M., Spinnler, B., Lankl, B.: Optical performance monitoring in digital coherent receivers. J. Lightwave Technol. **27**(16), 3623–3631 (2009)
24. Hayford-Acquah, T., Asante, B.: Causes of fiber cut and the recommendation to solve the problem. IOSR J. Electron. Commun. Eng. **12**, 46–64 (2017)

25. Hills, J., Lines, J., Baranauskas, E., Mapp, J., Bagnall, A.: Classification of time series by shapelet transformation. Data Min. Knowl. Disc. **28**(4), 851–881 (2014)
26. Kikuchi, K.: Fundamentals of coherent optical fiber communications. J. Lightwave Technol. **34**(1), 157–179 (2016)
27. Krogel, M.-A., Rawles, S., Železný, F., Flach, P.A., Lavrač, N., Wrobel, S.: Comparative evaluation of approaches to propositionalization. In: Horváth, T., Yamamoto, A. (eds.) ILP 2003. LNCS (LNAI), vol. 2835, pp. 197–214. Springer, Heidelberg (2003). https://doi.org/10.1007/978-3-540-39917-9_14
28. Krogel, M.-A., Wrobel, S.: Transformation-based learning using multirelational aggregation. In: Rouveirol, C., Sebag, M. (eds.) ILP 2001. LNCS (LNAI), vol. 2157, pp. 142–155. Springer, Heidelberg (2001). https://doi.org/10.1007/3-540-44797-0_12
29. Lachiche, N.: Propositionalization, pp. 812–817. Springer, Boston (2010). https://doi.org/10.1007/978-0-387-30164-8
30. Langley, P., Iba, W., Thompson, K.: An analysis of Bayesian classifiers. In: Proceedings of the Tenth National Conference on Artificial Intelligence (AAAI 1992), pp. 223–228 (1992)
31. Lavrač, N., Železný, F., Flach, P.A.: RSD: relational subgroup discovery through first-order feature construction. In: Matwin, S., Sammut, C. (eds.) ILP 2002. LNCS (LNAI), vol. 2583, pp. 149–165. Springer, Heidelberg (2003). https://doi.org/10.1007/3-540-36468-4_10
32. Layec, P., Dupas, A., Verchère, D., Sparks, K., Bigo, S.: Will metro networks be the playground for (true) elastic optical networks? J. Lightwave Technol. **35**(6), 1260–1266 (2017)
33. Lemaire, V., Salperwyck, C., Bondu, A.: A survey on supervised classification on data streams. In: Zimányi, E., Kutsche, R.-D. (eds.) eBISS 2014. LNBIP, vol. 205, pp. 88–125. Springer, Cham (2015). https://doi.org/10.1007/978-3-319-17551-5_4
34. Lines, J., Bagnall, A.: Time series classification with ensembles of elastic distance measures. Data Min. Knowl. Disc. **29**(3), 565–592 (2015)
35. Liu, X., Jin, B., Bai, Q., Wang, D., Wang, Y.: Distributed fiber-optic sensors for vibration detection. Sensors **16**, 1164 (2016)
36. Nokia white paper: Advances in optical layer restoration (2017). https://www.nokia.com/blog/optical-layer-restoration-improving-efficiency/
37. Pesic, J., Le Rouzic, E., Brochier, N., Dupont, L.: Proactive restoration of optical links based on the classification of events. In: Proceedings of the ONDM, pp. 1–6 (2011)
38. Pesic, J., Meuric, J., Le Rouzic, E., Dupont, L., Morvan, M.: Proactive failure detection for WDM carrying IP. In: Proceedings of IEEE INFOCOM, pp. 2971–2975 (2012)
39. Pesic, J.: Study of the mechanisms associated with the preventive network restoration in fiber optic core networks. Ph.D. thesis, Université de Bretagne-Sud (2012)
40. Project SENDATE-Tandem: Secure networking for a data center cloud in Europe - tailored network for data centers in the metro. https://www.celticnext.eu/project-sendate-tandem/
41. Rodríguez, J.J., Alonso, C.J., Boström, H.: Learning first order logic time series classifiers: rules and boosting. In: Zighed, D.A., Komorowski, J., Żytkow, J. (eds.) PKDD 2000. LNCS (LNAI), vol. 1910, pp. 299–308. Springer, Heidelberg (2000). https://doi.org/10.1007/3-540-45372-5_29
42. Schäfer, P., Leser, U.: Fast and accurate time series classification with WEASEL. In: Proceedings of the 2017 ACM on Conference on Information and Knowledge Management, pp. 637–646 (2017)

43. Shoemake, K.: Animating rotation with quaternion curves. ACM SIGGRAPH Comput. Graph. **19**(3), 245–254 (1985)
44. Simsarian, J.E., Winzer, P.J.: Shake before break: per-span fiber sensing with in-line polarization monitoring. In: Proceedings of OFC, p. M2E.6 (2017)
45. Time-series classification challenge: Workshop advanced analytics and learning on temporal data at ECML (2016). https://aaltd16.irisa.fr/challenge/
46. Warren Liao, T.: Clustering of time series data - a survey. Pattern Recognit. **38**(11), 1857–1874 (2005)

A Fully Automated Periodicity Detection in Time Series

Tom Puech[(✉)], Matthieu Boussard, Anthony D'Amato, and Gaëtan Millerand

craft ai, Paris, France
{tom.puech,matthieu.boussard,anthony.damato,gaetan.millerand}@craft.ai

Abstract. This paper presents a method to autonomously find periodicities in a signal. It is based on the same idea of using Fourier Transform and autocorrelation function presented in [12]. While showing interesting results this method does not perform well on noisy signals or signals with multiple periodicities. Thus, our method adds several new extra steps (hints clustering, filtering and detrending) to fix these issues. Experimental results show that the proposed method outperforms state of the art algorithms.

1 Introduction

A time series is defined by its 3 main components: the trend component, the periodic component and the random component. Trend analysis and prediction are topics that have been greatly studied [11] and will not be treated in the article, therefore every time series will be assumed stationary regarding its mean and variance, so this study focus the periodic component. The ability to detect and find the main characteristic of this component is not as easy as the trend component. Yet, the ability to detect periodicities in a time series is essential to make precise forecasts.

A periodicity is a pattern in a time series that occurs at regular time intervals. More precisely, the time series is said cyclical, if the time intervals at which the pattern repeats itself can't be precisely defined and is not constant. On the opposite, there are seasonal time series in which the pattern repeats itself at constant and well defined time intervals. Thus, cyclical patterns are more difficult to detect due to their inconsistency and the fact that they usually repeat themselves over large periods of time and therefore require more data to be identified. Nevertheless, seasonal patterns are very common in time series such as those related to human behaviour which usually have periodicities like hours and calendar (time of day, day of week, month of year). This kind of feature is well known and can be easily tested to see if they are beneficial or not. Unfortunately, when it comes to time series related to other phenomenons, the periodicities are not trivially found. For instance, tides level are multi-periodic time series correlated to both moon cycles and sun cycles; and females menstrual cycles are related to hormonal changes. The ability to detect periodicity in time series is fundamental when it comes to forecasting [6]. Once a periodic pattern has been

V. Lemaire et al. (Eds.): AALTD 2019, LNAI 11986, pp. 43–54, 2020.
https://doi.org/10.1007/978-3-030-39098-3_4

detected, numerous techniques can be used to model this later and improve forecasts [2]. However, periodicities detection is not easy and has been greatly studied in the existing literature, but most of current techniques are unable to detect periodicities without the need of preprocessing data [13] or have trouble detecting multiple periodicities [12]. This paper is organised as follow: we first present the Fourier transform and the Autoperiod algorithm [12] used to detect periodicities in a signal. Then we propose a new fully automated method, named Clustered Filtered Detrended Autoperiod (CFD-Autoperiod), which also combines the advantages of frequency domain and time domain while being robust to noise and able to handle multi periodicities. The frequency analysis provide a set of potential frequencies, called hints. Noise robustness is then achieved using a density clustering on those hints. Also, multi-periodicities are more precisely detected by both using detrending and filtering. Finally, we demonstrate that CFD-Autoperiod outperforms previous methods.

2   Related Works

Autocorrelation and Fourier transform are well known techniques used to find recurrent patterns in a given signal.

2.1   Fourier Transform

The Fourier transform decomposes the original signal $\{s(t_j)\}_{j \in [1,N]}$ in a linear combination of complex sinusoids, also called a Fourier series. Let N be the number of frequency components of a signal, P the periodicity of the signal and c_k the kth series coefficient then we have the Fourier series:

$$s_N(t) = \sum_{k=0}^{N-1} c_k \cdot e^{i\frac{2\pi kt}{N}}$$

Thus, the amplitude and phase of each sinusoids correspond to the main frequencies contained within the signal. The Fourier transform can easily detect the presence of frequencies in a signal. However, if we need the corresponding periodicities from each frequency then we have to return from the frequency domain to the time domain. Let DFT be the Discrete Fourier Transform of a discrete signal $\{s(t_j)\}$, then we can obtain the corresponding Periodogram $\mathcal{P}$ in the time domain as follow:

$$\mathcal{P}(f_k) = ||DFT(f_k)||^2 = ||c_k||^2 \text{ with } k = 0, 1, \ldots, \lceil \tfrac{N-1}{2} \rceil$$

where $f_k = \frac{2\pi k}{N}$ correspond to the frequency captured by each component.

However, in the frequency domain each bin is separated with a constant step of $\frac{1}{N}$, whereas in the time domain bins size is $\frac{N}{k(k+1)}$, thus the range of periods is increasingly wider. Therefore, the Fourier transform resolution for long periods is not sufficient to provide an accurate estimation of the periodicity.

2.2 Autocorrelation

Another way to find the dominant periodicities in a signal consists in calculating the autocorrelation function (ACF) of the given signal $s(t)$. The autocorrelation is the correlation between the elements of a series and others from the same series separated from them by a given interval Δt:

$$ACF(\Delta t) = \frac{1}{N} \sum_{j=0}^{N-t} s(t_j) \cdot s(t_j + \Delta t)$$

The ACF function provides a more accurate estimation of each periodicity, especially for longer periods as opposed to the Fourier transform [12]. However, it is not sufficient by itself due to the difficulty to select the most predominant peaks. Indeed, for a given periodicity p_1 the autocorrelation generates peaks for each p_1 multiple, hence the difficulty to select the relevant peaks when multiple periodicities composed a signal.

2.3 Hybrid Approach

A methodology combining both techniques advantages has been introduced by [12]. This method uses sequentially frequency domain (DFT) and time domain (ACF) in order to detect periodicity. The idea is to combine both methods in such a way that they complement each other. On the one hand, as mentioned earlier, due to its step inconstancy in the time domain, the Fourier transform resolution becomes insufficient to provide good estimations for long periods, where the autocorrelation has a constant resolution. On the other hand, according to [12], it is difficult to correctly detect periodicities using only the autocorrelation function.

They proposed the following steps: first, noise is discarded from possible periodicity hints using a threshold on the Periodogram. Then, these hints are refined using the ACF function. If a periodicity hint lies on a local maximum then it can be validated, otherwise, if it lies on a local minimum this latter is discarded. On top of that, thanks to the ACF resolution, a gradient ascent is used to refine the remaining hints (Fig. 1).

However, some issues such as multi-periodic signals, spectral leakage or presence of non-stationary periodicities are not addressed by the authors.

3 A New Methodology: CFD-Autoperiod

3.1 Spectral Leakage

The Fourier Transform is used to select periodicity hints. To do so, we use the 99% confidence [7,8,12] technique to compute the threshold distinguishing periodicity hints from noise in the Fourier transform. Firstly, it is necessary to find the maximum amount of spectral power generated by the signal noise. Let $\{s'(t_j)\}_{j \in [1,N]}$ be a permuted sequence of a periodic sequence $\{s(t_j)\}_{j \in [1,N]}$. s'

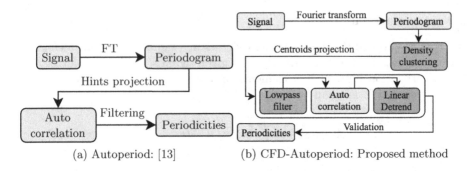

(a) Autoperiod: [13]   (b) CFD-Autoperiod: Proposed method

Fig. 1. Periodicity detection methods

should not exhibit any periodic pattern due to the random permutation process. Therefore, the maximal spectral power generated by s' should not be higher than the spectral power generated by a true periodicity in s. Thus, we can use this value as a threshold to eliminate the noise. To provide a 99% confidence level, this process is repeated 100 times and the $99th$ largest value recorded is used as a threshold (Fig. 2).

Unfortunately, for a given periodicity in X, rather than finding an unique corresponding hint, spectral leakage may produce multiple hints near the true periodicity. This phenomenon is due to the finite resolution of the Fourier Transform and can only be avoided knowing in advance the true periodicities of the signal.

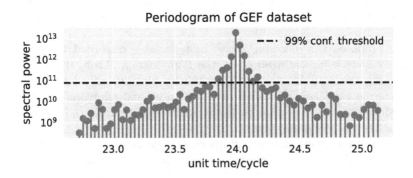

Fig. 2. Illustration of spectral leakage

Spectral leakage generates points with a spectral power higher than the threshold provided by the 99% confidence method (Fig. 2) and therefore generates imprecise periodicity hints. The autocorrelation might filter most of them but every imprecise periodicity hint increase the probability of false positives, therefore it is interesting to reduce the number of periodicity hints in order to achieve a higher precision score.

Density Clustering. Knowing that the distribution of spectral leakage is more dense around the true periodicity, performing a density clustering over periodicity hints and using the resulting centroids as periodicity hints can reduce the number of hints. A fundamental value in density clustering algorithms is the range in which it seeks for neighbours named ϵ. In our case, this value is not a constant because the accuracy of the hint is related to the resolution of the corresponding DFT bin size. A hint may have leaked from adjacent DFT bins, thus for a given hint of periodicity N/k, ϵ is set as the next bin value plus a constant width of 1 to avoid numerical issues when the difference from the current bin value to the next bin value is less than one:

$$\varepsilon_{N/k} = \frac{N}{(k-1)} + 1$$

The clustering is done by ascending periodicity order, hence a cluster made with small periodicities cannot be altered by bigger periodicity clusters.

Input: Hints - list of hints in ascending order
Output: Centroids - list of centroids
1 Clusters ← [] ;
2 cluster ← [] ;
3 ε ← Hints[0].nextBinValue + 1 ;
4 cluster.append(Hints[0]) ;
5 **for** *hint in Hints[1:]* **do**
6   **if** *hint ≤ ε* **then**
7   cluster.append(hint) ;
8   ε ← hint.nextBinValue + 1 ;
9   **else**
10   Clusters.append(cluster) ;
11   cluster ← [] ;
12 **end**
13 Centroids ← [] ;
14 **for** *cluster in Clusters* **do**
15   centroid ← mean(cluster) ;
16   Centroids.append(centroid) ;
17 **end**

Algorithm 1. Clustering pseudocode

As shown in the results (Fig. 3), the density clustering performed in the GEF dataset [4] drastically reduces the number of periodicity hints and the resulting centroids are close to the true periodicities (24 and 168). Once the centroids have been found, they are used as periodicity hints during the validation step.

Hints Validation. For the validation step, a search interval for each periodicity hint is needed to check if this latter lies on a hill or a valley of the ACF. [12]

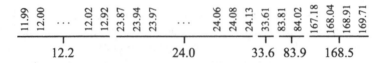

Fig. 3. Density clustering on GEF dataset. The bottom value shows the cluster mean.

used the DFT bin size to define this search interval but in order to get a better accuracy, we propose a different approach. A periodicity N generates hills on the ACF at each multiple of N and valleys at each multiple of $\frac{N}{2}$. Therefore, we defined the search interval R for a periodicity hint N as follow:

$$R = \left[\frac{N}{2}, ..., N + \frac{N}{2} \right]$$

Thereafter, a quadratic function is fitted to the ACR function in the search interval. In order to validate a hint, the function must have a negative second degree term and its derivative sign must change along the interval.

3.2 Multi-periodicities

The presence of multiple periodicities refutes the assumption that hills and valleys of the ACF are sufficient to validate or discard hints. Precisely, when validating a periodicity hint, correlations generated by both higher and lower frequencies than the hint can be problematic. These two problems are addressed in the following section.

Higher Frequencies. On the one hand, periodicities of higher frequencies induces sinusoidal correlations which may be in opposite phase with the correlation we are actually looking for (see Fig. 4). Let s be a multi-periodic signal composed of periodicities P_1 and P_2. Let P_1, a periodicity of length 20 and P_2, a periodicity of length 50. The periodicity P_1 produces on the signal ACF sinusoidal correlations of wavelength 20 and the periodicity P_2 produces sinusoidal correlations of wavelength 50. Thereby, at 50 lags on the ACF, the P_1 and P_2 periodicities will produce correlations in opposite phases and therefore nullify the hill at 50 used to validate or discard the periodicity hint P_2.

To tackle this issue, periodicity hints are analysed in ascending order. If a periodicity hint is validated, a lowpass filter with an adapted cutoff frequency is applied to the signal. Consequently, the following autocorrelations will be computed on this new signal. Thus, the resulting autocorrelations will not exhibit any correlation induced by frequencies higher than the cutoff frequency of the lowpass filter.

The cutoff frequency must be chosen carefully. Indeed, an ideal lowpass filter is characterised by a full transmission in the pass band, a complete attenuation in the stop band and an instant transition between the two bands. However, in practice, filters are only an approximation of this ideal filter and the higher the

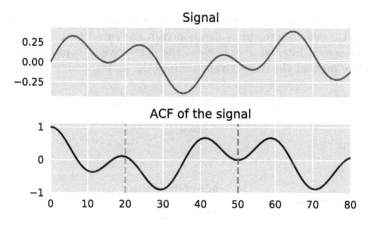

Fig. 4. Impact of multiple periodicities (20 and 50) on the ACF.

order of the filter is, the more the filter approximates the ideal filter, Fig. 5. In our case, we are studying the periodicities in the signal, therefore, we want a filter with a frequency response as flat as possible to avoid any negative impact on the periodicity detection. Thereby, a Butterworth filter has been chosen due to its flat frequency response with no ripples in the passband nor in the stopband.

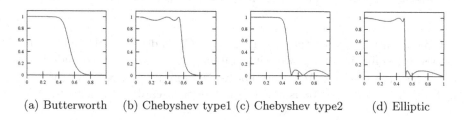

(a) Butterworth   (b) Chebyshev type1 (c) Chebyshev type2   (d) Elliptic

Fig. 5. Approximations of an ideal lowpass filter.

However, a Butterworth filter, despite all the good properties, has a slow roll-off attenuating frequencies nearby the cutoff frequency. For the validation step, we do not want to attenuate the periodicity hint, therefore the cutoff frequency must not be exactly equal to the frequency of the hint. For a given periodicity $\frac{N}{k}$, the frequency cutoff is equal to the previous bin value minus 1, to avoid the same numerical issues as described in the Density Clustering section:

$$f_c = \frac{1}{(\frac{N}{k+1} - 1)}$$

Lower Frequencies. On the other hand, low frequencies may induce a local trend in the autocorrelation that can be problematic when validating an hint.

Indeed, in order to validate a periodicity hint, a quadratic function is fitted to the ACF in the search interval as mentioned in the subsection Sec.17. Sadly, a trend in the search interval may prevent the derivative sign to switch (Fig. 6), and therefore prevent the correct validation of the corresponding hint.

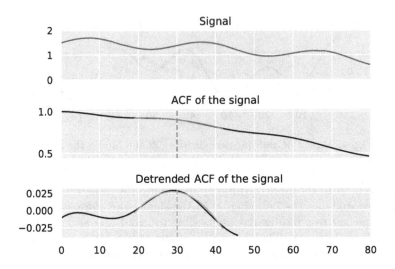

Fig. 6. Hint validation using the ACF on a multi-periodic signal (30, 500).

Consequently, to avoid this situation, the ACF is detrended by subtracting the best fitted line in the following interval $[0, \frac{N}{(k-1)} + 1]$ for a given period hint N/k. Thus, the resulting ACF does not exhibit any linear trend and therefore the fitted quadratic function is able to validate or discard hint efficiently.

4   Results

To evaluate the performances of the proposed method it is necessary to use time series datasets with periodicities. To do so, we perform our first evaluations on synthetic signals where the ground truth is known in order to compare raw performances and evaluations on real time series datasets.

4.1   Synthetic Signals

Signals of length 2000 with 1 to 3 periodicities have been generated. The periodicities have been chosen in the interval $[10, 500]$ using a pseudo-random process. For multi-periodic signals, this pseudo-random process ensures that periodicities are not overlapping each others by checking that one is at least twice as bigger as the previous one. Finally, in order to compute precision and recall metrics, a validation criterion has been established. We assumed that a periodicity P_d detected in a generated signal with a true periodicity P_t is valid if:

$$\lfloor 0.95 \times P_t \rfloor \leq P_d \leq \lceil 1.05 \times P_t \rceil$$

The metrics have been consolidated over 500 iterations for each generated periodicity. As shown in Table 1, for a non multi-periodic signal, autoperiod and CFD-Autoperiod method achieve high precision scores whereas the Fourier Transform achieves a high recall but a really low precision score. Indeed, the Fourier Transform method does not filter the hints using the autocorrelation. Nevertheless, the autoperiod method did not detect every periodicities even for non multi-periodic signals autoperiod. This is likely due to the absence of density clustering and the narrow interval search to find the corresponding hill on the ACF. For multi-periodic signals, both recall and precision are drastically decreasing for the autoperiod method and as it can be observed, the detrending step and the use of a lowpass filter by the CFD-Autoperiod method lead to better scores. Regarding the Fourier Transform scores, due to the lack of the filtering step its recall is high but its precision score is always the lowest.

Table 1. Precision/Recall comparison for pseudo-random and random process.

	Nb periods	Pseudo random			Random		
		1	2	3	1	2	3
Fourier transform	Precision	27.76	40.52	50.16	27.83	42.32	46.63
	Recall	80.40	78.20	**85.73**	77.80	**75.80**	**73.40**
Autoperiod	Precision	98.47	64.16	54.42	98.39	58.05	53.41
	Recall	77.20	51.20	32.87	73.20	35.70	26.13
CFD-Autoperiod	Precision	**100.00**	**91.10**	**86.93**	**100.0**	**71.78**	**68.07**
	Recall	**100.00**	**91.10**	78.93	**100.0**	55.20	43.07

Benchmarks have also been performed on synthetic signals generated via random process, without limitations on the periodicity values (Table 1). Naturally, the results with an unique periodicity are similar. However, for multi-periodic signals the autoperiod and CFD-Autoperiod methods achieve lower scores. This is due to the fact that both methods use the autocorrelation to filter hints and this latter is not able to distinguish very close periodicities. Therefore, the use of autocorrelation as a validation step does not allow the detection of periodicities near each others. Nevertheless, in real datasets, most of the periodicities are sufficiently spaced to be detected by the autocorrelation function and thus remains efficient as a validation step.

4.2   Real Datasets

Benchmarks have also been performed on real datasets (Table 2) and different types of time series have been chosen in order to test the validity of the proposed method.

– **GEF** ([4]): This dataset has been provided for the Global Energy Forecasting Competition 2014 (GEFCom2014) [4], a probabilistic energy forecasting competition. The dataset is composed of 6 years of hourly load data. This time series is multi-periodic with the following periodicities: daily (24), weekly (168) and bi-annual (4383). The CFD-Autoperiod method has detected and validated 4 periodicities with 3 of them correct. Whereas the autoperiod has detected 5 periodicities with only 2 valid and has missed the long term bi-annual periodicity.

– **Great Lakes** ([3]): This dataset contains monthly water level of the 5 great lakes and is provided by the National Oceanic and Atmospheric Administration [10]. This time series is mono-periodic with a periodicity of 12 months. The autoperiod method has detected 4 different periodicities with only one correct. Among these latter, 24 and 72 periodicities were detected and are only resulting correlations of the 12 periodicity. Whereas the CFD-Autoperiod has successfully filtered out the correlations of the 12 one. [9] used this dataset as well but did not write the exact periodicities detected by their method. In their plots, the segmentation for both Ontario and Clair lakes does not correspond to a periodicity of 12.

– **Pseudo periodic** ([5]): These datasets contain 10 pseudo periodic time series generated from 10 different simulation runs. The data appears to be highly periodic, but never exactly repeats itself. [9] did not write their exact results but the segmentation shown on their plot seems to correspond to a detected periodicity of 155. The CFD-Autoperiod method found a periodicity of 144 and the exact true periodicity seems to be 142.

– **Boston Tides** ([1]): This dataset contains water level records of Boston, MA from July 01 to August 31, with 6 min as sampling interval. It has been recently used by [13] to evaluate their method. They successfully detected 2 periodicities but their method required a preprocessing step whereas the CFD-Autoperiod method does not require any. The first detected periodicity is 12,4 h corresponding to the semi-diurnal constituent of 12 h and 25.2 min. They have also detected 28,5 days and 29 days periodicities which correspond to a lunar month. The CFD-Autoperiod method detected a periodicity of 24 h and 50 min whereas the autoperiod did not detect it. This value is interesting because it corresponds to the behaviour of a mixed tide (when there is a high high tide, a high low tide followed by a low high tide and a low low tide, in 24 h ans 50 min). However, it has not detected the lunar month periodicity but this might be due to the lack of data used. Indeed, [13] used 2 months of data and the CFD-Autoperiod can only detect periodicities of a length inferior or equal to the half of the signal length.

Table 2. Detected periodicities on real Dataset

		Detected periodicities	
		Values	Count
GEF	Fourier trans.	5.99, 11.99,...	44
	Autoperiod	24, 168, 192, 288, 528	5
	CFD-Autoperiod	24, 171, 496, 4118	4
Great lakes Clair	Fourier trans.	12.19, 23.27, 28.44, ...	7
	Autoperiod	12, 24, 35, 72	4
	CFD-Autoperiod	12, 505	2
Great lakes Ontario	Fourier trans.	12.2, 28.4, 36.6, ...	6
	Autoperiod	12, 35, 72	3
	CFD-Autoperiod	12	1
Pseudo 1	Fourier trans.	18.7, 35.1, 74.1, 142.9, ...	4
	Autoperiod	74, 146	2
	CFD-Autoperiod	144	1
Boston Tide	Fourier trans.	120.0, 120.9, 121.9, ...	11
	Autoperiod	124	1
	CFD-Autoper.	125, 246	2

5   Conclusion and Future Work

This paper describes an algorithm called CFD-Autoperiod detecting periodicities in time series and improving the autoperiod method proposed in [12]. CFD-
Autoperiod can be applied on noisy time series containing multiple periodicities
and output raw periodicities that can later be refined by external domain specific
knowledge (for instance 24 h for human daily activities). One case not treated in
this study concerns non-stationary series. A possible technique would consists
in tracking the evolution of the periodicities through time and using a Kalman
filter to track the apparition, disappearance or evolution of the detected periodicities. Using the confidence of the Kalman filter we could decide whether to
continue considering the presence of a particular periodicity in the signal even
if it is not detected for a while. This would strengthen the results obtained by
CFD-Autoperiod and give more reliable periodicities. Thus, even more complex
machine learning models can be built on top of them.

References

1. Boston Tides (2018). http://tidesandcurrents.noaa.gov/. Accessed 16 Aug 2018
2. Gooijer, J.G.D., Hyndman, R.J.: 25 years of time series forecasting. Int. J. Forecast. **22**(3), 443–473 (2006). Twenty five years of forecasting
3. Great lakes (2018). https://www.glerl.noaa.gov/data/dashboard/data/. Accessed 10 Aug 2018

4. Hong, T., Pinson, P., Fan, S., Zareipour, H., Troccoli, A., Hyndman, R.J.: Probabilistic energy forecasting: global energy forecasting competition 2014 and beyond. Int. J. Forecast. **32**(3), 896–913 (2016)

5. Keogh, E.J., Pazzani, M.J.: Pseudo periodic synthetic time series data set. https://archive.ics.uci.edu/ml/datasets/Pseudo+Periodic+Synthetic+Time+Series. Accessed 15 Aug 2018

6. Koopman, S.J., Ooms, M.: Forecasting daily time series using periodic unobserved components time series models. Comput. Stat. Data Anal. **51**(2), 885–903 (2006)

7. Li, Z., Ding, B., Rol, J.H., Nye, K.P.: Mining periodic behaviors for moving objects. In: Proceedings of the 16th ACM SIGKDD International Conference on Knowledge Discovery and Data Mining, pp. 1099–1108. ACM (2010)

8. Li, Z., Wang, J., Han, J.: Mining event periodicity from incomplete observations. In: Proceedings of the 18th ACM SIGKDD International Conference on Knowledge Discovery and Data Mining, KDD 2012, pp. 444–452. ACM, New York (2012). https://doi.org/10.1145/2339530.2339604

9. Parthasarathy, S., Mehta, S., Srinivasan, S.: Robust periodicity detection algorithms. In: Proceedings of the 2006 ACM CIKM International Conference on Information and Knowledge Management, Arlington, Virginia, USA, November, pp. 874–875 (2006)

10. Quinn, F.H., Sellinger, C.E.: Lake Michigan record levels of 1838, a present perspective. J. Great Lakes Res. **16**(1), 133–138 (1990)

11. Saad, E.W., Prokhorov, D.V., Wunsch, D.C.: Comparative study of stock trend prediction using time delay, recurrent and probabilistic neural networks. IEEE Trans. Neural Netw. **9**(6), 1456–1470 (1998)

12. Vlachos, M., Yu, P.S., Castelli, V.: On periodicity detection and structural periodic similarity. In: Kargupta, H., Srivastava, J., Kamath, C., Goodman, A. (eds.) Proceedings of the 2005 SIAM International Conference on Data Mining, SDM 2005, Newport Beach, CA, USA, 21–23 April 2005, pp. 449–460. SIAM (2005)

13. Yuan, Q., Shang, J., Cao, X., Zhang, C., Geng, X., Han, J.: Detecting multiple periods and periodic patterns in event time sequences. In: Proceedings of the 2017 ACM on Conference on Information and Knowledge Management, CIKM 2017, pp. 617–626, ACM, New York (2017)

Conditional Forecasting of Water Level Time Series with RNNs

Bart J. van der Lugt$^{(\boxtimes)}$ and Ad J. Feelders

Department of Information and Computing Sciences, Utrecht University,
Princetonplein 5, 3584 CC Utrecht, The Netherlands
b.j.vanderlugt@gmail.com

Abstract. We describe a practical situation in which the application of forecasting models could lead to energy efficiency and decreased risk in water level management. The practical challenge of forecasting water levels in the next 24 h and the available data are provided by a dutch regional water authority. We formalized the problem as conditional forecasting of hydrological time series: the resulting models can be used for real-life scenario evaluation and decision support. We propose the novel *Encoder/Decoder with Exogenous Variables* RNN (ED-RNN) architecture for conditional forecasting with RNNs, and contrast its performance with various other time series forecasting models. We show that the performance of the ED-RNN architecture is comparable to the best performing alternative model (a feedforward ANN for direct forecasting), and more accurately captures short-term fluctuations in the water heights.

Keywords: Time series · Conditional forecasting · Encoder/Decoder · Exogenous variables · Recurrent Neural Network

1 Introduction

In the Netherlands, water is all around us: knowing how to manage this water is key to sustaining our way of life. New technologies and an exponential increase in the amount of data available generate new possibilities in the field of hydrology. Accurate forecasts of weather, water levels and flow rates allow water boards (Waterschappen) to limit risk of flooding, drought damage and energy waste. Water boards are regional government bodies responsible for water quality, water levels and safety.

From this practice, the relevance of accurate *conditional forecasts* of time series data becomes especially clear. Conditional forecasts are a useful means of evaluating the impact of a hypothetical scenario. The goal is to predict the variables of interest conditioned on an *assumed future path* of one or more other variables in the system. These forecasts can be used to guide the decision making process by comparing various scenarios.

Made possible by Ynformed and Waterschap Zuiderzeeland.

Artificial Neural Network (ANN) models have become very popular in forecasting water level time series. They provide a good alternative to the traditional time series models (such as vector autoregressive (VAR) models) because ANNs do not assume linear dependencies. Recurrent Neural Networks (RNNs) were specifically designed to process sequential data, allowing for the model to retain short-term and long-term memory of the input series, thereby improving the performance of traditional feedforward ANNs on many machine learning tasks. Despite their great potential, the application of RNNs to conditional time series forecasting has not been extensively studied in the literature.

The method we propose in this paper is to use an Encoder/Decoder RNN architecture to generate conditional forecasts of time series data. Our approach distinguishes itself by considering the future path of the variables we conditioned on in the decoding step. It can therefore be characterized as an *Encoder/Decoder RNN with Exogenous Variables*. The resulting architecture is very flexible and can be used to model many real-world time series. In our experiments, we compare the performance of the ED-RNN with various other popular forecasting models in a conditional forecasting scenario. This forecasting problem, as well as the dataset of hydrological variables that is used for training and testing, is provided by the Waterschap Zuiderzeeland.

The rest of this paper is structured as follows. First, we present relevant literature regarding hydrological time series forecasting. We then provide a more in-depth description of our forecasting challenge, its relevance, and the various solutions to it. Lastly, we detail the results of our experiments and discuss their implications for the field.

2   Related Work

Traditionally, most of the research in water resource systems was done using hydrological models, which require significant amounts of domain knowledge. Studies showed that levels [19,24], flow dynamics [18] and quality [9] of surface water could be effectively modelled with this approach. However, a comparative study of such models for ground water by Konikow et al. [15] showed that it was impossible to scientifically verify and validate them, and argued that calibration procedures generate non-unique solutions with limited predictive accuracy.

Research into our geographical region of interest (the Noordoostpolder in Flevoland, The Netherlands) has been conducted in 2006 [5]. In this evaluation study, the authors studied the historical influx of water to the region, and contrasted it with its optimal value for different performance indicators using various hydrological models.

Modelling hydrological variables can also be done by applying time series models to a collection of historical data. Autoregressive (AR) models [16] fit a linear equation of previous measurements to predict the next value. The AR model is the special case of the Vector Auto Regressive (VAR) model [14], which is suited for multivariate instead of univariate time series. These models can be easily extended to include external regressors, moving averages, differencing, trends and seasonal components [16]. Limitation of VAR models include that they assume linear dependence between the variables, as well as linear dependence over time. Additionally, early studies [16,26] concluded that VAR models are unable to learn both short- and long-term dependencies between variables in a single model.

More recently, Artificial Neural Network (ANN) models have become very popular in forecasting hydrological variables, especially for water levels. An important advantage is that an ANN model creates a non-linear mapping from input to output. The challenge in using feedforward ANNs for time series data is finding a suitable way of incorporating past observations into the model, such that the temporal correlation is utilized. A comparative study of ANN models for groundwater level forecasting was conducted by Yoon et al. [25]. Their solution to modelling the time series data was to *lag* the variables, i.e., using a time-delayed version of the data as additional input. Another approach to modelling time series data is by applying a Fourier Transformation to the input space, which was first proposed and applied by Wang et al. [23]. Tiwari et al. [22] used a similar approach, using wavelet transforms, to develop an accurate model for predicting floods in an Indian river basin up to 10 h ahead.

Recurrent Neural Networks (RNNs) were specifically designed to process sequential data: their architecture allows them to consider network output of previous time steps in later iterations [6], thus retaining memory. The difficult task of learning both short-term and long-term dependencies without losing efficiency is a well-studied problem [3,13]. Various RNN architectures were compared and successfully applied by Groenen [7] for seasonality extraction, residual learning and accurate prediction of wastewater inflow at municipal wastewater treatment plants.

There are generally two approaches to forecasting multiple subsequent observations of a time series. A recursive forecasting (sometimes also called iterative forecasting) model repeatedly generates a prediction for a single period ahead, using a fixed window of observations and previous predictions. A direct forecasting model generates a prediction for variables multiple time steps ahead, and this predictions is independent of the (predictions of) observations in between. Various studies compared the performance of both approaches using ANNs, but the results are mixed and thus inconclusive [10,12,17].

3   Methodology

In this section, we first describe the conditional forecasting problem and the time series data that is available. Then, we describe several time series modelling approaches from literature, that we use to generate conditional forecasts for our data. Lastly, we propose our own method for conditional forecasting called the Encoder/Decoder RNN with Exogenous Variables.

3.1 Problem Description

The water management system in the Noordoostpolder is governed by employees of the Waterschap Zuiderzeeland. Their job is to manage the influx and efflux of water into the region. The influx of water to the polder consists of surface water from surrounding regions, groundwater seepage and precipitation. Water inside the polder flows along channels to one of 3 large pumping stations responsible for the efflux, which are operated manually.

Hydrologists at Waterschap Zuiderzeeland made an assessment of vital locations in the region based on connectivity, distance, flow directions and management practice. Surface water level series at 3 different locations were pointed out as target variables for the conditional forecast: predictions for these locations are informative and useful for the water managers. Besides this, it was decided that ground water level series for 2 locations, precipitation, and flow rates for the 3 large pumping stations would be the main descriptive variables for generating the prediction. Figure 1 shows a map of the Noordoostpolder, with the vital water system locations. Table 1 contains identifiers for each of the measurement series and a description of the location where these measurements were recorded.

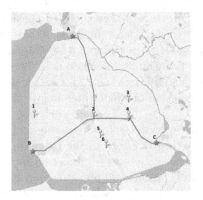

Fig. 1. Vital locations in the water management system of the Noordoostpolder. Numbers indicate water level measurement locations, letters indicate pumping stations. See Table 1 for a description of some of these points.

We derive using domain knowledge that ground and surface water measurements should be considered endogenous variables, because they are dependent upon each other and on other variables. Flow rates and precipitation can be treated as exogenous variables. Precipitation is the influx of water to the Noordoostpolder and is therefore independent of the water levels. Flow rates measure the amount of water that is displaced by the pumping stations and are defined by the pumping protocol. The available data consists of measurements every 15 min for all time steps between 2015 and 2018.

The conditional forecasting problem is formalized as follows. Let us denote the multivariate time series of length T with n endogenous variables as $\mathbf{y}_t \in \mathbb{R}^n$,

Table 1. Names for important measurement locations in this work, along with their official identifier defined by Waterschap Zuiderzeeland, type of measurement recorded at the location, and an indication of its position in the map of the Noordoostpolder shown in Fig. 1

Name	Identifier	Type	Unit	Location
WH2	NOP.PM4810.LT1	Surface water	cm NAP	2
WH3	MP6002	Surface water	cm NAP	3
WH5	NOP.ST4775.LT3	Surface water	cm NAP	5
GW1	21BN.093.01	Ground water	cm NAP	Near C
GW2	15HN.018.01	Ground water	cm NAP	Between 1 and A
FR2000	NOP.2000_TOT	Flow rate	m^3/hour	A
FR2100	NOP.2100_TOT	Flow rate	m^3/hour	C
FR2200	NOP.2200_TOT	Flow rate	m^3/hour	B
MWSP	KNMI Marknesse	Precipitation	mm/hour	Near 4

and the time series with m exogenous variables $\mathbf{x}_t \in \mathbb{R}^m$ for $0 \leq t < T$. Given a time step O called the *forecasting origin* and a parameter $h > 0$ called the *forecasting horizon*, we want a prediction for observations $y_{O+1}, \ldots y_{O+h}$. The model generating these predictions should use $y_t, \ldots y_O, x_t, \ldots x_O$ as well as $x_{O+1}, \ldots x_{O+h}$ as input, for some $t < O$. This generates a forecast of $\mathbf{y}$ conditioned on the future path of $\mathbf{x}$.

In our experiments, we split the time series data in two parts. The training set consist of all observations in 2015, 2016 and 2017, the test set of all observations in 2018. The former is used to tune the model parameters, the latter is only used to realistically evaluate the forecasting performance. For forecast evaluation, we choose forecast origins $O_i = 12{:}00{:}00$ (midday) for each day i in out test set, and we choose $h = 96$, which corresponds to forecasts up to 24 h ahead. The target variables are series WH2, WH3 and WH5, since the surface water levels provide relevant insight for the Waterschap Zuiderzeeland.

The modelling choices described above, made in consultation with Waterschap Zuiderzeeland, ensure that the forecasting models are useful and meaningful for the hydrologists and managers. The selected measurement series can be made accessible online, ensuring up-to-date forecasts. The choice of exogenous variables ensures that future paths can be easily constructed, using an assumption about actions of pumping station managers. By generating conditional forecasts for up to 24 h in the future, hydrologists can compare and evaluate various scenario's, and use these to adjust and improve their operations for the next day.

3.2 Forecasting Models

The first method we use to forecast the values in $\mathbf{y}_t$ is using VAR and VECM models [16], which are commonly used in time series analysis and are characterized by the assumption of linear dependencies. These models produce recursive forecasts, and their most important parameter is the lag parameter p for defining the number of past observations of $\mathbf{y}_t$ and $\mathbf{x}_t$ that are taken into account.

As a generalization of these linear models, we consider the feedforward Artificial Neural Network (ANN) [11], also called Multilayer Perceptron (MLP). The generic model architecture is used to learn a non-linear mapping from some input vector $\mathbf{I}$ to output $\mathbf{O}$. It consists of k layers L_i, with $i = 1, \ldots, k$, having l_i neurons in each layer. Neurons in the input layer are activated using input data, simply using $L_1 = \mathbf{I}$. Neurons in consecutive layers are activated through weighted connections with the previous layer, as follows:

$$L_{i+1} = \alpha(\mathbf{W}_i L_i + b_i) \qquad \text{for } i = 1, \ldots, k-1 \tag{1}$$

where L_i and L_{i+1} are vectors of size $l_i \times 1$ and $l_{i+1} \times 1$ respectively, $\mathbf{W}_i$ is an $l_{i+1} \times l_i$ matrix containing coefficients (weights) and b_i is a vector of size $l_{i+1} \times 1$ containing coefficients. The function $\alpha : \mathbb{R} \to \mathbb{R}$ is some non-linear *activation function* that is applied element-wise. The above is called the *feedforward step*, producing the output L_k: using a learning algorithm such as gradient descent backpropagation [11], the error between L_k and the desired output $\mathbf{O}$ is iteratively decreased.

We apply the generic feedforward ANN to time series forecasting in two ways. Recursive forecasting can be done using $\mathbf{I} = \{\mathbf{y}_{t-p}, \ldots \mathbf{y}_{t-1}, \mathbf{x}_{t-p}, \ldots \mathbf{x}_t\}$ as input, and $\mathbf{O} = \{\hat{\mathbf{y}}_t\}$. We thus have $l_1 = p(n+m) + m$ and $l_k = n$. This network can now be used recursively, using previous predictions as input, to generate forecasts for time steps $t+1, \ldots t+h-1$. Alternatively, we can implement an ANN for direct forecasting by choosing $L_1 = \{\mathbf{y}_{t-p}, \ldots \mathbf{y}_{t-1}, \mathbf{x}_{t-p}, \ldots \mathbf{x}_{t+h-1}\}$ as input, and $L_k = \{\hat{\mathbf{y}}_t, \ldots \hat{\mathbf{y}}_{t+h-1}\}$. In this case, we have $l_1 = p(n+m) + hm$ and $l_k = hn$. This network is not used recursively, but instead generates predictions for all desired time steps using a single feedforward operation.

Finally, we consider Recurrent Neural Networks (RNNs) and look at two common ways in which we can use these to generate conditional forecasts. RNNs provide an extension to feedforward ANNs, in that they are specifically designed to process sequences of observations. Instead of concatenating many observations into a single input vector like the ANN, the RNN takes a multivariate time series $\mathbf{I}_t \in \mathbb{R}^m$ for $1 \leq t \leq T$ as input, mapping it to the output series $\mathbf{O}_t \in \mathbb{R}^n$ by processing each time step t individually. What also distinguishes the RNN architecture is that a layer of RNN neurons uses the layer's activations at the previous time step as additional input. A single RNN layer L_{i+1} thus computes:

$$L_{i+1,t} = \alpha(\mathbf{W}_1 \sigma(L_{i+1,t-1}) + \mathbf{W}_2 L_{i,t} + b) \qquad \text{for } t = 1, \ldots, T \tag{2}$$

where the function $\sigma : \mathbb{R} \to \mathbb{R}$ is an element-wise function and the other terms are similar to the feedforward ANN case. The term $\sigma(L_{i,t})$ is called the hidden state of the i'th network layer: its initial state $\sigma(L_{i,0})$ can be specified by the user, set to 0 or be learned.

Learning the weights for an RNN could lead to several problems: since errors must be propagated over many time steps, the gradients could either *vanish* or *explode* (i.e., extreme decrease or increase in the norm). To counteract this, specialized RNN neuron architectures have been developed, such as the *Long Short-Term Memory* (LSTM) [6] and the *Gated Recurrent Unit* (GRU) [4].

Conditional time series forecasting using an RNN is not straightforward. The most common solution is to define an RNN that generates 1-ahead predictions, as seen in [8]. For this model, we choose $\mathbf{I}_t = \{\mathbf{y}_{t-1}, \mathbf{x}_t\}$ and $\mathbf{O}_t = \{\mathbf{y}_t\}$. However, for multi-step ahead forecasting, this recursive approach is counter intuitive. The RNN uses as input both its previous prediction and its previous hidden state: this could distort the memory management of the RNN and lead to extreme accumulation of errors for large h.

The second approach is to use $\mathbf{I}_t = \{\mathbf{y}_{t-h}, \mathbf{x}_t\}$ and $\mathbf{O}_t = \{\mathbf{y}_t\}$. This way, the RNN is not applied recursively and its memory is efficiently used. However, the input series is now composed of variables with substantial time shifts, which could lead to problems. To prevent the extraction of misleading patterns, we are required to use a moving average series of $\mathbf{y}_t$ instead of the actual measurements, resulting in a loss of information. Additionally, this approach forces us to use input sequences of $\mathbf{y}$ and $\mathbf{x}$ of the same length and we can not use $\mathbf{x}_t$ for $t < T$.

3.3   Encoder/Decoder RNN with Exogenous Variables

The above suggests that conditional forecasting using RNNs does not work very well, so we propose our own architecture for this problem. Requirements are that it allows us to use input sequences of $\mathbf{y}$ and $\mathbf{x}$ of varying length without time shifts, and that the memory management of the RNN is used efficiently during forecasting.

Our proposed approach to conditional forecasting with RNNs can be described as an *encoder/decoder approach with exogenous variables*. It consist of two steps: first, given origin O, horizon h and lag p, we encode the observations in $\mathbf{x}$ and $\mathbf{y}$ at times $O - p \leq t < O$ using an RNN layer of size l_1. This can simply be done using $\mathbf{I}_t^1 = \{\mathbf{y}_t, \mathbf{x}_t\}$, since all these observations are known. We only keep the last output of this RNN layer, instead of the entire series. The resulting output, which we call the encoding E, is a vector of values of size $l_1 \times 1$.

The second step is to turn the output of the first RNN layer, E, into predictions for $\mathbf{y}_{O+1}, ..., \mathbf{y}_{O+h}$. We do this by concatenating copies of the encoding to each time step in $\mathbf{x}_{O+1}, ..., \mathbf{x}_{O+h}$: the result is a new time series $\mathbf{z}_{O+1}, ..., \mathbf{z}_{O+h}$, with $\mathbf{z}_t = \{\mathbf{x}_t, E\}$. We use this combined time series as input to the second RNN layer, thus we write $\mathbf{I}_t^2 = \{\mathbf{x}_t, E\}$. This second RNN layer produces the predictions for $\mathbf{y}_{O+1}, ..., \mathbf{y}_{O+h}$, thus we write $\mathbf{O}_t = \{\mathbf{y}_t\}$. While the architecture appears to consist of two separate models, the encoder can not be trained without a decoder. In summary, our architecture generates predictions $\mathbf{O}_O, ... \mathbf{O}_{O+h-1}$ using an encoding of $\mathbf{I}_{O-p}^1, ... \mathbf{I}_{O-1}^1$ and using $\mathbf{I}_O^2, ... \mathbf{I}_{O+h-1}^2$ as additional information during decoding. Figure 2 contains a simplified, schematic representation of this RNN architecture.

The procedure of encoding and decoding a time series using RNNs is also called *sequence to sequence* (seq2seq) modelling, as proposed by Sutskever et al. [21]. In that work, it was not applied to measurement time series, but to words: translating sentences from one language to another, with good results.

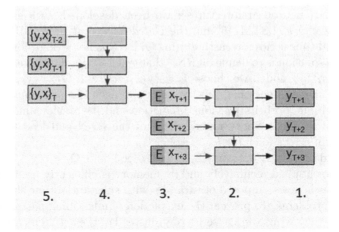

Fig. 2. Schematic representation of the Encoder/Decoder with Exogenous Variables RNN structure, with input data before the forecast horizon (5), first RNN layer (4), concatenation of exogenous variables after the forecast horizon and the copies of the encoding (3), second RNN layer (2) and the generated forecasts (1).

The most important difference with our application, and therefore the novelty of our approach, is that the initial seq2seq modelling was not conditional: there was no notion of exogenous values x_{O+1}, ..., x_{O+h}, but instead, only the copies of the encoding E were used as input to the second RNN layer.

4   Experimental Setup

As mentioned before, we use two parts of the available data: observations in 2015, 2016 and 2017 for tuning the model parameters, observations in 2018 to evaluate forecasts. The forecasting approach described, using $O_i = 12{:}00{:}00$ (midday) for each day i in 2018 and $h = 96$, results in a series of predictions $\hat{y}$ for all the water levels y in the testing set. We choose to evaluate the forecasts by determining the Root Mean Squared Error (RMSE) and Mean Average Percentage Error (MAPE) [2] of $\hat{y}$ and y. We also determine the squared Pearson correlation coefficient of $\hat{y}$ and y, sometimes referred to as the 'pseudo-R^2', which we shall simply reference as R^2. We show the results for the surface water level series WH2, WH3 and WH5, since these are the target variables of this study.

Methods for estimating VAR and VECM models, as well as generating their predictions on new data, are provided in the R package 'tsDyn'[20]. The package does not support the inclusion of lags of exogenous variables: the exogenous data thus had to be temporally transformed, creating new columns with time-delayed measurements.

All methods for defining and training ANN and RNN models are implemented in the 'Keras' python package, which can be controlled from the R environment using the R package called 'Keras' [1]. Implementing the feedforward

ANN models required temporal transformation of the data. To speed up training, measurements were normalized to the interval [0,1] using min-max scaling. Keras automatically uses the last 20% of observations in the training set as validation set: to prevent overfitting we defined an early stopping criterion based on the performance on the validation set. No other regularization techniques were used to generate the results in this paper.

To be able to efficiently reference the neural network model architectures, we introduce the following notation. 1-NN$_{i,j}(p)$ is used to describe a neural network generating 1-step ahead predictions, with two hidden layers of sizes i and j, and lag order p for the endogenous variables. Neural networks with only 1 hidden layer have no parameter j. D-NN$_{i,j}(p)$ is used to describe a direct forecasting ANN, with the same parameters. We reference the RNN architectures in a similar fashion. First, models are referenced by the types of neurons in the layers, namely, "LSTM" or "GRU". 1-LSTM$_{i,j}$ indicates an LSTM model that is trained for 1-ahead predictions with two layers of sizes i and j. XY-LSTM$_{i,j}$ is used to reference an LSTM model that implements the second RNN approach described: predicting $\mathbf{y_t}$ using $\mathbf{I}_t = \{\text{Mean}(\mathbf{y}_{t-h-192}, \ldots \mathbf{y}_{t-h}), \mathbf{x}_t\}$. If either of the two models above has only one layer, the variable j is omitted. Lastly, ED-LSTM$_{i,j}$ is used to reference an LSTM model that implements the encoder/decoder architecture with exogenous variables, which always requires at least two RNN layers.

5   Results

We begin by determining a baseline performance. This naive forecast is defined as follows: for each forecasting horizon $T_i = 12:00:00$ (midday) for every day i, we predict that the water levels in the next 24 h are equal to the average water level of the past 24 h. In Table 2, we show this baseline performance, expressed RMSE, MAPE and R^2.

Also in Table 2 are the RMSE, MAPE and R^2 of various VAR(p) and VECM(p) models. We observe that increasing the lag order p, and thereby increasing the model complexity, leads to a better performance. We also observe that even with the simplest VAR model, we are able to greatly improve the naive baseline performance.

Next, we evaluate the feedforward ANN architectures for both recursive and direct forecasting. We chose to present the models with lag order $p = 96$: lower values for p yielded worse results, and results for higher values of p were comparable or worse. The RMSE, MAPE and R^2 for the predictions on the test set are shown in Table 3. These ANN models are non-linear and contain many more parameters than the VAR models: the NN model complexity is therefore much higher. We observe that generating the recursive forecasts using ANNs yields bad results: it hardly improves the baseline model. This can likely be attributed to the accumulation of errors when forecasting multiple time steps ahead: for NN models, these negative effects are more extreme compared to the VAR/VECM models, due to the increased model complexity.

Table 2. Forecasting accuracy expressed as RMSE, MAPE and R^2 for the baseline predictor and various VAR(p) and VECM(p) models evaluated on the test set. In bold: for each target variable, its highest quality prediction with respect to RMSE, MAPE or R^2.

Model	WH2			WH3			WH5		
	RMSE	MAPE	R^2	RMSE	MAPE	R^2	RMSE	MAPE	R^2
Baseline	4.94	.0067	.45	5.17	.0064	.78	5.45	.0069	.37
VAR(8)	3.36	.0040	.84	3.65	.0043	.9	3.5	.0038	.77
VECM(8)	3.23	.0039	.83	3.51	.0040	.91	3.35	.0035	.78
VECM(24)	3.15	.0037	.84	3.35	.0038	**.92**	3.33	.0035	.78
VECM(48)	2.85	.0032	.86	3.26	**.0035**	**.92**	3.33	**.0034**	.79
VECM(96)	2.66	.0029	.86	3.28	.0036	.91	3.3	.0035	.78
VAR(192)	**2.50**	**.0028**	**.87**	3.22	.0037	**.92**	**3.13**	.0035	.78
VECM(192)	2.60	.0029	**.87**	**3.18**	**.0035**	**.92**	3.15	**.0034**	**.80**

We conclude from the D-NN results that generating direct forecasts using ANNs improves the performance of the VAR/VECM models, in particular for WH5. Nevertheless, the VAR/VECM model performance proves to be a reasonable baseline for model comparison. We also generated visualizations of the D-$NN_{96}(96)$ predictions for an informative subset of observations: these are shown in Fig. 3. We observe that the minimal and maximal water levels are properly predicted by the model, but the timing and steepness of the fluctuations is not very accurate. The performance metrics and visualizations for the D-NN model were presented to hydrologists at Waterschap Zuiderzeeland: they indicated that the forecasts are accurate enough to be used for decision support if they are generated for up to 24 h ahead.

The forecasting performance metrics of several models of the 1-RNN and XY-RNN architecture are shown in Table 4. These models were evaluated to be able to compare ANN and RNN architectures, to study the effect of using either LSTM neurons or GRU neurons, and to get an idea of the optimal RNN model size. We observe that recursive forecasting using RNNs (the 1-RNN models) yield even worse results than the recursive ANN models. A possible reason for this is that the error accumulation occurs both in the hidden states and in the input data for recursive forecasting RNNs. It also becomes clear that models with GRU neurons consistently yield better results than LSTM neurons. Lastly, we see that the results of the XY-RNN are slightly worse than the D-NN results. Moreover, the XY-RNN models are unable to yield better results than the VAR/VECM models. This is remarkable, because both the D-NN and XY-RNN models generate forecasts that do not suffer from an accumulation of error in the input data.

In Table 5 we show the forecasting performance of several RNN models with the proposed Encoder/Decoder RNN architectre. We conclude that the perfor-

Table 3. Forecasting performance expressed as RMSE, MAPE and R^2 for various ANN models with lag order $p = 96$. Performance was evaluated by generating forecasts on the test set. In bold: for each target variable, its highest quality prediction with respect to RMSE, MAPE or R^2.

Model	WH2			WH3			WH5		
	RMSE	MAPE	R^2	RMSE	MAPE	R^2	RMSE	MAPE	R^2
1-NN$_{24}$(96)	7.22	.0080	.36	16.17	.0231	.49	8.77	.0096	.24
1-NN$_{48}$(96)	4.23	.0051	.71	6.1	.0074	.78	5.86	.0076	.58
1-NN$_{48,16}$(96)	3.28	.0049	.78	4.73	.0059	.87	4.59	.0060	.70
1-NN$_{48,48}$(96)	4.18	.0052	.64	5.41	.0071	.82	5.2	.0069	.57
D-NN$_{24}$(96)	2.37	.0030	**.89**	3.2	.0040	.92	2.76	.0038	.84
D-NN$_{48}$(96)	**2.35**	**.0029**	.89	3.15	**.0037**	**.92**	2.85	.0038	.84
D-NN$_{96}$(96)	2.68	.0036	**.89**	**3.11**	.0038	**.92**	**2.49**	**.0033**	**.86**
D-NN$_{200}$(96)	3.05	.0040	.84	3.45	.0045	.91	3.64	.0047	.81
D-NN$_{48,16}$(96)	2.63	.0039	.86	4.23	.0053	.91	2.76	.0039	.85
D-NN$_{48,48}$(96)	3.03	.0043	.85	3.94	.0044	**.92**	3.35	.0047	.82
D-NN$_{96,16}$(96)	2.46	.0033	.88	4.16	.0049	.9	2.57	**.0033**	.85
D-NN$_{96,48}$(96)	2.98	.0040	.82	3.46	.0045	.91	3.39	.0043	.80

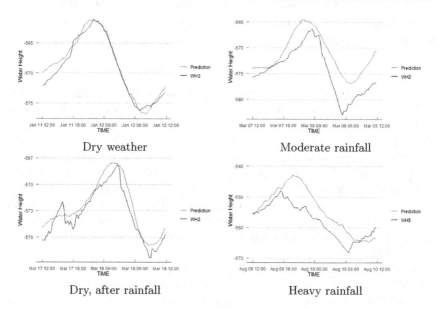

Dry weather   Moderate rainfall

Dry, after rainfall   Heavy rainfall

Fig. 3. Exemplary selection of WH2, WH3 and WH5 water levels, and the direct forecasts generated by the D-NN$_{96}$(96) model. Captions indicate the weather conditions on the day for which the forecast was generated.

Table 4. Forecasting performance expressed as RMSE, MAPE and R^2 of RNN models. Performance was evaluated by generating forecasts on the test set. In bold: for each target variable, its highest quality prediction with respect to either RMSE, MAPE or R^2.

Model	WH2			WH3			WH5		
	RMSE	MAPE	R^2	RMSE	MAPE	R^2	RMSE	MAPE	R^2
1-LSTM$_{25}$	7.00	.0091	.48	2.84	.0289	.55	6.65	.0067	.48
1-GRU$_{25}$	6.47	.0081	.57	7.32	.0121	.72	5.01	.0061	.64
1-LSTM$_{50}$	12.66	.0168	.00	24.83	.0210	.35	17.21	.0209	.00
1-GRU$_{50}$	4.04	.0047	.70	9.90	.0115	.41	3.97	.0042	.69
1-GRU$_{100}$	5.83	.0070	.40	11.09	.0163	.64	7.22	.0085	.35
1-GRU$_{50,50}$	9.50	.0122	.58	7.56	.0089	.54	6.16	.0075	.46
1-GRU$_{100,50}$	5.15	.0066	.69	8.96	.0113	.67	6.20	.0079	.52
XY-GRU$_{16}$	3.40	.0047	**.81**	3.79	.0047	.89	3.56	.0044	.71
XY-GRU$_{25}$	3.35	.0046	**.81**	**3.47**	**.0044**	**.91**	**2.83**	**.0037**	**.81**
XY-GRU$_{50}$	4.07	.0056	.78	4.43	.0057	.86	3.71	.0047	.76
XY-GRU$_{25,25}$	3.83	.0054	.78	4.03	.0051	.87	3.47	.0044	.74
XY-GRU$_{50,16}$	3.68	.0053	**.81**	3.83	.0051	.90	3.21	.0042	.77
XY-GRU$_{50,50}$	4.45	.0062	.74	4.17	.0055	.87	4.04	.0052	.70
XY-GRU$_{100,50}$	**3.01**	**.0042**	**.81**	3.94	.0054	.90	3.27	.0045	.78
XY-GRU$_{100,100}$	3.73	.0053	.80	3.89	.0049	.88	3.40	.0042	.74

mance of the ED-RNN model is comparable to the best performing alternative model (the D-NN) and better than the other results we have seen so far. Table 5 also contains the performance metrics for an ensemble model, containing the models ED-GRU$_{12,12}$, ED-GRU$_{25,50}$, D-NN$_{48}$(96) and D-NN$_{96}$(96). The predictions of the ensemble model are defined as the average of the 4 predictions from the individual models at each time step. The ensemble model shows that there is still room for improvement. Additionally, Fig. 4 contains informative visualizations of the predictions generated by the ED-GRU$_{25,50}$ model. From this, we conclude that the timing and steepness of fluctuations are more accurately predicted by the ED-RNN model compared to the D-NN, except for situations with heavy rainfall.

Lastly, we contrast the conditional forecasts generated by the D-NN$_{96}$(96) and ED-GRU$_{25,50}$ models in the case of an alternative path for the exogenous variables. Figure 5 contains, for a selected date in the test set, the original and alternative future paths for the variables on which we condition the forecasts. The alternative scenario has flow rates that are lower (less pumping) and with different timing (FR2000 is activated later, FR2200 is de-activated earlier). Hydrologists at Waterschap Zuiderzeeland indicated that, based on their domain experience, this alternative pumping scenario should result in higher water levels

Table 5. Forecasting performance expressed as RMSE, MAPE and R^2 of Encoder/Decoder RNNs with exogenous variables. Additionally, the performance for an ensemble model consisting of 2 ED-GRU models and 2 D-NN models. Performance was evaluated by generating forecasts on the test set. In bold: for each target variable, its highest quality prediction with respect to either RMSE, MAPE or R^2 by a single model.

Model	WH2			WH3			WH5		
	RMSE	MAPE	R^2	RMSE	MAPE	R^2	RMSE	MAPE	R^2
ED-GRU$_{8,8}$	2.98	.0039	.84	5.39	.0055	.78	3.01	.0038	.80
ED-GRU$_{8,12}$	2.51	.0032	**.87**	3.31	.0041	.92	**2.74**	**.0036**	.83
ED-GRU$_{12,12}$	**2.37**	**.0029**	**.87**	3.24	.0040	.92	2.79	**.0036**	.83
ED-GRU$_{25,25}$	2.85	.0036	.85	3.23	.0041	.92	3	.0038	.79
ED-GRU$_{25,50}$	2.95	.0038	.86	**3.04**	**.0037**	**.93**	2.85	**.0036**	**.84**
ED-GRU$_{50,25}$	3.28	.0044	.85	3.31	.0040	.92	2.84	**.0036**	.83
ED-GRU$_{50,50}$	3.04	.0039	.84	3.49	.0043	.91	2.87	**.0036**	.82
Ensemble	2.29	.0029	.91	2.71	.0032	.94	2.25	.0029	.89

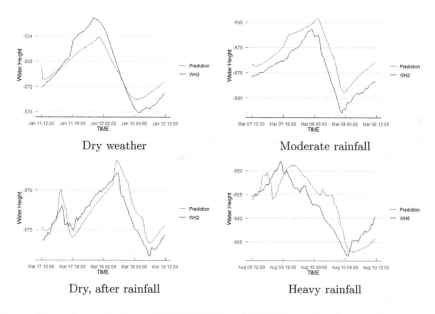

Dry weather   Moderate rainfall

Dry, after rainfall   Heavy rainfall

Fig. 4. Exemplary selection of WH2, WH3 and WH5 water levels, and the forecasts generated by the ED-GRU$_{25,50}$ model. Captions indicate the weather conditions on the day for which the forecast was generated.

with a delayed peak. Figures 6 and 7 contain the conditional forecasts generated for both the original and alternative scenario, and the original water levels. The alternative D-NN forecasts did not contain the expected delayed peaks, and for WH3 it has mostly lower water levels, which is unrealistic. The alternative ED-RNN forecasts did contain the expected changes compared to the original scenario. According to the knowledge and experience of the hydrologists at Waterschap Zuiderzeeland, the alternative forecasts of the ED-RNN model are therefore realistic and could be used for real-life scenario evaluation.

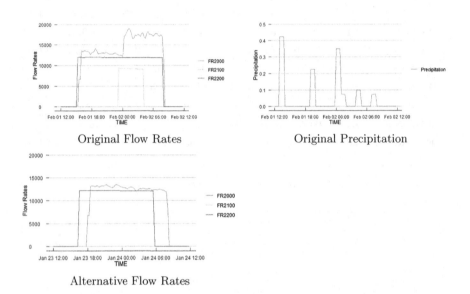

Original Flow Rates   Original Precipitation

Alternative Flow Rates

Fig. 5. Visualization of the exogenous variables used to generate the original (old) prediction above, and below for the alternative (new) prediction for February 2, 2018.

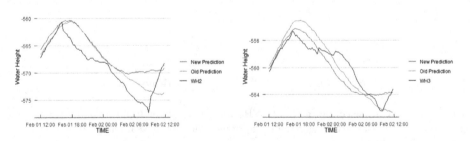

Fig. 6. Actual water height, original forecast (old) and alternative conditional forecast (new) on February 2, for target series WH2 and WH3. Predictions are generated by the D-NN$_{96}$(96) model.

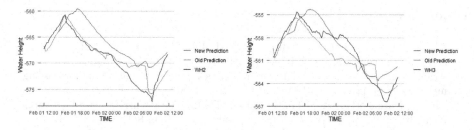

Fig. 7. Actual water height, original forecast (old) and alternative conditional forecast (new) on February 2, for target series WH2 and WH3. Predictions are generated by the ED-RNN$_{25,50}$ model.

6 Conclusion

This paper describes a practical situation in which the application of forecasting models could lead to energy efficiency and decreased risk in water level management. In consultation with the Waterschap Zuiderzeeland, we formalized the problem as a conditional forecasting problem using time series measurements of hydrological variables. Our modelling choices, e.g. the forecasting horizon and the inclusion of future paths of exogenous variables, ensure that the resulting forecasting problem imitates a real-life forecasting task.

We have proposed a novel architecture for conditional forecasting with RNNs. Our approach, described as an *Encoder/Decoder with Exogenous Variables* RNN (ED-RNN) model, is intuitive in its memory management, can be easily extended and is flexible in the inclusion of past observations and future paths of exogenous variables. It combines the ideas of sequence-to-sequence (Seq2Seq) RNN models with the conditional forecasting literature, resulting in a model architecture that can be used for modelling in all sorts of time series problems.

We showed that on this specific conditional forecasting problem, the results of the ED-RNN are comparable to the best performing alternative model (the D-NN), and better than the other alternatives considered. We observe that the predictions generated by the ED-RNN more accurately capture short-term fluctuations in the water heights than the predictions of the D-NN. Additionally, the ED-RNN generates realistic alternative conditional forecasts. Therefore, the model is applicable for real-life scenario evaluation and decision support by the Waterschap Zuiderzeeland.

Our search for model parameters, such as the model size, lag parameter, number of iterations and stopping criterion, was not exhaustive. Balancing the data and inclusion of additional measurement series were also not investigated. Hence, there is still room for improvement of our models. We conclude that our ED-RNN model architecture is a very interesting option for conditional forecasting with RNNs and that more empirical evaluation is needed to contrast the performance with alternative modelling techniques.

References

1. Alaire, J.J., Chollet, F., RStudio, Google: R Interface to Keras (2019). https://keras.rstudio.com/. Accessed 05 May 2019
2. Armstrong, J.S., Collopy, F.: Error measures for generalizing about forecasting methods: empirical comparisons. Int. J. Forecast. **8**(1), 69–80 (1992)
3. Che, Z., Purushotham, S., Cho, K., Sontag, D., Liu, Y.: Recurrent neural networks for multivariate time series with missing values. Sci. Rep. **8**(1), 6085 (2018)
4. Chung, J., Gulcehre, C., Cho, K., Bengio, Y.: Empirical evaluation of gated recurrent neural networks on sequence modeling. arXiv preprint arXiv:1412.3555 (2014)
5. FutureWater: Rapport Wateraanvoer Noordoostpolder (2006). https://www.futurewater.nl/downloads/2006_Immerzeel_FW50.pdf. Accessed 19 Oct 2018
6. Goodfellow, I., Bengio, Y., Courville, A., Bengio, Y.: Deep Learning, vol. 1. MIT Press, Cambridge (2016)
7. Groenen, I.: Representing seasonal patterns in gated recurrent neural networks for multivariate time series forecasting. Master thesis (2018). http://www.scriptiesonline.uba.uva.nl/657906. Accessed 20 Oct 2018
8. Guo, T., Lin, T., Lu, Y.: An interpretable LSTM neural network for autoregressive exogenous model. arXiv preprint arXiv:1804.05251 (2018)
9. Hamilton, D.P., Schladow, S.G.: Prediction of water quality in lakes and reservoirs. Part I-model description. Ecol. Model. **96**(1–3), 91–110 (1997)
10. Hamzaçebi, C., Akay, D., Kutay, F.: Comparison of direct and iterative artificial neural network forecast approaches in multi-periodic time series forecasting. Expert Syst. Appl. **36**(2), 3839–3844 (2009)
11. Haykin, S.S.: Neural Networks and Learning Machines, vol. 3. Pearson Education, Upper Saddle River (2009)
12. Hill, T., Marquez, L., O'Connor, M., Remus, W.: Artificial neural network models for forecasting and decision making. Int. J. Forecast. **10**(1), 5–15 (1994)
13. Hochreiter, S., Schmidhuber, J.: Long short-term memory. Neural Comput. **9**(8), 1735–1780 (1997)
14. Johansen, S.: Estimation and hypothesis testing of cointegration vectors in Gaussian vector autoregressive models. Econometrica: J. Econ. Soc. **59**, 1551–1580 (1991)
15. Konikow, L.F., Bredehoeft, J.D.: Ground-water models cannot be validated. Adv. Water Resour. **15**(1), 75–83 (1992)
16. Lütkepohl, H.: New Introduction to Multiple Time Series Analysis. Springer, Heidelberg (2005)
17. Mishra, A., Desai, V.: Drought forecasting using feed-forward recursive neural network. Ecol. Model. **198**(1–2), 127–138 (2006)
18. Nepf, H.: Drag, turbulence, and diffusion in flow through emergent vegetation. Water Resour. Res. **35**(2), 479–489 (1999)
19. Sophocleous, M.: Interactions between groundwater and surface water: the state of the science. Hydrol. J. **10**(1), 52–67 (2002)
20. Stigler, M.: tsDyn: nonlinear time series models with regime switching (2019). https://www.rdocumentation.org/packages/tsDyn/versions/0.9-44. Accessed 12 June 2019
21. Sutskever, I., Vinyals, O., Le, Q.V.: Sequence to sequence learning with neural networks. In: Advances in Neural Information Processing Systems, pp. 3104–3112 (2014)

22. Tiwari, M.K., Chatterjee, C.: Development of an accurate and reliable hourly flood forecasting model using wavelet-bootstrap-ANN (WBANN) hybrid approach. J. Hydrol. **394**(3–4), 458–470 (2010)
23. Wang, W., Ding, J.: Wavelet network model and its application to the prediction of hydrology. Nat. Sci. **1**(1), 67–71 (2003)
24. Yen, P.H., Jan, C.D., Lee, Y.P., Lee, H.F.: Application of Kalman filter to short-term tide level prediction. J. Waterw. Port Coast. Ocean Eng. **122**(5), 226–231 (1996)
25. Yoon, H., Jun, S.C., Hyun, Y., Bae, G.O., Lee, K.K.: A comparative study of artificial neural networks and support vector machines for predicting groundwater levels in a coastal aquifer. J. Hydrol. **396**(1–2), 128–138 (2011)
26. Zhang, G.P.: Time series forecasting using a hybrid ARIMA and neural network model. Neurocomputing **50**, 159–175 (2003)

Challenges and Limitations in Clustering Blood Donor Hemoglobin Trajectories

Marieke Vinkenoog[1,2]($\boxtimes$) ⓘ, Mart Janssen[1] ⓘ, and Matthijs van Leeuwen[2] ⓘ

[1] Department of Transfusion Technology Assessment,
Sanquin Research, Amsterdam, The Netherlands
m.vinkenoog@sanquin.nl
[2] Leiden Institute of Advanced Computer Science,
Leiden University, Leiden, The Netherlands

Abstract. In order to prevent iron deficiency, Sanquin—the national blood bank in the Netherlands—measures a blood donor's hemoglobin (Hb) level before each donation and only allows a donor to donate blood if their Hb is above a certain threshold. In around 6.5% of blood bank visits by women, the donor's Hb is too low and the donor is deferred from donation. For visits by men, this occurs in 3.0% of cases. To reduce the deferral rate and keep donors healthy and motivated, we would like to identify donors that are at risk of having a low Hb level. To this end we have historical Hb trajectories at our disposal, i.e., time series consisting of Hb measurements recorded for individual donors.

As a first step towards our long-term goal, in this paper we investigate the use of time series clustering. Unfortunately, existing methods have limitations that make them suboptimal for our data. In particular, Hb trajectories are of unequal length and have measurements at irregular intervals. We therefore experiment with two different data representations. That is, we apply a direct clustering method using dynamic time warping, and a trend clustering method using model-based feature extraction. In both cases the clustering algorithm used is k-means.

Both approaches result in distinct clusters that are well-balanced in size. The clusters obtained using direct clustering have a smaller mean within-cluster distance, but those obtained using the model-based features show more interesting trends. Neither approach results in ideal clusters though. We therefore conclude with an elaborate discussion on challenges and limitations that we hope to address in the near future.

Keywords: Time series · Clustering · Blood donation

1   Introduction

Sanquin is the national blood bank in the Netherlands. Every year, about 300 000 donors visit the blood bank, resulting in over 420 000 donations a year. Women are allowed to donate up to three times a year, men up to five times. There are many policies in place to ensure that the blood products that are collected are

© Springer Nature Switzerland AG 2020
V. Lemaire et al. (Eds.): AALTD 2019, LNAI 11986, pp. 72–84, 2020.
https://doi.org/10.1007/978-3-030-39098-3_6

safe for the patients they will be given to. Moreover, Sanquin has the responsibility to prevent volunteer blood donors from developing health problems related to blood donation. One big risk of regular blood donation is anemia due to low iron stores or iron deficiency. A whole blood[1] donation takes about 500 mL of blood from the donor, which contains 210 to 240 mg iron bound to hemoglobin (Hb). The total concentration of iron in the human body is approximately 38 mg/kg body weight for women and 50 mg/kg body weight for men, so a single blood donation constitutes a substantial loss of iron [5,6].

To prevent donors from becoming iron deficient, their Hb levels are checked before each blood donation. Based on the Hb measurement it is decided whether they may donate at that time: the lower limit for donation is 7.8 mmol/L for women, and 8.4 mmol/L for men. When a donor is below the threshold, they are sent home and can return for donation a few weeks later. This type of deferral occurs quite frequently: about 6.5% of female and 3.0% of male donors have too low Hb levels when they visit the blood bank.

The large number of deferrals is problematic, both for donors and the blood bank: being deferred from donation is demotivating for the donor, who may decide not to return in the future, and not efficient for the blood bank, leading to a higher cost per blood product.

Because of this, Sanquin and other blood banks internationally spend considerable resources on investigating ways to reduce the deferral rate while keeping donors healthy. One asset that can be exploited for this are the Hb measurements that blood banks have recorded in the past. In this paper we report on a preliminary study investigating whether we can distinguish groups of donors having different trends in their Hb trajectories; if this is the case, these trends could be used to devise more personalised invitation and deferral policies.

1.1 Approach and Contributions

We have data available on all blood bank visits in the Netherlands since 2006. For every donor, we have only two relevant background variables: year of birth and sex. It has long been known that age and sex affect Hb levels. Men's levels are higher than women's and decrease with age, while women's levels increase after menopause [7].

Apart from these factors, a large part of the variation in Hb levels can be attributed to diet and lifestyle: the iron richness of the donor's diet and their activity level play a substantial role here. However, we don't have large-scale data on this. The clusters of donors we hope to identify could be a proxy for these variables.

The more interesting part of the data are the Hb measurements taken every time the donor visits the blood bank. Each measurement has a time stamp, and together the individual measurements of a single donor form a time series; we will refer to these time series as Hb trajectories.

---

[1] Whole blood is standard blood; it is also possible to donate specific components.

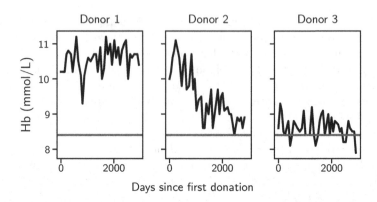

Fig. 1. Hemoglobin trajectories of three male donors. From left to right: a high stable Hb level, a declining Hb level, and a low stable Hb level. The red line is the Hb threshold for donation (8.4 mmol/L for male donors). (Color figure online)

We aim to find groups of donors whose Hb levels are similar throughout their donation history. More specifically, we would like to distinguish donors with a stable (high or low) Hb level from donors with a declining Hb level over time, as these require different donation policies. The three different trends that we expect to find in the data are illustrated in Fig. 1.

Finding groups of similar data points in an unsupervised manner is a typical clustering task and since Hb trajectories are time series, we naturally resort to time series clustering. Time series clustering can be applied in many fields and has been studied for a long time, as a result of which a large number of clustering methods for time series exist [1,8,11].

A big limitation, however, is that most existing algorithms require the time series to be sampled at fixed, equidistant time stamps. In our data, the sampling intervals are highly irregular on two levels. First, the intervals are not uniform across time series; an easy example is that women are allowed to donate three times a year, men five times. Second, the intervals are not uniform within the time series either: sometimes a donor returns for their next donation two months after the previous one, sometimes six months. Donors can also temporarily stop donating, and then return years later. A related limitation that is relevant to our data is that the time series have unequal lengths. Many donors in the data set have been regularly donating for over ten years, while others have just started.

Faced with these challenges, in this paper we will investigate whether we can transform our data for use with a standard clustering method without losing critical information. Specifically, we will employ two approaches: (1) direct clustering using re-sampling combined with dynamic time warping [2] as distance measure, and (2) trend clustering using model-based feature extraction combined with the Euclidean distance. As our main aim is to evaluate and compare the data representations, the choice of a clustering method is less important; we will use k-means [9] because it is straightforward, effective, and well-known.

The main contributions of our preliminary study are (1) a proof-of-concept showing that clustering of Hb trajectories of Dutch blood donors is feasible, and (2) the identification of challenges and limitations of using time series clustering for Hb trajectories. We consider these to be important first steps towards an effective clustering method for irregular time series in which the irregularities itself may contain useful information.

The remainder of the paper is organised as follows. Section 2 provides more details about the data, after which Sect. 3 describes the pre-processing, data representations, and clustering method. Section 4 presents the results, after which we conclude with an elaborate discussion in Sect. 5.

2   Data

Our data consists of all blood donations made at any of Sanquin's locations between January 2006 and June 2018, extracted from the blood bank's database system eProgesa. In total, there are 6 945 611 donations by 688 665 unique donors. Because we are interested in donors' Hb trajectories from their first donation onward, we selected for our analyses all donors that did not visit the blood bank before 2010. It is possible that there are donors in the data set that donated before 2006 and returned after a gap of at least four years, but we expect this number to be low, and their Hb levels similar to actual new donors.

Many types of blood donation take place at Sanquin, the most common being plasma donation and whole blood donation. During plasma donation, red cells are returned to the donor and only the plasma is collected. As hemoglobin is contained in the red blood cells, this type of donation does not have a substantial effect on Hb levels. Therefore, we only look at donors that donate whole blood, during which no blood components are returned to the donor.

We take into account donors that have donated whole blood at least eight times in our time window—once a year on average. There are 23 856 female and 20 299 male donors that fit these criteria. To decrease computation time, we randomly selected 5 000 women and 5 000 men for our experiments. Within this data set, the deferral rate due to low Hb is 7.8% among female donors and 3.3% among male donors.

The two data sets contain 5 000 individual univariate time series each, consisting of the Hb measurements during the visits to the blood bank. Hb is measured in mmol/L. The median number of Hb measurements per time series is 12 for women (interquartile range, IQR 10–14) and 14 for men (IQR 11–19).

The time intervals between measurements differ both within and between time series. The minimum required interval between two donations is 122 days for women and 56 days for men, but it can even be a few years. The median interval for women is 133 days (IQR 112–169) and for men 79 days (IQR 64–114). Aside from the Hb measurements, the only variable used is the sex of the donor. Clustering methods will be applied separately to the female and male subsets.

3   Methods

We will experiment with two data representations and compare the results of the k-means clustering algorithm on both representations. The methods will be compared on cluster tightness using mean within-cluster distance, and visually on the informativeness of the cluster using the graphs of the cluster centroids.

The first method employs direct clustering using dynamic time warping based on the Hb levels at each time point, the second method employs trend clustering using model-based feature extraction. Preprocessing is the same for both.

3.1   Preprocessing

When time series are of equal length and have the same measurement intervals, clustering is relatively straightforward. At each time point, we can calculate the difference between measurements in two time series, and group time series with smaller differences in the same cluster. However, from this perspective our data is rather messy: time series are all of differing lengths and have different measurement intervals, both within and between individuals. While there are more sophisticated ways to handle this (see Sect. 5), none of the existing algorithms that we found are perfectly suited to our data. Therefore, for this first trial we decided to side-step the problem of unequal intervals by resampling the time series to regular intervals by linear interpolation.

We take each donor's first donation since 1 January 2010 as the starting point of their time series. All time stamps are relative to the first time stamp, recorded as days since first donation. Hb values are then resampled to weekly measurements using linear interpolation. This gives a maximum of 439 observations per donor, one for each week between 1 January 2010 and 1 June 2018. Donors that started donating later in the time window will have fewer measurements, and thus have a number of missing values at the tail of the time series. For the first 140 weeks, the number of donors with missing values is almost zero, but then the number of donors that still has measurements starts dropping at a steady rate. We chose to use Hb measurements up to 286 weeks after the first donation, at which time half of our 5000 donors has no missing values, and the other half misses at most 50% of observations.

3.2   Direct Clustering Using Dynamic Time Warping

For this method, the features that we will feed to the clustering algorithm are the resampled Hb measurements as described in the previous section. As a distance measure, we use dynamic time warping (DTW) [2] with the window parameter set to $w = 5$. This algorithm is better-suited to our data than for instance the Euclidean distance, because it takes into account varying speeds and time shifts. Because the time series vary in length, we compare time series only up to the last data point in the shortest series.

The algorithm can be summarized as follows:

1. Calculate the Euclidean distance between the first point in the first series, and every point within the window of $w = 5$ in the second series;
2. Store the minimum distance calculated;
3. Repeat steps 1–2 for all points in the first series;
4. Add all the minimum distances to get the DTW distance.

3.3   Trend Clustering Using Model-Based Feature Extraction

The second method takes as input for the clustering algorithm not the (resampled) time series itself, but rather a set of features that should summarize the time series in such a way that similar time series will have similar feature values. We are interested in distinguishing three types of Hb trajectories: high stable, low stable, and declining. We therefore choose to cluster the trajectories based on the intercept and slope of the linear trend.

The intercept and slope are calculated using linear least-squares regression on the resampled time series described in the previous section, to allow for a direct comparison between the two methods. Because the slope and intercept values are on different scales, we normalize them using a min-max scaler before clustering. The values are then all between 0 and 1, 0 being the minimum value among the time series and 1 the maximum.

3.4   Clustering Algorithm

For the actual clustering, we use k-means clustering [9], a heuristic algorithm that is usually quite fast at finding a local optimum. It requires the user to specify the number of desired clusters k. We chose this well-known algorithm for its wide applicability and straightforward implementation.

For the direct clustering, the input to the algorithm contains the resampled time series. Because of the differing lengths of the time series, we chose to initialise the clusters randomly from a uniform distribution, instead of choosing k time series as initial cluster centroids. The distance measure used is DTW.

For the trend clustering, the input consists of two features per trajectory: the intercept and the slope of the linear trend. As distance measure the Euclidean distance is used.

In general, k-means clustering returns the best results if the algorithm stops when the difference between the cluster centroids in two subsequent iterations is smaller than some ϵ. Because the program is computationally expensive due to the DTW calculations, we opted to let it run for at most five iterations for the first clustering method.

The algorithm is as follows:

1. Initialize k cluster centroids;
2. Assign each time series to the cluster to which it is most similar, based on the specified distance;
3. Recalculate the cluster centroids by taking the average value for each feature;
4. Repeat steps 2–3 for 5 iterations or until convergence.

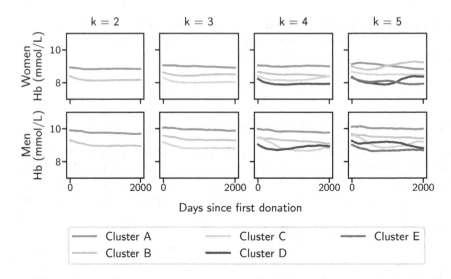

Fig. 2. Cluster centroids after clustering resampled Hb trajectories of 5000 female and 5000 male donors with the k-means clustering algorithm ($k = \{2, 3, 4, 5\}$) and DTW distance as distance measure.

3.5   Evaluation

We compare the clusters based on the two data representations in two ways: cluster tightness and cluster informativeness. The first is a numerical comparison, the second graphical. Cluster tightness is assessed by the mean within-cluster distance. For each cluster, we calculate the distance from the cluster centroid to the individual time series by taking the DTW distance between the two. The mean of these distances is the mean within-cluster distance. We also calculate the sum of the within-cluster distance for each value of k, which is the sum of the DTW distances between the individual time series and the cluster centroids, summed over all clusters. As the number of clusters increases, we expect the sum of the within-cluster distances to decrease.

Cluster informativeness is assessed visually by looking at the graphs of the cluster centroids. We hope to see centroids that are different in slope, and not just horizontal lines with different average Hb values.

4   Results

We will first present the results from both methods separately, then compare the two on cluster tightness and informativeness.

Table 1. The mean distance from the centroid to the time series ($\bar{d}$) and the number of time series in each cluster (N) after direct clustering. Dynamic time warping is used as distance measure. The rightmost column shows the sum of the within-cluster distances.

Sex	k	Cluster A $\bar{d}$ (N)	Cluster B $\bar{d}$ (N)	Cluster C $\bar{d}$ (N)	Cluster D $\bar{d}$ (N)	Cluster E $\bar{d}$ (N)	Sum
Female	2	7.1 (1613)	6.3 (3387)	–	–	–	32670
	3	5.7 (2128)	7.0 (986)	5.9 (1886)	–	–	30135
	4	5.4 (1197)	5.2 (1205)	5.9 (1671)	6.9 (927)	–	29049
	5	6.3 (475)	6.5 (413)	5.5 (1379)	5.9 (1766)	5.4 (967)	28840
Male	2	7.2 (2020)	6.3 (2980)	–	–	–	33260
	3	6.1 (1997)	5.6 (1851)	6.9 (1152)	–	–	30508
	4	7.1 (1600)	5.8 (1589)	5.5 (835)	5.1 (976)	–	30222
	5	4.9 (896)	5.9 (1424)	5.2 (906)	5.5 (871)	6.8 (903)	28567

4.1 Direct Clustering

Figure 2 shows the centroids of the clusters after direct clustering with DTW. At $k = 2$ and $k = 3$, we see that the clusters are based mostly on the mean Hb level in the donors, and cluster centroids are almost parallel. At higher numbers of clusters, we start to see some differences in trends as well, with centroids intersecting each other. At $k > 5$, we saw that centroids start overlapping for longer periods of time and are no longer distinct enough to be informative. These graphs are not included in the paper. In almost all centroids, there is a decrease in Hb value at the beginning of the Hb trajectory.

To assess the tightness of the clusters, Table 1 shows the mean within-cluster distances, with DTW used as distance measure. The total sum of the within-cluster distances decreases as the number of clusters increases, which is expected because the same distance measure was used to create the clusters. The names of the clusters correspond to those in Fig. 2. Table 1 also shows the number of time series assigned to each cluster. We see that in size, the clusters are quite well-balanced: the smallest cluster has size 413 where size 1000 would be expected if all clusters were the same size (female donors, $k = 5$, cluster B).

4.2 Trend Clustering

Figure 3 shows the cluster centroids after clustering on trend features. As after the direct clustering, the centroids are distinct from each other and do not intersect at $k = 2, 3$. From $k = 4$ and up, cluster B shows an interesting new trend in male donors: the slope of the line is much steeper than those of the other clusters.

In Table 2, we see that the mean distance from the centroid to the individual time series is larger than in the clusters obtained using the first method. The sum of the within-cluster distances does not decrease as k increases, and for female donors it even increases substantially. This can happen because in this method, the clusters are decided based on the Euclidean distances between the trend features of the time series, rather than the DTW distance between time series as in the first method.

The number of time series per cluster is mostly well-balanced, although there are some cases of small clusters: at $k = 5$, in male donors, cluster A only contains 386 time series where 1000 would be expected if all clusters were of equal size.

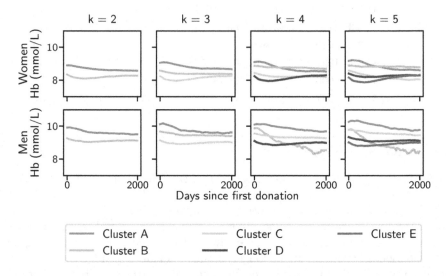

Fig. 3. Cluster centroids after clustering resampled Hb trajectories of 5000 female and 5000 male donors based on the intercept and slope of the linear trend, using the k-means clustering algorithm ($k = \{2, 3, 4, 5\}$). The limits on the y-axis are equal to those of Fig. 2 for comparison.

4.3   Comparison

From the within-cluster distances, it is clear that the direct clustering method leads to tighter clusters. Figure 4 illustrates this well. It shows the result of both direct and trend feature clustering on male donors with $k = 4$ clusters. Each subplot shows the cluster centroid in red, and 100 randomly selected individual time series within the cluster in grey. Although after both direct and trend clustering the cluster centroid lies in the middle of the individual time series, the spread is much smaller in direct than in trend clustering.

In both methods, cluster centroids vary mostly in the average Hb value over time, and not as much in trend, which is what we are mostly interested in. The exception is cluster B in the trend clustering method, which shows a relatively steep downward trend.

Table 2. The mean distance from the centroid to the time series ($\bar{d}$) and the number of time series in each cluster (N) after trend clustering. Dynamic time warping is used as distance measure for evaluation. The rightmost column shows the sum of the within-cluster distances.

Sex	k	Cluster A $\bar{d}$ (N)		Cluster B $\bar{d}$ (N)		Cluster C $\bar{d}$ (N)		Cluster D $\bar{d}$ (N)		Cluster E $\bar{d}$ (N)		Sum
Female	2	8.1	(2028)	6.8	(2972)	–		–		–		36689
	3	10.1	(1075)	6.5	(1727)	9.6	(2198)	–		–		43195
	4	8.2	(602)	10.8	(1181)	6.7	(1362)	10.5	(1855)	–		46318
	5	6.2	(839)	14.1	(1016)	8.5	(881)	11.9	(1761)	8.8	(503)	52431
Male	2	11.0	(2843)	11.1	(2157)	–		–		–		55156
	3	9.5	(831)	6.5	(1924)	8.7	(2245)	–		–		40113
	4	10.8	(389)	15.3	(961)	7.0	(2104)	6.4	(1546)	–		43392
	5	6.0	(386)	6.3	(1071)	7.1	(1378)	7.9	(445)	8.6	(1720)	37234

To verify the stability of the cluster centroids obtained by the k-means algorithm, we ran it several times with different random initialisation values. Visual inspection of the results showed that the algorithm consistently converged to the same centroids.

5   Discussion

The clusters obtained by the two methods are clearly very different. The centroids of the clusters are much more linear when the direct clustering is applied, compared to the trend feature clustering. The mean within-cluster distances are much smaller in the first method, which indicates denser clusters. However, this comparison is biased, because the first method used the same distance measure during clustering, so it is expected to minimise this distance. The second method minimised the Euclidean distance between the linear trend features of the time series, and not the DTW distances.

The results from the direct clustering are in line with our expectations. The clusters suit the time series relatively well, and the total sum of within-cluster distances decreases as the number of clusters increases. However, the time series are clustered together mostly on average Hb level, which is not what we are looking for in this context. We would prefer to identify clusters based on the overall trends of Hb values in each donor, so that we can distinguish donors with a high stable Hb level, a low stable Hb level, and decreasing Hb levels from each other.

This is what we expected to see after clustering time series based on trend. It is partly what we see in the cluster centroids: in male donors, for $k = \{4, 5\}$, cluster B is very distinct from the others and has a steep downward slope. We know that declining Hb trajectories are highly prevalent in female donors as well, but none of those centroids have a slope close to the one in male donors.

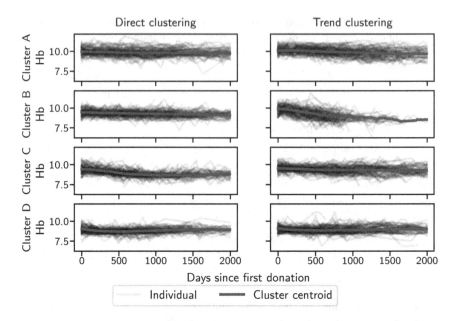

Fig. 4. Cluster centroids after clustering resampled Hb trajectories of 5000 male donors, using direct (left) or trend clustering (right) and k-means clustering with $k = 4$. Red lines are the cluster centroids. 100 randomly sampled individual Hb trajectories from each cluster are also plotted to show the fit. (Color figure online)

An interesting observation is that in almost all clusters, the Hb level is decreasing in the first ±500 days and then plateaus. This indicates that there is an initial effect of blood donation on average Hb levels, but after the initial effect the Hb reaches a new steady state. However, this is only based on the average Hb levels of 5000 donors, and individual Hb trajectories still show a lot of variation over time, making it hard to predict.

Limitations. There are some features in the data that were ignored in this first exploration in Hb trajectory clustering. There is a seasonal component to Hb levels: in warm seasons, levels are lower than in cold seasons. Because we used the number of days since first donation as time points and not the actual dates, we lost this information. An improvement would be to correct for seasonal variations before transforming the time variable. The same applies for the time of day Hb was measured: it is highest in the morning and then drops steadily throughout the day.

A very clear feature of the data that was not used is the unequal sampling interval. Both methods required the intervals to be equal, so we resampled the time series using linear interpolation to satisfy this requirement. This means that we lose the information contained within the sampling intervals, and the resampled data points are of lower accuracy than the original measurements.

The third feature of the data that we would like to include in further analyses is whether or not a donation followed the Hb measurement. If the Hb level is below the threshold of 7.8 mmol/L for women or 8.4 mmol/L for men, no donation is made, and it is likely that the next Hb measurement is higher. There is also an interaction with the interval length: if a donor has donated blood, the next measurement has to be at least 56 days later, but if the Hb level was too low, it can be shorter.

Other Irregular Time Series Frameworks. There are many more fields in which irregular time series are observed (astronomy, medicine, economics, etc.), and in which the irregularities contain information we don't want to lose by transforming the data to equally spaced data. Some algorithms focus on calculating rolling time series operators such as simple moving averages or exponential moving averages [4]. This is a more elegant form of interpolation than what we have applied here, but the information contained in the intervals themselves is still lost.

A more fitting approach for our data might be a framework that takes two time series as input for each donor: one containing the Hb measurements and one containing the interval lengths. We might consider a move to more complex algorithms, such as recurrent neural networks (RNNs) in combination with long short-term memory (LSTM) cells [12]. While the majority of RNN implementations still uses fixed time steps, the Phased LSTM model, which introduces an additional time gate, handles irregular intervals without losing the information contained within the time steps [10]. A similar approach is Time-LSTM, which has been used to model website users' sequential actions by taking into account the sampling intervals [13].

Another deep learning model that looks at informative missingness is GRU-D [3], which is based on gated recurrent units (GRU). It has been applied to real-world clinical data sets, where the missingness rate is highly correlated with variables of interest. This model has achieved good results in supervised classification tasks, and may also have useful applications for our unsupervised clustering task.

Future Work. By clustering donors' Hb trajectories we hope to find clusters of donors that respond similarly to frequent blood donation. We assume that the clusters are a proxy for unobserved donor characteristics, such as iron intake, diet, physical activity levels and iron needs. If clustering is successful, we want to search for correlations between the cluster and donor information collected in questionnaires in previous studies carried out at Sanquin (Donor InSight). Eventually, the goal is to predict as early as possible in a donor's donation career which cluster they belong to, and to assign an optimal donation frequency based on this information. That way, deferral due to low Hb may be minimised, and donors will stay healthy and motivated.

References

1. Aghabozorgi, S., Shirkhorshidi, A.S., Wah, T.Y.: Time-series clustering-a decade review. Inf. Syst. **53**, 16–38 (2015)
2. Berndt, D.J., Clifford, J.: Using dynamic time warping to find patterns in time series. In: Proceedings of the 3rd International Conference on Knowledge Discovery and Data Mining, pp. 359–370. AAAI Press (1994)
3. Che, Z., Purushotham, S., Cho, K., Sontag, D., Liu, Y.: Recurrent neural networks for multivariate time series with missing values. Sci. Rep. **8**(1), 6085 (2018)
4. Eckner, A.: Algorithms for unevenly-spaced time series: moving averages and other rolling operators. In: Working Paper (2012)
5. Finch, C.A., Cook, J., Labbe, R., Culala, M.: Effect of blood donation on iron stores as evaluated by serum ferritin. Blood **50**(3), 441–447 (1977)
6. Gropper, S.S., Smith, J.L.: Advanced Nutrition and Human Metabolism. Cengage Learning, Boston (2012)
7. Hawkins, W., Speck, E., Leonard, V.G.: Variation of the hemoglobin level with age and sex. Blood **9**(10), 999–1007 (1954)
8. Liao, T.W.: Clustering of time series data-a survey. Pattern Recogn. **38**(11), 1857–1874 (2005)
9. Lloyd, S.: Least squares quantization in PCM. IEEE Trans. Inf. Theory **28**(2), 129–137 (1982)
10. Neil, D., Pfeiffer, M., Liu, S.C.: Phased LSTM: accelerating recurrent network training for long or event-based sequences. In: Advances in Neural Information Processing Systems, pp. 3882–3890 (2016)
11. Rani, S., Sikka, G.: Recent techniques of clustering of time series data: a survey. Int. J. Comput. Appl. **52**(15), 1–9 (2012)
12. Sak, H., Senior, A.W., Beaufays, F.: Long short-term memory recurrent neural network architectures for large scale acoustic modeling. In: INTERSPEECH (2014)
13. Zhu, Y., et al.: What to do next: modeling user behaviors by time-LSTM. In: IJCAI, pp. 3602–3608 (2017)

Localized Random Shapelets

Mael Guillemé[1,2]([✉]), Simon Malinowski[2], Romain Tavenard[3],
and Xavier Renard[4]

[1] Energiency, Rennes, France
[2] Univ Rennes, Inria, CNRS, IRISA, Rennes, France
{mael.guilleme,simon.malinowski}@irisa.fr
[3] Univ Rennes, CNRS, LETG, IRISA, Rennes, France
[4] AXA, Paris, France

Abstract. Shapelet models have attracted a lot of attention from researchers in the time series community, due in particular to its good classification performance. However, such models only inform about the presence/absence of local temporal patterns. Structural information about the localization of these patterns is ignored. In addition, end-to-end learning shapelet models tend to generate meaningless shapelets, leading to poorly interpretable models. In this paper, we aim at designing an interpretable shapelet model that takes into account the localization of the shapelets in the time series. Time series are transformed into feature vectors composed of both a distance and a localization information. Then, we design a hierarchical feature selection process using regularization. This process can be tuned to select, for each shapelet, either only its distance information or both distance and localization information. It is hence possible for every selected shapelet to analyze whether only the presence or the presence and the localization contributed to the decision process improving interpretability of the decision. Experiments show that this feature selection process has competitive performance compared to state-of-the-art shapelet-based classifiers, while providing better interpretability.

Keywords: Time series · Machine learning · Shapelets

1 Introduction

Time series classification has recently gained an increasing attention from researchers, due in particular to its possible application in various domains such as economics, agriculture, and health for instance. There are two main families of methods for that task: some deal with raw time series and use or design dedicated (dis-)similarity measures, while others rely on feature extraction to embed time series in metric spaces in which standard machine learning tools can be considered. The work presented in this paper is part of this latter category. Feature-based methods include works relying on hand-crafted features [3,12] as

© Springer Nature Switzerland AG 2020
V. Lemaire et al. (Eds.): AALTD 2019, LNAI 11986, pp. 85–97, 2020.
https://doi.org/10.1007/978-3-030-39098-3_7

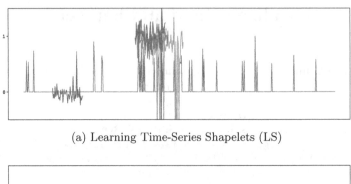

(a) Learning Time-Series Shapelets (LS)

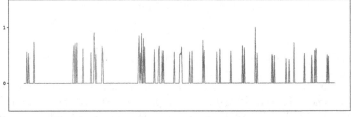

(b) Localized Random Shapelets (LRS)

Fig. 1. Comparison between shapelets extracted by the *Learning Time-Series Shapelets* (LS) algorithm and our Localized Random Shapelets (LRS) approach. This Figure has been generated using `tslearn` implementation of LS [14].

well as learning-based approaches, among which the shapelet model plays an important role. Shapelets have first been introduced in [19]. They correspond to subsequences that are able to discriminate classes. The concept of shapelet transform has then been proposed in [7]. It consists in transforming time series into a vector whose components represent the similarity between the time series and shapelets that have been selected beforehand (or learned, as in [5]). After this transformation, time series are embedded in a Euclidean space where classifiers like Multi-Layer Perceptron or Support Vector Machines can be used. Techniques based on the shapelet transform are amongst the most accurate ones for time series classification (an interesting survey and comparison of time series classification methods can be found in [1]). However, they have three main drawbacks. First, the step of generating (or learning) shapelets that lead to accurate classification is computationally demanding (especially when dealing with large time series datasets). Some works have been proposed in order to fasten this step, by relying on time series approximation [8] or by drawing random shapelets [10,18]. Second, no information about the localization of the shapelets in the time series is available after the transformation. Classical shapelet transform only makes use of the similarity between a shapelet and a time series. Information about when the shapelet occurs in the time series might be of importance to discriminate classes. This can be related to previous works that have shown that localization of extracted features in time series improve classification accuracy [15]. To better understand why, let us consider, for example, a sign language sentence recognition task. In this use case, being able to recognize salient patterns (gesture atoms) is key, but localizing them in the sentence is also important in order to understand the meaning of the sentence. Third, most shapelet-based models suffer from a lack of interpretability in the sense that (i) it is difficult to understand the impact of each shapelet on the final classification decision and/or (ii) extracted shapelets might not always be related to original time series. Figure 1 compares shapelets learned by the Learning Shapelet (LS) algorithm [5] on the EARTHQUAKES dataset and those extracted (at random) by our algorithm. Time series are rescaled to lie in the [0, 1] range before learning the shapelets. However, we can see that LS-extracted shapelets have very little in common with the time series and do not even fit in the [0, 1] range. In other words, shapelets cannot be seen as realistic time series patterns. For methods based on the shapelet transform [7], shapelets are extracted from original time series. But they then feed an ensemble of classifiers, which makes it difficult to understand relationship between shapelets and class belongings.

In this paper, we propose a novel shapelet model that tackles these drawbacks. First, in order to reduce the computing cost of selecting the most discriminant shapelets, our model selects shapelets randomly from training data. Hence, extracted shapelets are, by definition, closely related to the time series. Moreover, this random shapelet framework allows us to easily take the shapelet localization information into account. Second, we propose a dedicated feature selection method called Semi-Sparse Group Lasso (SSGL) capable of either ignoring a shapelet, keeping only its distance information or using both the distance and localization information. Third, we show that obtained shapelets are meaningful and the resulting model can be easily analyzed to get insights about which are the important features (for the classification task) in the dataset and for each of these features, what kind of information (presence only or presence and localization) contributed to the decision. Overall, we show that we are able to reach competitive performance w.r.t. Learning Shapelets [5] (even outperforming this baseline when larger datasets are considered) with a more interpretable model. The rest of this paper is organized as follows. Our Localized Random Shapelet model is detailed in Sect. 2 and its interpretability is discussed in Sect. 3. Section 4 evaluates the benefit of the proposed model on time series classification.

2 Localized Random Shapelet Model

2.1 Background on Shapelets and Shapelet Transform

A shapelet $S = s_1, \ldots, s_l$ is a temporal sequence (that can be extracted from existing time series or not). Given a time series $T = t_1, \ldots, t_L$, the distance between s and T is defined as:

$$d(T, S) = \min_{1 \leq j \leq L-l+1} \sqrt{\sum_{i=1}^{l}(s_i - t_{i+j-1})^2}. \tag{1}$$

In other words, euclidean distances between s and every subsequence of T (of length l) are computed and only the best match (minimum distance) is kept.

Given a set $\mathcal{S} = \{S_1, \ldots, S_K\}$ of K shapelets, the shapelet transform of T is defined as the vector $v_1, \ldots, v_K$ such that $v_k = d(T, S_k)$ for all k. The original way to select a set of shapelets for a classification task is to evaluate the discriminatory power of a shapelet candidate by using for instance the information gain [7,19], and to keep the ones with the higher gain. A strategy based on learning the shapelets that minimize an objective function was proposed in [5]. Other works consider the use of random shapelets and then rely on classical feature selection algorithms together with the classification step. In [10], it has been shown that with this idea, a few thousands subsequences are enough to reach state-of-the-art classification performance on a standard benchmark [2].

2.2   Localized Random Shapelet Model

In this framework, no information about the localization of the shapelets in the time series is used, while it has been shown that this kind of information helps improving classification performance [15]. In this section, we explain how we can integrate such information in the shapelet transform framework and derive a feature selection algorithm that keeps localization information only when needed.

In our Localized Random Shapelet (LRS) model, each shapelet S is drawn uniformly at random from the set of all training time series snippets. Each shapelet leads to two features for each time series T. The first feature is the same as in the classical shapelet transform, i.e. the shapelet distance[1] $d(T, S)$ between T and s as defined in Eq. (1). The second feature corresponds to the first time instant at which this distance is reached. It is computed as

$$l(T, S) = \operatorname*{argmin}_{1 \leq j \leq L-l+1} \sqrt{\sum_{i=1}^{l} (s_i - t_{i+j-1})^2}. \tag{2}$$

Let $\mathcal{T} = T_1, \ldots, T_N$ be a dataset of N time series. This set is transformed by the localized random shapelet model into a feature matrix $\mathbf{X}$, such that:

$$\mathbf{X} = \begin{pmatrix} d(T_1, S_1) \; l(T_1, S_1) \; \cdots \; d(T_1, S_K) \; l(T_1, S_K) \\ \vdots \qquad \vdots \qquad \qquad \vdots \qquad \vdots \\ d(T_N, S_1) \; l(T_N, S_1) \; \cdots \; d(T_N, S_K) \; l(T_N, S_K) \end{pmatrix}. \tag{3}$$

Once this feature matrix computed, we feed it to a standard multi-layer perceptron classifier as shown in Fig. 2. This model takes as input a $2 \times K$-dimensional vector and outputs probabilities for the different classes at stake. The number of hidden layers can be adapted to application needs. We denote the whole set of parameters of this model by $\boldsymbol{\theta}$, and inside this set of parameters, we isolate the parameters of the first layer in the model and denote them $\boldsymbol{\beta}$.

---

[1] Note that the term distance is an abuse of notation since $d(T, S)$ is not a distance, mathematically speaking.

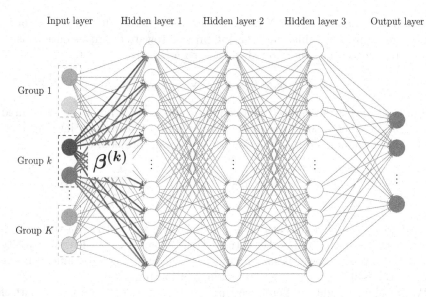

Fig. 2. Overview of our localized random shapelet model. Blue circles indicate distance features while orange ones correspond to location features. For each shapelet, a group is formed whose weights are denoted $\beta^{(k)}$ (where k is the shapelet index). Note that the number of hidden layers may vary from one application to the other. (Color figure online)

2.3   Structured Feature Selection

As explained above, the proposed shapelet model relies on random shapelets (taken from the original time series) in order to fasten the shapelet generation step. When dealing with such shapelets, a feature selection strategy should be applied before (or jointly with) the classification step, in order to simplify the resulting representation, which tends to improve overall accuracy [9]. It can be seen in Eq. (3) that the extracted features are structured. Distance features tell how well a shapelet matches a time series, while localization features inform about the location of the match. Classical feature selection strategies are hence not adapted to this kind of feature matrix. Indeed, it does not seem reasonable to exclude a distance feature related to a shapelet while keeping the associated localization feature. However, removing a localization feature and keeping the associated distance feature might be meaningful in cases where the localization of a shapelet does not impact the class belonging of the times series. In the following, we design a feature selection strategy adapted to the kind of features extracted from the localized random shapelet model. This strategy, based on regularization, is described below.

Regularization Strategy. In the following, we assume that we have a prediction problem with a loss function $\mathcal{L}$ to be minimized. This loss function is computed over a dataset $\mathbf{X}$ of N observations associated with a target vector $\mathbf{y}$. A standard approach to bias the learning process towards sparse solutions is to derive a regularized loss function, as done for Lasso regression [16]:

$$\mathcal{L}^{\text{Lasso}}(\mathbf{X}, \mathbf{y}, \boldsymbol{\theta}) = \mathcal{L}(\mathbf{X}, \mathbf{y}, \boldsymbol{\theta}) + \lambda \|\boldsymbol{\beta}\|_1 \tag{4}$$

Simon et al. [13] introduced Sparse-Group Lasso (SGL), a more structured regularization scheme that could take feature group information into account. The resulting regularized loss function for a K-group problem is:

$$\mathcal{L}^{\text{SGL}}(\mathbf{X}, \mathbf{y}, \boldsymbol{\theta}) = \mathcal{L}(\mathbf{X}, \mathbf{y}, \boldsymbol{\theta}) + \alpha \lambda \|\boldsymbol{\beta}\|_1 + (1 - \alpha) \lambda \sum_{k=1}^{K} \sqrt{p_k} \|\boldsymbol{\beta}^{(k)}\|_2 \tag{5}$$

where p_k is the number of features in group k and $\boldsymbol{\beta}^{(k)}$ is the sub-vector of $\boldsymbol{\beta}$ made of features from group k. Here, the $\|\boldsymbol{\beta}\|_1$ term enforces per-feature sparsity while $\|\boldsymbol{\beta}^{(k)}\|_2$ pushes towards sparsity at the group level. The α parameter hence acts as a trade-off between these two regularization terms.

We consider a slightly different setting in which, inside a group, only part of the features can be dropped. In our case, each group corresponds to a shapelet. For each shapelet, two features are available: one for the distance and one for localization of the match. We aim at designing a strategy that can, for each shapelet (or group), either:

- drop all information related to that shapelet (if the shapelet is useless for prediction),
- keep only the distance information (if the location of the shapelet does not help for prediction),
- keep both the distance and localization information.

In order to meet these constraints, we introduce the Semi-Sparse-Group-Lasso (SSGL) framework, which consists in minimizing the following loss function:

$$\mathcal{L}^{\text{SSGL}}(\mathbf{X}, \mathbf{y}, \boldsymbol{\theta}) = \mathcal{L}(\mathbf{X}, \mathbf{y}, \boldsymbol{\theta}) + \alpha \lambda \|\mathbf{M}_{\text{ind}} \boldsymbol{\theta}\|_1 + (1 - \alpha) \lambda \sum_{k=1}^{K} \sqrt{p_k} \|\boldsymbol{\beta}^{(k)}\|_2 \tag{6}$$

where $\mathbf{M}_{\text{ind}}$ is an indicator diagonal matrix made of ones and zeros, the latter corresponding to variables that should be kept as soon as the group is not zeroed-out (i.e. variables that will not be considered for ℓ_1 regularization). In the case of our localized shapelet model, $\mathbf{M}_{\text{ind}}$ has a diagonal that alternates between zeros for dimensions corresponding to distances and ones for those related to the localization information.

Optimization in Practice. In practice, minimization of such a regularized loss function can be tackled by several means. First, building on [13], one can derive a block-wise procedure that considers feature groups one at a time and starts by deciding on whether it should be zeroed-out or not. In the case of an

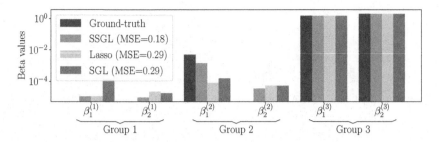

Fig. 3. Coefficients learned using different regularization schemes for a linear regression problem. Ground-truth coefficients are reported in blue. (Color figure online)

ordinary least square regression setting, it gives the following sufficient condition for zeroing-out group k (*i.e.* dropping all the information from the corresponding shapelet):

$$\left\| \mathbf{M}_{\mathrm{ind}} S \left(\frac{\mathbf{X}^{(k)\top} \mathbf{r}_{-k}}{N}, \alpha\lambda \right) \right\|_2 \leq \sqrt{p_k}(1 - \alpha)\lambda, \tag{7}$$

where $\mathbf{X}^{(k)}$ is the submatrix of $\mathbf{X}$ in which only variables from group k are kept, $\mathbf{r}_{-k}$ is the partial residual of $\mathbf{y}$, substituting all group fits other than group k and $S(\cdot, \cdot)$ is the coordinate-wise soft thresholding operator:

$$(S(\mathbf{z}, \alpha\lambda))_j = \mathrm{sign}(z_j)(|z_j| - \alpha\lambda)_+. \tag{8}$$

If this condition is satisfied, all $\boldsymbol{\beta}^{(k)}$ coefficients are set to zero and the process goes on to the next group. Otherwise, optimization of the coefficients inside group k should be performed, either using subgradient equations in a coordinate-wise algorithm or by performing gradient descent steps inside group k.

In all the experiments presented in this paper, we rather use full gradient descent on the regularized loss, in order not to face known limitations of block-wise gradient descent algorithms such as slow convergence and low parallelism capabilities. This strategy was already successfully applied in [11].

Toy Example: Structured Linear Regression. Figure 3 presents a comparison of the three regularization schemes described in this section. For this comparison, we used the following model to draw samples:

$$\mathbf{y} = \mathbf{X} \cdot \boldsymbol{\beta} + \boldsymbol{\varepsilon}, \tag{9}$$

where $\mathbf{X}$ and $\boldsymbol{\varepsilon}$ are drawn from centered normal distributions of standard deviation 1 and 0.01 respectively and $\boldsymbol{\beta} = \left[\beta_1^{(1)}, \beta_2^{(1)}, \beta_1^{(2)}, \beta_2^{(2)}, \beta_1^{(3)}, \beta_2^{(3)} \right]$ has only three non-zero components: $\beta_1^{(2)}$, $\beta_1^{(3)}$ and $\beta_2^{(3)}$ (*cf.* Fig. 3).

We assume to have a problem similar to the shapelet setting, *i.e.* we have groups of two variables among which only $\beta_2^{(k)}$ is concerned by ℓ_1-norm regularization (for group k). This structural information is used for SGL and SSGL variants in the experiments, while Lasso is blind to such structure.

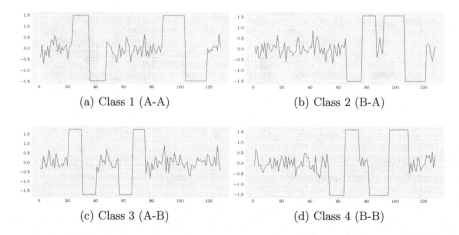

(a) Class 1 (A-A)   (b) Class 2 (B-A)

(c) Class 3 (A-B)   (d) Class 4 (B-B)

Fig. 4. An example of each class of TwoPatterns dataset.

For this example, we use a simple model without any hidden layer. First, SSGL outperforms both SGL and Lasso in terms of mean squared error (MSE), showing the benefit of taking variable structure into account in the model. Second, from a more qualitative perspective, the structure of the ground truth coefficients is better preserved with SSGL (all three null coefficients have low value estimators and $\beta_2^{(1)}$ is better estimated thanks to the intra-group specific regularization scheme).

3   Model Interpretability

In this section, we illustrate the interpretability of our method through a simple use-case. We consider the TwoPatterns dataset from the UCR & UEA time series classification repository. TwoPatterns is a synthetic dataset in which each time series is made of two pattern occurrences surrounded by noise. There are two different patterns (named A and B in the following) in the dataset and the classification problem is hence made of four classes, corresponding to all possible permutations of patterns A and B, as shown in Fig. 4. For this illustration, we rely on a simple variant of our model in which we have no hidden layer and draw $K = 2,000$ shapelets to build our feature space. We show that, once trained, our model can be easily analyzed by scrutinizing its weights.

More precisely, in the following, we aim at answering the following questions:

– Which shapelets are the most important for classification?
– For each of these shapelets, is the localization information important for the decision ?

Note that, in this simple setting where no hidden layer is used, this information comes in a straight-forward manner by analyzing weights, but the same

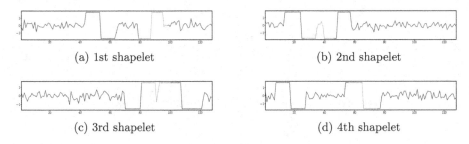

(a) 1st shapelet   (b) 2nd shapelet

(c) 3rd shapelet   (d) 4th shapelet

Fig. 5. Four most important shapelets (in red) extracted by our method from the TwoPatterns dataset. (Color figure online)

analysis could be performed in the multi-layer case through gradient descent in the shapelet transform space.

First, we can extract most important shapelets (in terms of classification power) by ranking them with respect to the ℓ_2-norm of their associated weight matrix $\beta^{(k)}$. Top-4 shapelets for dataset TwoPatterns are presented in Fig. 5. They fully match expectations since they focus on discriminative parts of the time series and cover both patterns A and B, as well as successions of these.

Then, for a shapelet that is considered discriminant, we can wonder whether its localization and distance are both used by the model or not. To assess the importance of the distance feature for a shapelet, we compute the ℓ_2-norm of the coefficients of $\beta^{(k)}$ that are associated with its distance feature. We call this value distance coefficient. Similarly, to assess the importance of the localization feature for a shapelet, we compute the ℓ_2-norm of the coefficients of $\beta^{(k)}$ that are associated with its localization feature. We call this value localization coefficient.

The first shapelet of Fig. 5 has the 4th highest localization coefficient amongst the 2,000 shapelets, together with the 14th highest distance coefficient. This means that for this shapelet both the distance and the localization are important. It is coherent as this shapelet corresponds to a B pattern. The distance feature enables to discriminate class 1 from the others, while the localization features enables to discriminate class 2 and class 3. This is confirmed by the histograms of Fig. 6. The second shapelet of Fig. 5 has the 2nd highest distance coefficient amongst the 2,000 shapelets. However, its localization coefficient is not as important as its distance coefficient (217th out of 2,000). This means that for this shapelet the distance feature is important but not the localization. This is coherent as this shapelet corresponds to the end of a pattern A followed by the beginning of a pattern B, which only occurs in class 3, hence distance feature is enough to discriminate class 3 from the others, as confirmed by Fig. 6. Similar conclusions can be drawn for shapelets 3 and 4.

We have seen in this section that our model allows easy extraction of the shapelets that have more contributed to discriminate classes. One can also easily analyze whether the localization of these shapelets was used by the model. This kind of information is very important as it brings a richer interpretability in the decision process. Conversely, state-of-the-art shapelet-based algorithms tend to

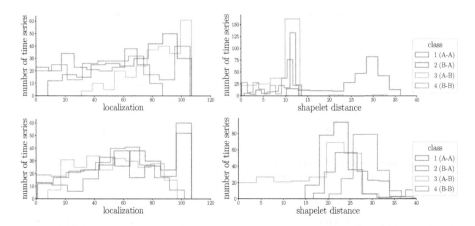

Fig. 6. The distribution of the localization (left) and distance (right) for the most important (first row) and second most important (second row) shapelet in TwoPatterns dataset.

suffer from lack of interpretability. Shapelet Transform is a weighted ensemble of several standard classifiers, which makes it difficult to assess the importance of shapelets in the decision process. In the Learning Shapelet (LS) framework, obtained shapelets are not constrained to be similar to training time series (cf. Fig. 1), which limits the interpretability of such framework.

4   Experiments

In this section, we present experimental results to assess the performance of the proposed Localized Random Shapelet (LRS) model and compare it to state-of-the-art shapelet-based methods.

4.1   Experimental Setup

The proposed LRS is compared to the following state-of-the-art baselines: Shapelet Transform (ST) [7], the Learning Shapelet (LS) model [5] and the Fast Shapelet (FS) one [8]. Experiments are based on the datasets from the UCR & UEA time series classification repository [2], a classical benchmark in the time series classification field. It is composed of 85 datasets with diverse time series classification problems. A description of the datasets can be found in [1]. Classification performance for baseline methods is retrieved from the website associated to this dataset.

For each dataset, we draw $K = 2,000$ shapelets uniformly at random from the time series training set. For the length of the shapelets, we followed the procedure described in [5]. All time series are represented by a feature vector which size is twice the number of shapelets (cf. Eq. (3)). This feature vector embeds information about shapelet distance and localization.

We use a 3-hidden-layer model with 256, 128 and 64 units in the hidden layers and each internal layer is followed by a batch normalization layer as suggested in [6]. We add some dropout in the second and third layer. We use ReLU activations [4] for all internal layers and softmax activation for the final layer. The regularization in LRS requires two more hyper-parameters: λ that controls the regularization strength, and α that controls the trade-off between lasso and group-lasso terms. We cross-validated the dropout from the set $\{0.0, 0.3, 0.5, 0.7\}$, λ from the set $\{10^{-1}, 10^{-}, \dots 10^{-7}\}$ and α from the set $\{0.1, 0.3, 0.5, 0.7, 0.9\}$. Models are learned using RMSPROP optimizer [17] with a learning rate of 0.001.

4.2   Runtime and Memory Cost

Experiments are run on a Laptop with a Fedora 24 system, 16 GB DDR4 RAM and dual core CPU (i7-6600U 2.6 GHz). Python code used for these experiments is publicly available[2]. As an indication of the low computing and memory cost of our method, it requires 66 seconds and 1.5 GB of memory to learn a model (for a given set of hyper-parameters) on the ELECTRIC DEVICES dataset that is the largest in the UCR & UEA archive.

4.3   Evaluation of the Impact of the SSGL Regularization

Figure 7 shows the error rates on 85 datasets for two different regularization strategies: Lasso [16] and SSGL. It can be seen that the SSGL regularization strategy (that allows selection for each shapelet of either distance feature, or distance and localization features, or none of these) slightly improves classification performance over Lasso (that makes the selection for each features independently).

4.4   Performance Comparison Against Baselines

Critical diagrams show the average ranks of the classifiers in order, and cliques, represented by a solid bar. A clique represents a group of classifiers within which there is no significant pairwise difference. Figure 8 presents critical diagrams of the performance against the baselines when considering all datasets, and when considering only datasets with more than 300 training instances.

Overall, in terms of classification performance, only Shapelet Transform outperforms our approach. As already stated, ST is a weighted ensemble of several standard classifiers, hence suffering from lack of interpretability about the decision process. The performance of LRS is slightly better than LS (but not significantly). When we only consider large datasets (the 42 datasets with more than 300 training instances, which are better suited to the characteristics of our method), performance of LRS is better than LS and FS and gets closer to that of ST. This seems to indicate that taking the localization information into account enables to improve classification performance provided that sufficient training data is available to correctly fit the model.

---

[2] https://github.com/rtavenar/localized_random_shapelets.

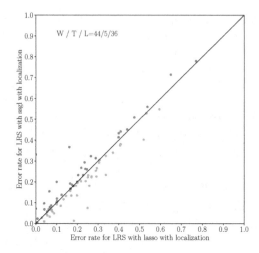

Fig. 7. Error rates comparison on 85 UCR datasets between LRS with ssgl regularization against LRS with lasso regularization.

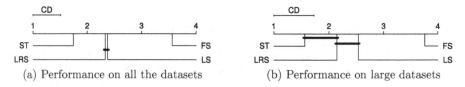

(a) Performance on all the datasets   (b) Performance on large datasets

Fig. 8. Critical diagrams of the performance against the baselines.

5   Conclusion

In this paper, we have proposed a novel shapelet model that has low computing cost, competitive performance and better interpretability compared to traditional shapelet-based methods. This model uses shapelet localization in addition
to the traditional shapelet transform representation in a random shapelet framework. As such a framework needs many shapelets as input, we have designed
a dedicated hierarchical regularization framework (SSGL) to fit our application needs. Experiments show that our model produces a ranking of realistic
shapelets, and is able to explain their importance both in terms of distance and
localization. This enables an easy and rich interpretability of the classification
process. Moreover our classification performance is competitive with state-of-
the-art shapelet-based classifiers.

References

1. Bagnall, A., Lines, J., Bostrom, A., Large, J., Keogh, E.: The great time series
   classification bake off: a review and experimental evaluation of recent algorithmic
   advances. Data Min. Knowl. Disc. **31**, 606–660 (2016)
2. Bagnall, A., Lines, J., Vickers, W., Keogh, E.: The UEA & UCR time series classification repository. www.timeseriesclassification.com

3. Bailly, A., Malinowski, S., Tavenard, R., Chapel, L., Guyet, T.: Dense bag-of-temporal-SIFT-words for time series classification. In: Douzal-Chouakria, A., Vilar, J.A., Marteau, P.-F. (eds.) AALTD 2015. LNCS (LNAI), vol. 9785, pp. 17–30. Springer, Cham (2016). https://doi.org/10.1007/978-3-319-44412-3_2. https://hal.archives-ouvertes.fr/hal-01252726

4. Glorot, X., Bordes, A., Bengio, Y.: Deep sparse rectifier neural networks. In: Proceedings of the Fourteenth International Conference on Artificial Intelligence and Statistics, pp. 315–323 (2011)

5. Grabocka, J., Schilling, N., Wistuba, M., Schmidt-Thieme, L.: Learning time-series shapelets. In: Proceedings of the ACM SIGKDD International Conference on Knowledge Discovery and Data Mining, pp. 392–401 (2014)

6. Ioffe, S., Szegedy, C.: Batch normalization: accelerating deep network training by reducing internal covariate shift. arXiv preprint arXiv:1502.03167 (2015)

7. Lines, J., Davis, L.M., Hills, J., Bagnall, A.: A shapelet transform for time series classification. In: Proceedings of the ACM SIGKDD International Conference on Knowledge Discovery and Data Mining, pp. 289–297 (2012)

8. Rakthanmanon, T., Keogh, E.: Fast shapelets: a scalable algorithm for discovering time series shapelets, pp. 668–676, May 2013

9. Renard, X., Rifqi, M., Erray, W., Detyniecki, M.: Random-shapelet: an algorithm for fast shapelet discovery. In: IEEE International Conference on Data Science and Advanced Analytics, pp. 1–10 (2015)

10. Renard, X., Rifqi, M., Fricout, G., Detyniecki, M.: EAST representation: fast discriminant temporal patterns discovery from time series. In: ECML/PKDD Workshop on Advanced Analytics and Learning on Temporal Data (2016)

11. Scardapane, S., Comminiello, D., Hussain, A., Uncini, A.: Group sparse regularization for deep neural networks. Neurocomputing **241**, 81–89 (2017)

12. Schäfer, P.: The BOSS is concerned with time series classification in the presence of noise. Data Min. Knowl. Disc. **29**(6), 1505–1530 (2015)

13. Simon, N., Friedman, J., Hastie, T., Tibshirani, R.: A sparse-group lasso. J. Comput. Graph. Stat. **22**(2), 231–245 (2013)

14. Tavenard, R.: tslearn: a machine learning toolkit dedicated to time-series data (2017). https://github.com/rtavenar/tslearn

15. Tavenard, R., Malinowski, S., Chapel, L., Bailly, A., Sanchez, H., Bustos, B.: Efficient temporal kernels between feature sets for time series classification. In: Ceci, M., Hollmén, J., Todorovski, L., Vens, C., Džeroski, S. (eds.) ECML PKDD 2017. LNCS (LNAI), vol. 10535, pp. 528–543. Springer, Cham (2017). https://doi.org/10.1007/978-3-319-71246-8_32. https://halshs.archives-ouvertes.fr/halshs-01561461

16. Tibshirani, R.: Regression shrinkage and selection via the lasso. J. R. Stat. Soc. Ser. B (Methodol.) **58**, 267–288 (1996)

17. Tieleman, T., Hinton, G.: Lecture 6.5-rmsprop: divide the gradient by a running average of its recent magnitude. COURSERA: Neural Netw. Mach. Learn. **4**(2), 26–31 (2012)

18. Wistuba, M., Grabocka, J., Schmidt-Thieme, L.: Ultra-fast shapelets for time series classification. CoRR abs/1503.05018 (2015). http://arxiv.org/abs/1503.05018

19. Ye, L., Keogh, E.: Time series shapelets: a new primitive for data mining. In: Proceedings of the ACM SIGKDD International Conference on Knowledge Discovery and Data Mining, pp. 947–956 (2009)

Poster Presentation

Feature-Based Gait Pattern Classification for a Robotic Walking Frame

Christopher M. A. Bonenberger, Benjamin Kathan, and Wolfgang Ertel[⊠]

Institut für Künstliche Intelligenz,
Ravensburg-Weingarten University of Applied Sciences, Weingarten, Germany
{bonenbch,kathanb,ertel}@rwu.de
http://iki.hs-weingarten.de

Abstract. This paper presents a system for fast detection of gait patterns of walking frame users, where the challenge is to recognize a change in activity before the signal behaves stationary. The system is used as a basis for inferring the user's intention in order to develop an improved shared-control strategy for an electric-driven walking frame. The data required for gait pattern identification is recorded by a set of low budget infrared distance sensors. We compare different sliding window based feature extraction methods in combination with classical machine learning algorithms in order to realize a fast real-time online gait classification. Moreover, a simple hierarchical feature extraction method is proposed and evaluated on our data-set.

Keywords: Multivariate time-series · Feature extraction · DWT · FFT · Shared control · Elderly care

1 Introduction

Machine Learning with applications in care of the elderly has recently found great interest in science as well as in commercial products and services. There are applications ranging from social companion robots to smart-home-systems, adapted to the needs of elderly people. We describe the development of a machine learning driven solution for control of an electric-driven walking frame. The existing system, on which we build in the following, is supporting the user by a fifth wheel as driving element. This wheel is controlled via the momentum inserted by the user, following a simple control strategy (perpetuating the momentum). This way of control is intuitive, as the user does not need to give any input by means of handles or buttons. However, in some situations the walking frame does not behave as it is supposed to. In one example, the walking frame will continue driving until it is explicitly stopped by a counter-force (the user actively impeding or an obstacle stopping the walking frame). This behavior is not desirable, because elderly people may not give such distinct inputs. Beyond that, the forces acting on the frame are ambiguous, i.e. they can be either a consequence of the user's motions or of the environment (e.g. up-/downhill route). To counter this

© Springer Nature Switzerland AG 2020
V. Lemaire et al. (Eds.): AALTD 2019, LNAI 11986, pp. 101–109, 2020.
https://doi.org/10.1007/978-3-030-39098-3_8

problem we need to infer the user's intention to walk or to stop from it's actual activity. An obvious solution is to develop a fast gait classifier for the given system. In the following, several ways to implement such a multivariate time-series classifier are described and evaluated.

There are, however, numerous methods to approach time-series classification. We do not claim to provide a full survey-like comparison of all state-of-the-art algorithms. In order to facilitate potential marketability, we try to avoid high computational complexity and to develop a narrow system (few low-cost sensors). We demonstrate the performance and feasibility of several important methods for our application. Specifically, we focus on feature-based interval methods in combination with standard classifiers.

2   Related Work

There are many machine learning projects aiming for an enhanced functionality of walking frames. Often the applications focus on navigation and/or inferring user intention (user-modeling). To name just a few: [14] describes a system that provides navigational aid to the elderly using probabilistic models; [7] presents a robotic walker that learns a user-model from navigational activity in assisted living environment. [8] describes the use of handles with sensors capturing linear forces in order to grasp the user's intention; additionally, the walking aid uses a path planner for obstacle avoidance. In [17] an ADL-assistance system (Activities of Daily Living) is described; one of the topics addressed is gait monitoring and analysis. The gait monitoring system is used to detect pathological gait patterns in order to handle such. The user data is recorded via a laser range finder (LRF) mounted to the walking frame and analyzed using Hidden Markov Models to classify the different gait stages. [4] describes a method to control "Mobility Assistive Devices" based on gait analysis. They extract features such as velocities, positions and distances from the LRF data, and use it for a conceptual gait analysis. In [3] a LSTM-based method for on-line gait stability analysis based on RGB-D and LRF sensors is described. In [22] a robotic walker for gait rehabilitation of stroke patients is implemented as a shared-control system using wearable motion sensors and force/torque sensing. [18] use hierarchical Hidden Markov Models and point out the advantages of such compared to Support Vector Machines (especially for inferring user activities). A "complex distributed home automation and robotics system providing health monitoring and (socially interactive) assistance in daily living tasks to the elderly (and their caregivers) at home" is presented in [10], furthermore the technological challenges in development of such a system are pointed out. [24] recently presented the evaluation of a gait-analysis system for shared-control based on pressure sensor data at the handle of a walking aid and draw positive conclusions concerning the applicability of such a system.

Regarding time-series classification there are numerous algorithms (cf. [2]) that perform either feature, distance or model based classification [21]. In the following we focus on the first category.

Feature based methods have been successfully applied for many time-series classification tasks (see [1,9,15,16,20]). We focus on simple statistical feature extraction methods inspired by PAA and SAX [11,12], Wavelet features (theory in [6,13,19], for applications see e.g. [5,23]) and Fourier features.

3   System Description

Our system is comprised of multiple functions (similar to the ones listed above), among which we focus on gait analysis as input to a shared-control system. For this purpose we use six infrared distance sensors positioned to capture objects in the region of interest. We use force sensors in the handles (force sensitive resistor pads) to gain more information about the user's behavior. Additionally, the walking frame is equipped with an inertia measurement unit and an odometer at the rigid wheels, such that forces acting on the walking frame and the resulting velocities as well as the covered distance are monitored. For localization and navigation we use several other hardware components. Yet, in the following we consider only the data obtained by the infrared sensors pointing to the user's legs. In Fig. 2 sample data is given.

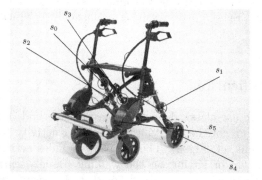

Fig. 1. The walking frame used for data acquisition. The sensors are all directed to the expected position of the user's legs (s_4 and s_5 are attached to the rods holding the rigid wheels, pointing to the user's feet).

3.1   Sensory System Details

Figure 1 shows the prototype used for all the experiments. We use infrared sensors with ranges of 20 cm–150 cm (s_0, s_1), 10 cm–80 cm (s_2, s_3) and 4 cm–30 cm (s_4, s_5) to monitor the user's leg movements. The infrared sensors output analog distance values, coded as voltage, which is converted to a 10 bit digital signal. The sampling interval is $T_s = 0.0165$ s. Although the prototype offers several other sensors, in the following we restrict to infrared sensor data. This is mainly because we are striving for an economic solution. An obvious cheap alternative would be ultrasonic sensors, yet such turned out to be unsatisfying. The main reasons for this are low spacial resolution, high sensitivity to fading and losses due to absorption in material (especially cloth).

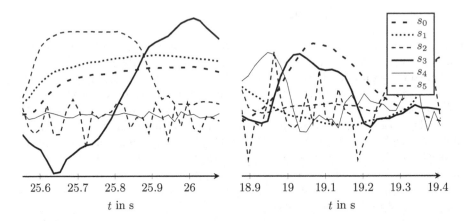

Fig. 2. Scaled sample data recorded by the infrared sensors (left: a person sitting down on the walking frame, right: a person walking, scaling only for visualization).

4   Gait Classification

For gait analysis we use classical machine learning methods to detect whether the user is walking or not, i.e. carrying out another activity (e.g. sitting down on the walking frame, cf. Fig. 2). The data set includes activities such as sitting down, getting up or sitting on the walking frame's seating, standing in front of the walking frame (resting or moving), technical failures (covered sensors, sporadic sensor failure) and different kind of walking data (slow, fast, crooked, smallandtallpersons, ...). We compare several algorithms applied to this binary classification problem, namely Support Vector Machines (SVM), XGBoost (XGB), Random Forests (RF), Gaussian Naive Bayes (NB) and as a baseline for comparison 1-Nearest-Neighbor (based on Dynamic Time Warping, 1NN-DTW and using euclidean distance, 1NN-ED).

4.1   Feature Extraction

The data consists of a d-dimensional time series (restricted to at maximum 6 infrared sensors, i.e. $d \leq 6$), which is processed using a sliding window (we use a Tukey-window with $\alpha = 0.1$ which proved to be a good choice). Thus a data window of width w is a multivariate time series (batch) $s \in \mathbb{R}^{d \times w}$. In order to enable a fast classification of incoming events, the sliding window must be as narrow as possible. On the other hand a narrow window makes classification more difficult, i.e. there is a trade-off between reactivity and accuracy. In order to capture the shape of the current signal, we compare several methods:

- computing the Discrete Wavelet Transform (DWT, using Daubechies-Wavelets) for each variable/dimension and pick the k largest coefficients (value and position/translation)
- extraction of Fourier coefficients as features (considering k largest Fourier coefficients and their position/frequency)
- statistical features (mean and extrema on "dyadic" intervals for each variable)

Capturing k largest values is advantageous compared to using a threshold, because it results in a lower dimension of the input space, yet the most relevant information is kept (assuming the transformed data to be sparse). That this assumption holds up can be seen from Fig. 3, where some sample data and the sparse Wavelet and Fourier representation are depicted.

In the following we use a window of width $w = 32$ (corresponding to 0.528 s, cf. Fig. 2), which is the smallest possible size that is still leading to an acceptable accuracy. We use overlapping windows (50% overlap) in order to speed up the system further. A dyadic window size is convenient to avoid the necessity of (zero) padding.

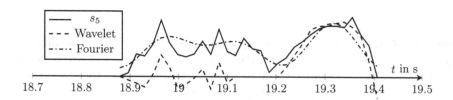

Fig. 3. Visualization of feature extraction via Fourier and Wavelet transform. The graphs show windowed sample data (Tukey-window, $\alpha = 0.1$) and the information given in the feature vectors, when using Fourier or Wavelet features (inverse transforms of sparse coefficient vectors). Here $k = 2$, hence for Fourier features the two largest coefficients and their frequencies are kept (4 features). The Wavelet representation results from a two level Wavelet transform ($k = 2$ and $n = 2$ resulting in 8 features)

Wavelet Features. We use the n-th level discrete Wavelet transform and extract the largest coefficients on each decomposition level as features. This means we transform the multivariate time series—for each variable separately—and from the coefficients on each decomposition level we extract the position and amplitude of the k largest detail and approximation coefficients (for example, when $k = 3$ and $n = 3$ we get 54 features for each multivariate batch s, with $s \in \mathbb{R}^{6 \times w}$). We use the "db3"-wavelet (Daubechies-Wavelet with three vanishing moments), which—in an empirical analysis—turned out to be a good choice.

Wavelets of wider support are not useful, because those are leading to strong border effects. Beyond that, higher order wavelets are weak in peak detection, which is important for our purpose.

Fourier Features. Another way to capture the shape of gait pattern is the Fourier transform. To extract the relevant data the Fast Fourier transform (FFT) is computed and again k largest coefficients are extracted (position/frequency and amplitude). The resulting features are easy to interpret, as the DC-part (which is usually the largest coefficient) is the mean distance of the leg to the respective sensor and the higher frequencies render the speed and amplitude of the leg movement.

Hierarchical Statistical Features. Besides the feature extraction methods listed above we propose the extraction of basic statistical features in a hierarchical manner (closely related to a discrete Haar-Wavelet transform), especially the interval-wise extraction of local mean (similar to PAA) and local extrema. The basic idea is, to compute the mean of 2^i sub-sequences and from that recursively the mean of 2^{i-1} up to the whole series mean (see Fig. 4). Additionally, the minima and maxima of the respective sub-sequences are captured. This is computationally efficient (the computation of the mean yields a sparse matrix factorization, cf. Wavelet-Analysis) and leads to effective features. We refer to this as *Dyadic Statistical Features* (DSF).

Feature Scaling. To scale data we either use standard scaling or min-max normalization based on the training data $\mathcal{X}_T$, i.e. either $x' = (x - \bar{x}_T)/s_T$ (where sample mean $\bar{x}_T$ and sample variance s_T are determined from the training set) or $x' = (x - \min_i x)/(\max_i x_i - \min_i x_i)$, where $x_i \in \mathcal{X}_T$.

4.2 Classification Results

As mentioned above we compare common classifiers in combination with the previously introduced feature extraction methods for our problem. Although XGBoost, Random Forests and Support Vector Machines usually outperform Naive Bayes, we consider it for better comparability and in order to "rank" the classification problem. For all classifiers we find—if necessary—optimized parameters by cross validated ($k = 5$) grid search and use 50% of the data as training set. The classes are balanced. For each classifier we use the one feature scaling method out of the above mentioned with best performance. Beyond that we optimized the number of used coefficients (the parameter k used along with FFT and DWT feature extraction) for each experiment separately. We use the accuracy on the test set as a score to compare our classifiers. To characterize the data set we computed the accuracy using 1NN-DTW, which is 0.898, and 1NN-ED, which is 0.876. Although especially 1NN-DTW this is too slow for application in our system, it is a good baseline for comparison. The results of our experiments are given in Table 1 and Fig. 5.

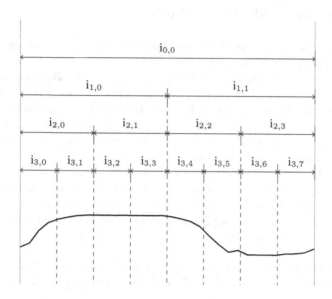

Fig. 4. Dyadic statistical feature extraction: for each of the intervals $i_{m,n}$ the mean along with the extrema are extracted ($\{\text{mean}(i_{m,n}), \text{max}(i_{m,n}), \text{min}(i_{m,n})\} \forall m, n$). Applying a recursive scheme, the complexity reduces to $\mathcal{O}(n \log n)$.

Table 1. Comparison of Support Vector Machines (SVM), XGBoost (XGB), Random Forests (RF)—all with best performing parameters—and Gaussian Naive Bayes (NB) using the feature extraction methods listed above. The accuracy using 1NN-DTW is 0.898, the accuracy with 1NN-ED is 0.875.

Accuracy	SVM	XGB	RF	NB
Wavelets	0.955	**0.981**	**0.978**	**0.882**
Fourier	0.944	0.962	0.945	0.892
Statistical	**0.964**	0.944	0.941	0.703

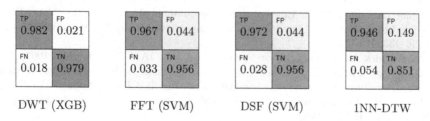

| DWT (XGB) | FFT (SVM) | DSF (SVM) | 1NN-DTW |

Fig. 5. Confusion matrices for different feature extraction methods (with best performing classifier) and 1NN-DTW.

5   Conclusion and Future Work

The presented methods were tested on the running system under realistic conditions, leading to satisfactory results, yet there is need for further improvements. The system's response is fast (i.e. an accurate classification is achieved with a narrow window), but for best usability of the walking frame, the user's desired speed should be estimated. Beyond that the user's specific state should be inferred from the gait data, where especially a fall detection is of interest.

The results of statistical feature extraction on dyadic intervals are promising. The method should be evaluated on benchmark data-sets.

Finally, the presented data-set is eligible for testing variable selection, whereat the application motivates this attempt. It has to be investigated whether the number of sensors can be reduced, i.e. only a subset of sensors (e.g. s_0, s_1, s_3) can be used for classification without substantial decrease in accuracy in order to increase the efficiency of the system.

Acknowledgments. This work was supported by a grant from the German Ministry of Education and Research (BMBF; KMU-innovativ: Medizintechnik, 13GW0173E).

References

1. Bagnall, A., Davis, L., Hills, J., Lines, J.: Transformation based ensembles for time series classification. In: Proceedings of the 2012 SIAM International Conference on Data Mining, pp. 307–318. SIAM (2012)
2. Bagnall, A., Lines, J., Bostrom, A., Large, J., Keogh, E.: The great time series classification bake off: a review and experimental evaluation of recent algorithmic advances. Data Min. Knowl. Disc. **31**(3), 606–660 (2017)
3. Chalvatzaki, G., Koutras, P., Hadfield, J., Papageorgiou, X.S., Tzafestas, C.S., Maragos, P.: On-line human gait stability prediction using LSTMs for the fusion of deep-based pose estimation and LRF-based augmented gait state estimation in an intelligent robotic rollator. arXiv preprint arXiv:1812.00252 (2018)
4. Chalvatzaki, G., Papageorgiou, X.S., Maragos, P., Tzafestas, C.S.: User-adaptive human-robot formation control for an intelligent robotic walker using augmented human state estimation and pathological gait characterization. In: 2018 IEEE/RSJ International Conference on Intelligent Robots and Systems (IROS), pp. 6016–6022. IEEE (2018)
5. Chan, K.P., Fu, A.W.C.: Efficient time series matching by wavelets. In: Proceedings 15th International Conference on Data Engineering (Cat. No. 99CB36337), pp. 126–133. IEEE (1999)
6. Daubechies, I.: Ten Lectures on Wavelets, vol. 61. SIAM, Philadelphia (1992)
7. Glover, J., Thrun, S., Matthews, J.T.: Learning user models of mobility-related activities through instrumented walking aids. In: 2004 Proceedings of the IEEE International Conference on Robotics and Automation, ICRA 2004, vol. 4, pp. 3306–3312. IEEE (2004)
8. Graf, B.: Reactive navigation of an intelligent robotic walking aid. In: Proceedings 10th IEEE International Workshop on Robot and Human Interactive Communication, ROMAN 2001 (Cat. No. 01TH8591), pp. 353–358. IEEE (2001)

9. Kampouraki, A., Manis, G., Nikou, C.: Heartbeat time series classification with support vector machines. IEEE Trans. Inf Technol. Biomed. **13**(4), 512–518 (2008)
10. Kearney, K.T., Presenza, D., Saccà, F., Wright, P.: Key challenges for developing a socially assistive robotic (SAR) solution for the health sector. In: 2018 IEEE 23rd International Workshop on Computer Aided Modeling and Design of Communication Links and Networks (CAMAD), pp. 1–7. IEEE (2018)
11. Lin, J., Keogh, E., Lonardi, S., Chiu, B.: A symbolic representation of time series, with implications for streaming algorithms. In: Proceedings of the 8th ACM SIGMOD Workshop on Research Issues in Data Mining and Knowledge Discovery, pp. 2–11. ACM (2003)
12. Lin, J., Keogh, E., Wei, L., Lonardi, S.: Experiencing SAX: a novel symbolic representation of time series. Data Min. Knowl. Disc. **15**(2), 107–144 (2007)
13. Mallat, S.: A Wavelet Tour of Signal Processing. Elsevier, Amsterdam (1999)
14. Montemerlo, M., Pineau, J., Roy, N., Thrun, S., Verma, V.: Experiences with a mobile robotic guide for the elderly. In: AAAI/IAAI 2002, pp. 587–592 (2002)
15. Mörchen, F.: Time series feature extraction for data mining using DWT and DFT (2003)
16. Nanopoulos, A., Alcock, R., Manolopoulos, Y.: Feature-based classification of time-series data. Int. J. Comput. Res. **10**(3), 49–61 (2001)
17. Papageorgiou, X.S., Chalvatzaki, G., Dometios, A.C., Tzafestas, C.S.: Human-centered service robotic systems for assisted living. In: Aspragathos, N.A., Koustoumpardis, P.N., Moulianitis, V.C. (eds.) RAAD 2018. MMS, vol. 67, pp. 132–140. Springer, Cham (2019). https://doi.org/10.1007/978-3-030-00232-9_14
18. Patel, M., Miro, J.V., Dissanayake, G.: A hierarchical hidden Markov model to support activities of daily living with an assistive robotic walker. In: 2012 4th IEEE RAS & EMBS International Conference on Biomedical Robotics and Biomechatronics (BioRob), pp. 1071–1076. IEEE (2012)
19. Strang, G., Nguyen, T.: Wavelets and Filter Banks. SIAM, Philadelphia (1996)
20. Timmer, J., Gantert, C., Deuschl, G., Honerkamp, J.: Characteristics of hand tremor time series. Biol. Cybern. **70**(1), 75–80 (1993)
21. Xing, Z., Pei, J., Keogh, E.: A brief survey on sequence classification. ACM SIGKDD Explor. Newsl. **12**(1), 40–48 (2010)
22. Ye, J., et al.: An adaptive shared control of a novel robotic walker for gait rehabilitation of stroke patients. In: 2018 IEEE International Conference on Intelligence and Safety for Robotics (ISR), pp. 373–378. IEEE (2018)
23. Yen, G.G., Lin, K.C.: Wavelet packet feature extraction for vibration monitoring. IEEE Trans. Industr. Electron. **47**(3), 650–667 (2000)
24. Zhang, Q., Fan, W., Sun, B., Li, Z., Song, L.: Research on movement law of walking-aid robot. In: 2018 IEEE International Conference on Intelligence and Safety for Robotics (ISR), pp. 227–231. IEEE (2018)

How to Detect Novelty in Textual Data Streams? A Comparative Study of Existing Methods

Clément Christophe[1,2(✉)], Julien Velcin[1], Jairo Cugliari[1], Philippe Suignard[2], and Manel Boumghar[2]

[1] Université de Lyon, Lyon 2, ERIC, Lyon, France
{julien.velcin,jairo.cugliari}@univ-lyon2.fr
[2] EDF R&D, Palaiseau, France
{clement.christophe,philippe.suignard,manel.boumghar}@edf.fr

Abstract. Since datasets with annotation for novelty at the document and/or word level are not easily available, we present a simulation framework that allows us to create different textual datasets in which we control the way novelty occurs. We also present a benchmark of existing methods for novelty detection in textual data streams. We define a few tasks to solve and compare several state-of-the-art methods. The simulation framework allows us to evaluate their performances according to a set of limited scenarios and test their sensitivity to some parameters. Finally, we experiment with the same methods on different kinds of novelty in the New York Times Annotated Dataset.

Keywords: Novelty Detection · Text mining · Evaluation framework · Natural Language Processing

1 Introduction

This work has been mainly driven by an industrial use case, in which our aim is to detect as soon as possible emerging issues in data related to customer returns (e.g., emails, complaints). "Ranking plans" (meaning, predefined categories) are already used to classify these data but the partners have realized that classes can evolve over time. This raises the problem of detecting new classes (our "novelty") in textual data streams.

It is a complex issue that can be related to several domains (e.g., signal processing, data mining), and which, because of its usefulness and its many fields of application, is particularly interesting to study. Although this issue has attracted attention in several critical areas: video-surveillance, physiological monitoring, cancer detection, immunology, its development in textual data is still limited outside of event detection [14,20]. The lack of development of these approaches at the level of textual data can be due to the specific nature of these data type and the difficulty of choosing the best representation for the task.

V. Lemaire et al. (Eds.): AALTD 2019, LNAI 11986, pp. 110–125, 2020.
https://doi.org/10.1007/978-3-030-39098-3_9

It is common to use topic modeling techniques to represent textual data, such as LDA [3] or its temporal variants [2,5]. These methods are particularly used to study the appearance of concept drifts [13,18].

Different applications consider novelty in different ways: some compare it to a single time event and therefore use event detection methods [12], others define it as an outlier detection task [17] or first story detection (FSD) task [1]. Besides, these methods are rarely tested on the same types of data (e.g., Twitter data, scientific abstract, press articles). In this work, we aim at comparing different families of method on a common dataset, and on different tasks and controlled scenarios.

It turns out that, after studying the literature on novelty detection, we notice that despite the fact that the general idea remains more or less the same, the formalism is not identical depending on the application cases. We notice few studies that analyze different methods of novelty detection. The work of Markou and Singh [10] distinguishes between statistical approaches and neural network approaches, which may not be very modern given the convergence of these two domains. Marsland's work [11] gives us a description of the novelty in biological organisms and points out the lack of precise definition in the literature. Finally, the work of Pimentel [16] allows the creation of a taxonomy related to methods of novelty detection; it classifies the approaches according to 5 major categories. (1) The probabilistic approach tries to estimate the density of the "normal" class. (2) The distance-based approach includes nearest-neighbour and clustering techniques. (3) The reconstruction-based approach involves a regression model that would fit the training data with the intuition that a high reconstruction error is a sign of novelty. (4) The domain-based approach consists of defining a boundary between "normal" and "abnormal" data. Finally, (5) the information-theoretic techniques are based on the idea that novel data will significantly alter the information content in a dataset. Here, we want to apply novelty detection methods to textual data streams. We realized that even if some works exist today, we can say that there is no unique definition of novelty and that these methods regularly use information in addition to plain text (e.g., ReTweet relation in Twitter, citation network).

In order to shed light on the available approaches, we study novelty detection by defining a common framework. In other words, we use a general definition of novelty that allows us to define specific tasks to solve. Then, we select a number of previous works addressing tasks close to novelty detection and extend them to solve our tasks. We perform experiments to determine which methods are the most effective in which cases, and what are the parameters that influence the performance. The rest of our work is organized as follows. In Sect. 3, we describe our simulation framework. In Sect. 4 we give information on the benchmark methodology and on the tested algorithms. Finally, in Sect. 5 we present our results on simulated datasets and on the New York Times Annotated Dataset.

2   Definition of Novelty

In this section, we review the definitions adopted in the literature before bringing them together into a common framework.

2.1   Novelty in the Literature

The term "novelty" is often referred to "anomalies" or "outliers", but all these refer to a fixed observation over time. The novelty to detect is related to a signal: a novelty is an abnormal or unexpected change in a signal, which means that the observed state is different from what we can expect. It can be defined to deal with various types of signal: electronic systems, network logs, medical diagnostics, monitoring of industrial equipment or textual data. In each of these cases, the novelty is materialized by a change in the nature of the signal that is considered as abnormal or unexpected. It is therefore necessary to pay attention to the temporal aspect of this signal in order to characterize it. This characterization depends on what we want to detect concretely. In order to evaluate our methods, we have to structure the different novelty types. For textual data, the word or topic frequency over time can stand for the signal we want to monitor.

One type of novelty we want to detect corresponds to weak signals whose frequency increases over time before becoming strong signals. It is a distinction between novelty and noise: the novelty becomes a strong signal while the noise remains a weak signal that has little interest for us. The work of [6] gives us a definition of a weak signal: a weak "new" signal must come or be recognized by an expert group (see Fig. 1). This signal anticipates phenomena having impacts on the future and may include features that must be detected as soon as possible. A new weak signal is growing by itself over time and it is an early warning of an emerging trend. Mannermaa [9] defines a weak signal as a phenomenon that is unlikely to appear but has a large potential for influence. These two definitions are not clear enough to develop an automatic detection system. Actually, it is mentioned that a weak signal needs to be recognized by a group of experts. This does not remove the human from the loop.

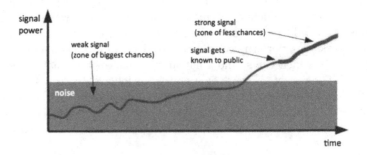

Fig. 1. Evolution of a weak signal over time [4].

A novelty can also correspond to the sudden increase of a signal during a very short time: we observe a "peak". Another type of novelty may correspond to an unusual change in frequency. Actually, the usual periodicity of a signal can be modified and this can be considered as a novelty. Finally, the analysis of concept drifts can also be considered as a novelty detection task. In these works [13,18], the methods aim at detecting a change in the parameters of the targeted classes.

2.2 Our Definition of Novelty

We now present what we consider as a novelty, i.e. what signal types can potentially interest us. Figure 2 summarizes the 3 types we focus on in this paper. We find the type of weak signal that evolves into a strong signal slowly over time (the most interesting one for our industrial use case), the event type signal that shows a sudden burst, and finally the cyclical signal.

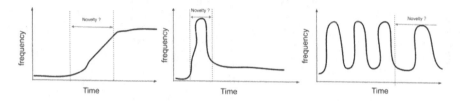

Fig. 2. Three possible types of novelty.

The cyclical signal is not necessarily considered as a novelty. Actually, it depends on the users and what they want to detect. However, we choose to keep it nonetheless for broadening the scope of our experiments. The main question remains the same: from when can we consider a signal as being novel? Finally, we mention the definition of [9] that introduces the concept of influence. Several methods in the literature model this influence [5] by applying it to data from scientific articles. We realized that this influence was not synonymous with novelty. Actually, some scientific papers can be extremely quoted and influential for a field without being the first innovative method of a domain. This explains why we choose not to consider the structural information provided by the links between documents (e.g., quotes, ReTweet), and consider only raw textual data.

3 Simulating Novelty in Textual Data

In this section, we see how to generate textual data corresponding to our novelty typology constructed in the previous section. Then, we explain how we use a mixture model to simulate these data. These textual data are simulated using the concept of topic: namely, a probability distribution over the vocabulary.

3.1 General Framework

Our main goal is to test the ability of different algorithms to detect novelty in textual data streams. We propose a precise methodology that allows us to measure the influence of various parameters on the results. In this part, we explain how we set up the datasets to create different novelty dynamics. In order to account for different novelty types, we build different scenarios. These scenarios correspond to three main types: cyclical, emergent and event. For each type, we vary some parameters to study the algorithms' performances. These scenarios are shown in Fig. 3. To measure the sensitivity of the algorithm, we define a dataset as a set of topics: one novel topic has a temporal dynamics defined in one of the scenarios of Fig. 3 and the 9 others are constant over time (our "normal" data).

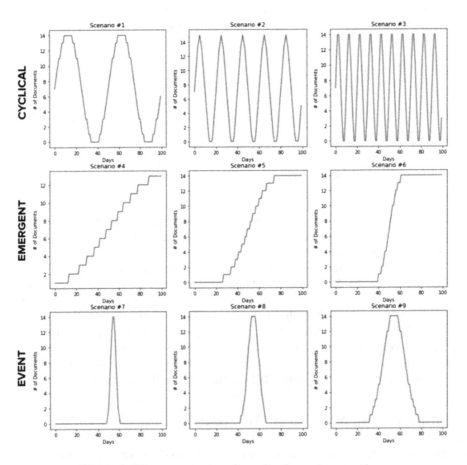

Fig. 3. 9 different scenarios of novelty dynamics over time.

3.2   Simulating

To simulate textual data, we use a mixture model[1] [15]. For each document d we assign a topic z and then sample 100 words from its probability distribution over the 10,000 words of the vocabulary. It should be noted that we use a bag-of-words approach and that the order with which our words are generated is not important. We do not really simulate documents strictly speaking but rather sets of bag-of-words that are drawn from the topic distribution. The mixture model that allows us to generate these probability distributions depends on a hyperparameter α that controls the sparsity of the vocabulary distribution. It gives us the ability to generate topics that are more or less close in terms of Kullback-Leibler Divergence (KL-Div). This is an important feature to test the different algorithms. When using topic models or probability distributions over a vocabulary, it is common to use the Kullback-Leibler Divergence to have an idea of the proximity between two topics.

We have simulated probability distributions on the vocabulary for each topic and assigned one topic per document. This allows us to create a simulated dataset. To add the temporal dimension, we sort the documents in the desired order. This order is given by the dynamics in Fig. 3. These scenarios give us the ability to test how an algorithm performs for each of them.

4   Experiments

In this section, we present the algorithms we study, the tasks they originally solve and how we adapt them for our evaluation framework.

4.1   Tasks to Resolve

In order to evaluate the methods originally designed for different applications, we define several tasks to be solved, with evaluation measures specific to each of these tasks. We measure the performance of the different methods on three tasks:

- Task 1: The goal is to raise an alert as soon as the novelty appears in the dataset. The evaluation measure corresponds to the delay between the day of novelty appearance and the day of the alert.
- Task 2: The goal is to detect words associated with novelty. As the topics in our documents are entirely simulated, we know the words associated with the novel topic. By using the 100 most likely words of the novel topic, we build a ground truth and we can use precision/recall measures.
- Task 3: The goal is to detect the documents responsible for the appearance of novelty. Thanks to our simulation, we know the topic associated with each document. We have a ground truth and we can also use precision/recall measures for the evaluation.

---

[1] The code for simulation is available at https://github.com/clechristophe/NoveltySimulator.

4.2 Evaluated Algorithms

The chosen algorithms come from different application fields: some are used for event detection, especially on Twitter, others for the detection of first stories, and others to observe the evolution of the language over time. In this section, we explain the main idea behind each of these methods, which task it is expected to solve in the first place, and finally how we adapt it to solve other tasks related to novelty detection.

Detections, bounds, and timelines: Umass and tdt-3 [1] (**TF-IDF**): this paper is among the first in the field of First-Story-Detection. This method represents the documents in a space corresponding to the TF-IDF score associated to document words. Then it uses a k-nearest-neighbor-based search with the cosine dissimilarity (1-cos) to identify new documents. This work makes the assumption that a document appearing far from its nearest neighbors is new.

Structured event retrieval over microblog archives [12] (**BS**): this paper focuses on the detection of sudden bursts in Twitter data. It develops a metric named *Burstiness Score* based on the word frequencies over each day. To detect new words, we consider the words with the most important BS score every day and compare them to our ground truth of words coming from our simulated topics.

Towards effective event detection, tracking and summarization on microblog data [8] (**DF**): this paper uses the *Document Frequency* feature and a Jaccard distance to form "new words clusters" every day that we compare with our ground truth.

On-line trend analysis with topic models: twitter trends detection topic model online [7] (**OLDA**): this paper presents a method that detects events over time slices. It is a variant of LDA that updates the proportion of word/topic every day. The new topics are identified via a Jensen-Shannon distance with the topics of the previous days. For word detection, we can compare the most likely words of a topic identified as new with our ground truth.

Topicsketch: Real-time bursty topic detection from twitter [19] (**TopicSketch**): this paper presents a method adapted to event detection on Twitter data. The proposed model monitors the speed and acceleration of word frequencies to detect novelty. Every day, the model can raise an alert for one or more words that we can compare to our ground truth.

Table 1 gives us information about what tasks the algorithms are originally designed to solve. In order to evaluate these methods, we need to adapt them for other tasks and measure their performances on these new tasks. Even if the adaptation is not optimal and does not represent the best way to resolve a specific task, it gives us insight on how the method or feature or even just the representation helps. Now, we describe how we adapt these algorithms.

In order to adapt the TF-IDF [1] method to new word detection, we use the IDF of each word (traditionally associated with rarity) to see if the most important values of each day is a good indicator of novelty. For the method based

Table 1. Which tasks the algorithms are originally designed to solve?

Algorithm	Task 1	Task 2	Task 3
TF-IDF			X
BS		X	
DF		X	
OLDA		X	
TopicSketch	X	X	

on the Burstiness Score [12], we aggregate the burstiness score of each word in the document to create a burstiness score for the document. This aggregation can be done in several way (mean, median, percentile). To use the Document Frequency [8] feature to detect new documents, we were inspired by [1] and we use a search for k-nearest neighbors in a representation space for documents built from their *Document Frequency*. When using OLDA [7] to detect new topics, we compare the documents belonging the most to the topic identified as novel with our ground-truth documents. The TopicSketch [19] method is used to raise alerts when a term frequency is detected as abnormal. For the document detection, we observe the documents that are responsible for the alert as well as previous documents containing the detected term.

5   Results

In this section, we present the performance results of the evaluated algorithms on the tasks defined earlier. First, we enumerate specific results that help us determine the ideal parameters and understand their influence on the performance. We present these results on specific scenarios and trace the temporal evolution of precision/recall measures over time as well as the evolution of the number of new documents. Finally, we test each of these methods on an excerpt of the New York Times Annotated Dataset.

5.1   Influence of the Distance Between Topics

First we study the influence of the distance between topics on the performance of novelty detection algorithms. As a reminder, we generated datasets where we control the Kullback-Leibler divergence (KL-Div) between topics. We generated 6 datasets with the following KL-Div values: $0.01, 0.05, 0.1, 0.5, 09, 0.99$. Our intuition is the following: since most algorithms are based on similarity measure between documents and/or on the evolution of term frequencies in the corpus, we assume that novelty detection becomes more difficult with the reduction of the distance between topics. We test this hypothesis by observing the evolution of the performance on the document detection task. We see on Fig. 4 that our hypothesis is globally true, especially for the two research-based methods compared to nearest neighbors and TopicSketch. Finally, it is interesting to note that, although the detection level is very low for the DF and OLDA methods, they both have optimal results for KL-Div = 0.1.

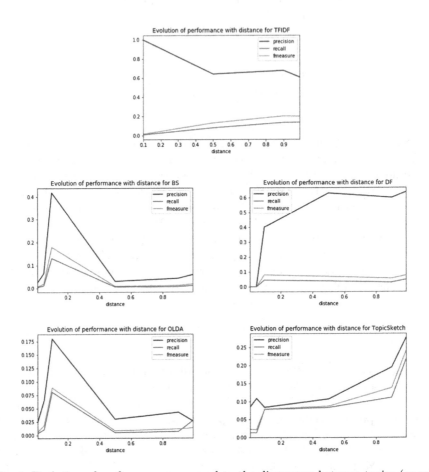

Fig. 4. Evolution of performance compared to the divergence between topics (as calculated with KL-div) for each tested algorithm.

5.2   Influence of the Choice of K for KNN-Based Algorithms

Several tested algorithms are based on a k-nearest-neighbors search. The choice of the value of the best k can greatly influence the results. Actually, the method of Allan [1] is originally thought to carry out a first story detection task, i.e. detect the first document far from all its neighbors in the representation space. The aggregation of several similar documents in the same subspace can be interesting to detect. It is necessary to modify the value of k to observe this type of phenomenon. Since we aim at correctly classifying the maximum number of novel documents, we focus on recall. We observe on Fig. 5 that, the higher the value of k, the longer good performances last over time, which is what we expect. Actually, the new documents appear in the same part of the representation space and the performance starts to decrease as soon as k documents have appeared. This is what we can expect for a first story or anomaly detection method.

5.3   Influence of the Speed of Novelty Appearance

Some methods that we are evaluating in this work have been initially developed to address event detection. Events are associated to topics that appear very quickly and in large quantities before disappearing almost as quickly. It is a typical behavior we can observe in Twitter data. This idea corresponds to the scenarios 7, 8 and 9 that we simulate in our data. Here we evaluate the influence of the speed at which new topics appear on two methods (OLDA and TopicSketch) on the document detection task.

We observe on Fig. 6, as expected, that the two tested methods are more sensitive to a steep slope and therefore better detect the novelty when it appears quickly. We can conclude that these methods are more suited to event detection tasks than to the detection of novelty appearing slowly over time.

5.4   General Results

In this section, we present the general results for the detection of new words (Task 2) and new documents (Task 3).

On Table 2, we see that, despite the overall low results, it is still the method based on TopicSketch that achieves the most competitive performance. For all the measures relating to Task 2, the latter is better. We also see that the OLDA method does not work at all for detecting new words in the case of cyclical scenarios. Finally, it is generally the recall that is very weak, which means that few words really new are correctly found by the algorithms. In terms of document detection, the results are more diverse, only the TopicSketch and TF-IDF methods stand out. We note that the two research-based methods compared to the nearest neighbors (TF-IDF & DF) work very poorly on the cyclical scenarios, which is in line with our initial intuition. This table shows that the results are quite low but it also highlights the fact that tested algorithms work differently on different scenarios.

5.5   Evaluation on the New York Times Annotated Dataset

To illustrate the performances of the different algorithms, we tested them on a real dataset[2] corresponding to articles published by the New York Times. It is a dataset of 1.8 million items (20 years of data) manually annotated by topic. We decided to carry out our experiments on the first 4 years and on topics with specific temporal behaviors. In order to evaluate our methods, we need

---

[2] https://catalog.ldc.upenn.edu/LDC2008T19.

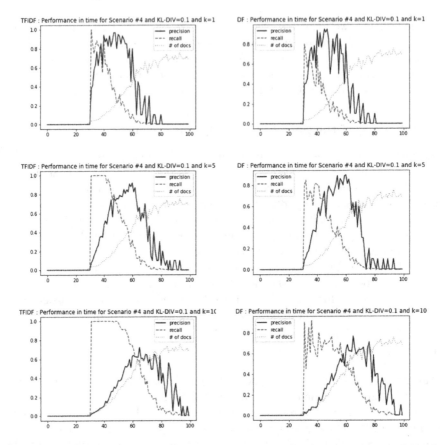

Fig. 5. Evolution of Precision and Recall measure with the appearance of novelty depending on the value of k. The curve representing the number of documents per day is normalized.

to artificially incorporate novelty into our data. For each of the topics, whose temporal evolution is presented in Fig. 7, we completely deleted its associated documents in 1987. This year of data thus forms our historic. For the next three years (1988–1989–1990), the topic is present in the data and the documents associated with it forms our ground truth.

We now test the ability of different algorithms to detect the targeted "new" topic. The representation spaces (TF-IDF, DF) or topics (OLDA) are initialized with data containing no text of the targeted topic. We then launch the methods *with* the documents corresponding to the new topic. This way, we have a ground truth and we know what we want to detect. For evaluation measures, that we present below, we use Area Under Curve (AUC) to check whether the algorithms have a good tendency to classify the really novel documents first. We use AUC instead of precision-recall because we find it more relevant for this real dataset. Contrary to the simulated data, we have not such a strong ground truth and AUC provides a more relevant summary of the method ability to rank (tagged)

Table 2. Precision (P), Recall (R) and F-Measure (F) results for each evaluated algorithms on 9 scenarios for Tasks 2 & 3.

Results for task 2: detection of new words								
Methods	Scenario 1			Scenario 2			Scenario 3		
	P	R	F	P	R	F	P	R	F
TF-IDF	0.073	0.005	0.010	0.085	0.004	0.009	0.089	0.006	0.012
BS	0.044	0.004	0.007	0.025	0.006	0.010	0.007	0.009	0.008
DF	0.186	0.005	0.010	0.179	0.004	0.008	0.205	0.006	0.013
OLDA	0	0	0	0	0	0	0	0	0
TopicSketch	**0.239**	**0.106**	**0.138**	**0.286**	**0.104**	**0.153**	**0.281**	**0.106**	**0.151**
Methods	Scenario 4			Scenario 5			Scenario 6		
	P	R	F	P	R	F	P	R	F
TF-IDF	0.247	0.006	0.012	0.400	0.003	0.007	0.496	0.009	0.017
BS	0.173	0.005	0.010	0.308	0.003	0.006	0.375	0.010	0.020
DF	0.330	0.005	0.011	0.504	0.003	0.006	0.594	0.008	0.017
OLDA	0.130	0.006	0.011	0.197	0.002	0.005	0.420	0.010	0.021
TopicSketch	**0.483**	**0.105**	**0.172**	**0.552**	**0.103**	**0.170**	**0.716**	**0.109**	**0.187**
Methods	Scenario 7			Scenario 8			Scenario 9		
	P	R	F	P	R	F	P	R	F
TF-IDF	0.456	0.008	0.015	0.466	0.005	0.011	0.499	0.010	0.021
BS	0.352	0.008	0.017	0.366	0.005	0.010	0.377	0.011	0.021
DF	0.543	0.007	0.015	0.604	0.006	0.012	0.621	0.010	0.020
OLDA	0.302	0.009	0.017	0.248	0.006	0.013	0.341	0.010	0.022
TopicSketch	**0.608**	**0.108**	**0.182**	**0.641**	**0.106**	**0.179**	**0.762**	**0.111**	**0.193**
Results for task 3: detection of new documents								
Methods	Scenario 1			Scenario 2			Scenario 3		
	P	R	F	P	R	F	P	R	F
TF-IDF	0	0	0	0.062	0.001	0.003	0.093	0.002	0.005
BS	0.028	0.005	0.008	0.083	0.013	0.023	**0.125**	0.018	0.032
DF	0	0	0	**0.193**	0.052	**0.071**	0	0	0
OLDA	0.029	0.005	0.008	0.084	0.014	0.024	0.109	0.018	0.029
TopicSketch	**0.051**	**0.036**	**0.040**	0.062	**0.056**	0.043	0.096	**0.078**	**0.083**
Methods	Scenario 4			Scenario 5			Scenario 6		
	P	R	F	P	R	F	P	R	F
TF-IDF	0.600	0.023	0.04	**0.825**	0.055	0.103	**0.856**	0.046	0.085
BS	0.048	0.005	0.010	0.102	0.011	0.019	0.258	0.027	0.049
DF	**0.638**	**0.026**	0.050	0.650	0.029	0.056	0.741	0.046	0.087
OLDA	0.048	0.005	0.010	0.077	0.011	0.019	0.108	0.027	0.043
TopicSketch	0.150	0.096	**0.114**	0.165	**0.123**	**0.139**	0.229	**0.155**	**0.183**
Methods	Scenario 7			Scenario 8			Scenario 9		
	P	R	F	P	R	F	P	R	F
TF-IDF	**0.818**	0.278	0.375	**0.843**	0.167	**0.259**	**0.852**	0.085	0.149
BS	0.604	**0.481**	**0.536**	0.326	0.133	0.189	0.170	0.034	0.057
DF	0.770	0.054	0.100	0.710	0.071	0.122	0.838	0.052	0.090
OLDA	0.104	0.181	0.132	0.069	0.080	0.070	0.061	0.045	0.038
TopicSketch	0.216	0.186	0.197	0.209	0.128	0.150	0.221	**0.142**	**0.166**

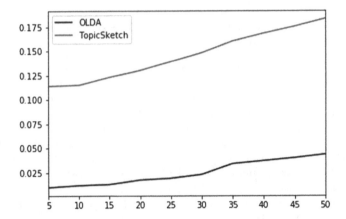

Fig. 6. Evolution of F-Measure with the slope parameter of the novelty appearance.

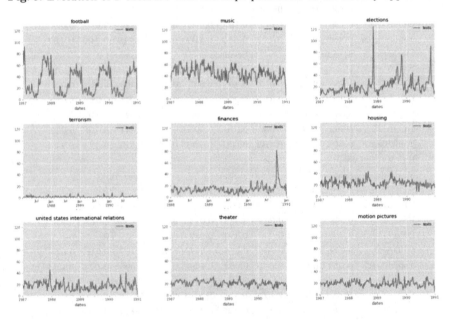

Fig. 7. Temporal evolution of some categories in the NYT.

novel documents before other (less relevant) documents. An AUC score close to 1 is better (Tables 3 and 4).

Note that each method does not necessarily perform well on the same topics. For example, only the TopicSketch method achieves interesting results for *Football*. This is a typical cyclical topic and therefore the words associated with these events occur a lot in the corpus, especially during matches such as the Superbowl. Some topics like *Terrorism* are more complicated to detect. This is explained by the fact that they still remain at the weak signal level in the corpus.

Table 3. AUC scores on some categories of the NYT Annotated Corpus.

	Football	Finances	Theater	Art	Elections
TF-IDF	0,257	0,292	**0,744**	0,514	0,334
BS	0,281	0,312	0,412	0,474	0,51
DF	0,241	0,242	0,614	**0,534**	0,378
OLDA	0,294	0,411	0,531	0,521	0,671
TopicSketch	**0,641**	**0,524**	0,514	0,531	**0,751**

Table 4. AUC scores on some categories of the NYT Annotated Corpus.

	USA intl. relations	Music	Motion pictures	Housing	Terrorism
TF-IDF	0,301	**0,588**	0,675	0,300	0,553
BS	0,14	0,201	0,254	0,145	0,341
DF	0,286	0,514	0,612	0,241	0,513
OLDA	0,561	0,54	**0,712**	**0,610**	0,491
TopicSketch	**0,614**	0,485	0,631	0,524	**0,540**

6   Conclusion and Future Works

In this work, we have built a common framework for the task of novelty detection.
We have shown that several works of the literature studied this field but not
necessarily from the same angle: the novelty was not defined the same way, the
tasks were not identical and no common benchmark exists in the literature. We
proposed our own definition of novelty with different novelty types. Working on
simulated data allowed us to control the data creation process and, thus, to better
measure the performances of the different methods according to each situation.
Although artificial data was useful for challenging the chosen algorithms when
confronted to archetypal situations, attention should be paid on the conclusion
we can draw from the experiments. Actually some concerns may be raised about
the global low scores we achieved. This can be due to a simplified data generation
process, the adaption of the existing methods designed for solving close but
different tasks, or the choice we made for the competing algorithms.

This work allowed us to draw conclusions on the features and metrics to use
according to the novelty type we aim to detect. Actually, methods using metrics
based on a simple count of words, like TopicSketch (speed and acceleration) [19],
seem to be able to detect novelty more easily than methods based on a representation space of words or documents Even if the results are globally low, the goal
of this paper was to show that: (a) there is no clear consensus around the definition of novelty, (b) a method designed for one scenario (e.g., event detection)
may be adapted to solve another scenario (e.g., emergent trend identification),
(c) different novelty scenarios need different types of methods, which is related
to the well-known No Free Lunch theorem.

However, working with simulated bag-of-word data prevents us from using context information and therefore using embeddings-based methods. In the future, we will focus on these methods applied to novelty detection and we also plan to evaluate methods based on more recent topic modeling models. Also, some more complex novelty types are interesting to study such as the disappearance of a topic or the fusion of two topics.

References

1. Allan, J., Lavrenko, V., Malin, D., Swan, R.: Detections, bounds, and timelines: UMass and TDT-3. In: Proceedings of Topic Detection and Tracking Workshop, pp. 167–174. SN (2000)
2. Blei, D.M., Lafferty, J.D.: Dynamic topic models. In: Proceedings of the 23rd International Conference on Machine Learning, pp. 113–120. ACM (2006)
3. Blei, D.M., Ng, A.Y., Jordan, M.I.: Latent Dirichlet allocation. J. Mach. Learn. Res. **3**(Jan), 993–1022 (2003)
4. Eckhoff, R., Markus, M., Lassnig, M., Schon, S.: Detecting weak signals with technologies overview of current technology-enhanced approaches for the detection of weak signals. Int. J. Trends Econ. Manag. Technol. (IJTEMT) **3**(5) (2014)
5. Gerrish, S., Blei, D.M.: A language-based approach to measuring scholarly impact. In: ICML, vol. 10, pp. 375–382. Citeseer (2010)
6. Hiltunen, E., et al.: Weak signals in organizational futures learning. Helsinki School of Economics (2010)
7. Lau, J.H., Collier, N., Baldwin, T.: On-line trend analysis with topic models: \# Twitter trends detection topic model online. In: Proceedings of COLING 2012, pp. 1519–1534 (2012)
8. Long, R., Wang, H., Chen, Y., Jin, O., Yu, Y.: Towards effective event detection, tracking and summarization on microblog data. In: Wang, H., Li, S., Oyama, S., Hu, X., Qian, T. (eds.) WAIM 2011. LNCS, vol. 6897, pp. 652–663. Springer, Heidelberg (2011). https://doi.org/10.1007/978-3-642-23535-1_55
9. Mannermaa, M.: Heikoista signaaleista vahva tulevaisuus. Wsoy (2004)
10. Markou, M., Singh, S.: Novelty detection: a review–part 1: statistical approaches. Signal Process. **83**(12), 2481–2497 (2003)
11. Marsland, S.: Novelty detection in learning systems. Neural Comput. Surv. **3**(2), 157–195 (2003)
12. Metzler, D., Cai, C., Hovy, E.: Structured event retrieval over microblog archives. In: Proceedings of the 2012 Conference of the North American Chapter of the Association for Computational Linguistics: Human Language Technologies, pp. 646–655. Association for Computational Linguistics (2012)
13. Murena, P.A., Al-Ghossein, M., Abdessalem, T., Cornuéjols, A.: Adaptive window strategy for topic modeling in document streams. In: 2018 International Joint Conference on Neural Networks (IJCNN), pp. 1–7. IEEE (2018)
14. Ng, K.W., Tsai, F.S., Chen, L., Goh, K.C.: Novelty detection for text documents using named entity recognition. In: 2007 6th International Conference on Information, Communications & Signal Processing, pp. 1–5. IEEE (2007)
15. Nigam, K., McCallum, A.K., Thrun, S., Mitchell, T.: Text classification from labeled and unlabeled documents using EM. Mach. Learn. **39**(2–3), 103–134 (2000)
16. Pimentel, M.A., Clifton, D.A., Clifton, L., Tarassenko, L.: A review of novelty detection. Signal Process. **99**, 215–249 (2014)

17. Ritter, G., Gallegos, M.T.: Outliers in statistical pattern recognition and an application to automatic chromosome classification. Pattern Recogn. Lett. **18**(6), 525–539 (1997)
18. Suzuki, Y., Fukumoto, F.: Detection of topic and its extrinsic evaluation through multi-document summarization. In: Proceedings of the 52nd Annual Meeting of the Association for Computational Linguistics (Volume 2: Short Papers), vol. 2, pp. 241–246 (2014)
19. Xie, W., Zhu, F., Jiang, J., Lim, E.P., Wang, K.: Topicsketch: real-time bursty topic detection from Twitter. IEEE Trans. Knowl. Data Eng. **28**(8), 2216–2229 (2016)
20. Yang, Y., Zhang, J., Carbonell, J., Jin, C.: Topic-conditioned novelty detection. In: Proceedings of the eighth ACM SIGKDD International Conference on Knowledge Discovery and Data Mining, pp. 688–693. ACM (2002)

Seq2VAR: Multivariate Time Series Representation with Relational Neural Networks and Linear Autoregressive Model

Edouard Pineau[1,2(✉)], Sébastien Razakarivony[1], and Thomas Bonald[2]

[1] Safran Tech, Signal and Information Technologies, Châteaufort, France
pineau.edouard@gmail.com
[2] Telecom Paris, Institut Polytechnique de Paris, Paris, France

Abstract. Finding understandable and meaningful feature representation of multivariate time series (MTS) is a difficult task, since information is entangled both in temporal and spatial dimensions. In particular, MTS can be seen as the observation of simultaneous causal interactions between dynamical variables. Standard way to model these interactions is the vector linear autoregression (VAR). The parameters of VAR models can be used as MTS feature representation. Yet, VAR cannot generalize on new samples, hence independent VAR models must be trained to represent different MTS. In this paper, we propose to use the inference capacity of neural networks to overpass this limit. We propose to associate a relational neural network to a VAR generative model to form an encoder-decoder of MTS. The model is denoted Seq2VAR for Sequence-to-VAR. We use recent advances in relational neural network to build our MTS encoder by explicitly modeling interactions between variables of MTS samples. We also propose to leverage reparametrization tricks for binomial sampling in neural networks in order to build a sparse version of Seq2VAR and find back the notion of Granger causality defined in sparse VAR models. We illustrate the interest of our approach through experiments on synthetic datasets.

Keywords: Multivariate time series · Vector linear autoregression · Relational neural networks · Granger causality

1 Introduction

Nowadays, more and more data come as multivariate time series (MTS) and finding understandable and meaningful feature representation of observed MTS samples is needed for information mining and downstream machine learning tasks. Among standard MTS representation and modeling [3], vector linear auto-regression (VAR) [21] captures dynamical and causal information contained in the data. Yet, VAR does not have representation inference mechanism: one model fits all samples. Consequently, to represent different MTS, independent

© Springer Nature Switzerland AG 2020
V. Lemaire et al. (Eds.): AALTD 2019, LNAI 11986, pp. 126–140, 2020.
https://doi.org/10.1007/978-3-030-39098-3_10

VAR models must be trained. This operation becomes very expensive when VAR parameters are constrained, for example with sparsity [1] or symmetry, since there are no closed-form nor simple regularization to solve it. In contrast, efficient and powerful inference is a key advantage of neural networks based representation learning.

Many recent works on neural generative models have been used for representation learning, with particular attention on variational autoencoders (VAE) [8,22]. The VAE, as a latent variable model, finds the joint distribution between observed data and a set of latent variables. With appropriate assumptions on the variational distribution and regularization, one hopes to uncover and disentangle independent causal sources of variations in the data, with a certain form of interpretability and a good representation power. However, finding such disentangled representation cannot be successfully done without an appropriate inductive bias [12].

In this context, a specialized VAE architecture, called neural relational inference (NRI), has recently been developed for interaction inference in MTS [9]. NRI uses the concept of relational learning [18] to explicitly capture the variable interactions that explain the data dynamics. The inferred binary interaction graph is used as a variable selection preceding a nonlinear auto-regressive decoding scheme. The objective, with an appropriate setting, is both to help the generative decoder with sparsity and to uncover the real interactions in an unsupervised manner.

Nevertheless, despite good inductive bias, this approach suffers from its powerful decoder, that does not necessarily need meaningful latent representation to recover data. In our experiments, we show that with NRI, this problem manifests when the interactions to discover are heterogeneous, i.e., the latent interaction graph is weighted. As a result, the unsupervised interaction discovery does not correspond anymore to true physical reality while the model still decodes properly. We note that the problem of information vanishing in the presence of a too expressive decoder is classical [14,20]: in extreme cases, the inference part becomes meaningless, transforming the VAE into a standard generative auto-regressive model [10].

Finally, by construction, NRI is built to consider only the previous time step for each prediction. Therefore, it needs lagged information as explicit input, which mechanically increases the number of parameters to train.

In this paper, we propose an alternative, simple MTS representation learning framework that exploits both VAR generative models and neural network inference capacities. As in [9], we assume that MTS are the observation of a system that can be represented with causal information. Following the classical framework of encoder-decoder, we build the Seq2VAR model, whose architecture presents three main advantages. First, we prevent information vanishing by representing our MTS samples as the parameters of a VAR instead of the input of a neural auto-regressive decoder. Second, we leverage recent advances in neural networks binary sampling [7,11,13] to build explicit sparse representations; this way, non-zero entries of the inferred representation can be interpreted as

Granger causalities. Third, we help our model generalizing over the notion of interactions by using a relational inference neural network (RINN) [9] as MTS encoder. These three properties make Seq2VAR able to find meaningful MTS representations.

After presenting Seq2VAR model and assumptions, we perform some experiments to assess its different advantages. We then discuss (1) the interest of using RINN encoder instead of recurrent neural networks (RNN), that are explicitly made for time series modeling, and (2) the relations and differences between Seq2VAR and the NRI model.

2   Model Description

2.1   Notations and Assumptions

Let $\mathcal{X} \subseteq \mathbb{R}^{d \times T}$ be some finite set of n d-dimensional MTS defined over the time range $t = 1, \ldots, T$. We assume that each MTS $X^{(s)}$, $s = 1, \ldots, n$ is generated by some dynamical system. Specifically, we assume that each MTS follows a K-order linear auto-regressive model, i.e., there exists some tensor $A^{(s)} \in \mathbb{R}^{K \times d \times d}$ such that the MTS $X^{(s)} = (X_1^{(s)}, \ldots, X_T^{(s)}) \in \mathcal{X}$ satisfies $X_t^{(s)} = \sum_{k=1}^{K} A_k^{(s)} X_{t-k}^{(s)}$ for all $t = K+1, \ldots, T$. Both the tensor $A^{(s)}$ and the initial values $(X_1^{(s)}, \ldots, X_K^{(s)})$ are unknown and can change from one sample to the other. Some additive observation noise can be added to the samples. In this paper, we assume that the set of tensors $\{A^{(s)}, s = 1, \ldots, n\}$ belongs to $\mathcal{A}$, the set of acceptable dynamical systems. This set $\mathcal{A}$ is also unknown.

2.2   General Problem Setup

We place ourselves in the encoder-decoder framework. We use a relational inference neural network (RINN) as MTS encoder [9], which takes a sample $X^{(s)}$ as input and outputs a tensor $\hat{A}^{(s)}$. The decoder is a VAR model parametrized by $\hat{A}^{(s)}$. This tensor is therefore the latent representation of the MTS, with respect to the linear decoding assumption. We denote the encoder by F_ϕ, where ϕ are a parameter in some finite-dimensional space. Observe that F_ϕ is a mapping from $\mathbf{R}^{d \times T}$ to $\mathbb{R}^{K \times d \times d}$. The parameter ϕ is optimized for the objective function:

$$\sum_{s=1}^{n} \left\{ \sum_{t=K+1}^{T} \left\| X_t^{(s)} - \sum_{k=1}^{K} F_\phi(X^{(s)})_k X_{t-k}^{(s)} \right\|_2^2 + \lambda \Omega \left(F_\phi(X^{(s)}) \right) \right\}. \qquad (1)$$

Here Ω is a regularizing penalty function and λ a positive coefficient of penalization. These can be used to control the sparsity of the output (number of non-zero entries of the tensor $F_\phi(\cdot)$). We call our model Seq2VAR (sequence-to-VAR).

2.3   Sparsity in Seq2VAR

Seq2VAR offers the possibility to modify the encoding posterior distribution and the regularization depending on the task of interest. In particular, the output of the encoder F_ϕ may be made sparse [1,5,23]. For such constraint, we use the recent advances in sparse representation learning based on derivations of Gumbel-Softmax trick [6,15].

In theory, true sparse learning rely on L_0 regularization. In practice L_0 norm cannot be directly used as penalty in the objective function since it is non-differentiable. General approaches uses Ridge, LASSO or group-LASSO regularization [5] as proxy for L_0 regularization. This sparsity becomes implicit and is difficult to control. As an alternative and to obtain explicit sparsity, we propose to use stochastic gates determining for each samples $X^{(s)}$ which entries of $F_\phi(X^{(s)})$ are set to zero [13]. The probability of each gate is an additional output of the RINN encoder. Gates are sampled using a continuous relaxation of binomial sampling [6,15], to let the gradient flow. The encoder outputs the probability of opening the gates, denoted $P_\phi(X^{(s)})$. We denote $G_\phi(X^{(s)})$ the binary gates that are sampled with the following derivation of Gumbel-softmax trick proposed in [11]:

$$G_\phi(X^{(s)}) = \sigma\left(\frac{P_\phi(X^{(s)}) + \log U - \log(1-U)}{\tau}\right), \qquad (2)$$

with σ the sigmoid function, τ the temperature of the relaxation (the higher, the smoother the approximated binary sampling) and $U \sim \mathcal{U}(0,1)$. The σ, log and $+$ are matrix element-wise operators, U has the same dimensions than $P_\phi(\cdot)$, with all entries sampled independently. Depending on the task, $G_\phi(\cdot)$ lives either in $\mathbb{R}^{K \times d \times d}$ or in $\mathbb{R}^{1 \times d \times d}$. The latter corresponds to variable selection, while the former corresponds to variable and lag selection. The collection of gates forms a binary mask that is directly applied to the dense tensor $F_\phi(\cdot)$.

We can now control the sparsity of the model with an appropriate penalty function Ω applied to $G_\phi(\cdot)$ in the following sparse problem:

$$\sum_{s=1}^{n}\left\{\sum_{t=K+1}^{T}\left\|X_t^{(s)} - \sum_{k=1}^{K}\left(G_\phi(X^{(s)}) \odot F_\phi(X^{(s)})\right)_k X_{t-k}^{(s)}\right\|_2^2 + \lambda\Omega\left(G_\phi(X^{(s)})\right)\right\},$$

$$(3)$$

where $\odot$ denotes the Hadamard product.

In [13], the authors propose a method for creating sparse neural networks with a similar method, in a Bayesian deep learning setting. They regularize the sparsity with the norm of the probability of the gates. In (3) we generalize this method to representation inference. We use the number of positive gates, i.e., the sum of all the entries of the (almost) binary mask as a proxy for the norm L_0 on encoder output. Thanks to the continuous relaxation of the binary sampling (2), this sum is differentiable with respect to ϕ and can be used as a penalization in the objective function.

Remark 1. A particular case of sparse approach for Seq2VAR is the pure binary, i.e., by using only $G_\phi(\cdot)$ as a VAR parameters. This case is studied in the Experiment Sect. 3.2.

2.4 Symmetry in Seq2VAR

Another constraint that can be easily imposed to Seq2VAR is the symmetry of the tensor $\hat{A}^{(s)}$. Thanks to the inference mechanism, we can force $\hat{A}^{(s)}$ to be symmetric by imposing $\hat{A}^{(s)} = 1/2(F_\phi(X^{(s)}) + F_\phi(X^{(s)})^{T(1,2)})$, where $T(1,2)$ is the transposition of dimensions 1 and 2 of the tensor. This setting can be particularly important in the case where the interactions between variables are physical links. We experiment more specifically this constraint in Sect. 3.3, where this model is referred to as symmetric-Seq2VAR. Note that symmetry can be easily coupled with sparsity.

3 Experiments

3.1 Methodology

As a preliminary experimental work, we illustrate our approach on several synthetic datasets, each with several levels of difficulty to illustrate generalization capacity, causality discovery and representation power. First, in order to assess the generalization capacity of Seq2VAR, we use a test set with intrinsic parameters (causality graphs, interaction intensities) that differ from those of the train set in all experiments. Second, causality discovery is assessed through the F1-score between inferred and ground truth causality graphs. When $\hat{A}^{(s)}$ is dense, we keep the most significant entries, i.e., those above a certain percentile of all entries in absolute value. This percentile is chosen with a priori knowledge. Third, since the set $\mathcal{A}$ is finite, we can assess unsupervisely learned representation with a standard downstream task like classification. We classify the systems with the inferred tensors $\hat{A}^{(s)}$. The classification is a 1-nearest-neighbor on the tensors with l^2 norm. The classification is completed in test set representation. Test set is divided in train and test subset for the classification task.

For each experiment, we compare Seq2VAR to NRI [9] and VAR [21], from which we respectively inspire for encoder and decoder. We remind that NRI learning relies on variational inference, whose objective function contains a Kullback Leibler divergence between variational posterior and a certain prior distribution [8]. In binary and sparse setting, the prior of each latent graph is the proportion of 1 wanted in the whole latent graph, since all latent entries are independently sampled, by the mean-field assumption of VAEs. We always give NRI the true proportion as prior. For Seq2VAR, eventual usage of sparsity or regularization is specified when existing.

To provide fair comparison benchmarks, the experiments are built such that both VAR and NRI model fit in. Technical details about neural network architectures and parameters are given in Appendix A. We used the *Statsmodel* python library [19] for the VAR. The code used for the experiments is available at:

https://github.com/edouardpineau/Seq2VAR. Experiments on real datasets, in particular in the context of system health monitoring at Safran, will be the developed as a future work.

3.2 Assessing Seq2VAR in Binary Linear Setting

For our first experiment, we aim at (1) showing that binary sampling approach is relevant for Seq2VAR model and (2) analysing how Seq2VAR behaves in the presence of noise. We place ourselves in a favorable setting for VAR, NRI and Seq2VAR. We generate samples from a stationary 1-order linear autoregressive model, where the linear transition matrix is a permutation matrix. We add several level of additive Gaussian noise to the observations (see Fig. 1 for an illustration).

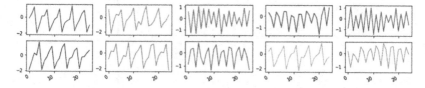

Fig. 1. 10-dimensional permutation MTS with observation noise $\mathcal{N}(0, 0.3)$.

We chose $d = 10$, $T = 50$, $K = 1$. Taking $\#\mathcal{A} = 20$, we generate 10 permutation matrices for the train set and 10 other permutation matrices for the test set. From each matrix we generate 100 samples with random $\mathcal{N}(0, 1)$ initial conditions. We train two versions of the Seq2VAR: dense with no penalty and binary. After training, Seq2VAR has generalized the notion of permutation. We note that the binary version is naturally the only one to find the real permutation matrices. Figure 2 shows the outputs of different versions of Seq2VAR encoder at test time, with different level of observation noise.

We see in Fig. 2 an illustration of the problems created by an increase of observation noise variance. While signal-to-noise ratio decreases, disentanglement of the permutations from the noise becomes harder. VAR overestimate the density of the matrix. Optimal mean-square solution (closed form) of VAR decodes noisy signal by mixing noisy signals. On the contrary, Seq2VAR (without regularization) is parsimonious (but not sparse), i.e. it it gathers many entries of $\hat{A}^{(s)}$ around zero (see Fig. 3).

We explain this behavior by two facts. First the inference mechanism of Seq2VAR is shared by all samples and has integrated the noise by seeing numerous noisy examples. Second, the low expressive decoder cannot integrate noise nor deal with complex mixture of noisy signals. This second point explains why Seq2VAR resists better to noise than NRI.

We present in Table 1 the classification accuracy and causality recovery in the presence of different level of observation noise. Seq2VAR approaches outperform VAR and NRI when noise gets stronger. binary-Seq2VAR give also better results, as its assumption fits the data better.

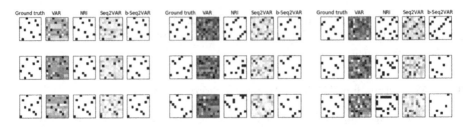

Fig. 2. Inferred transition matrices for different test samples, using VAR, NRI, Seq2VAR and binary Seq2VAR, compared to ground truth, depending on the level of observation noise: $\mathcal{N}(0, 0.1)$ (left), $\mathcal{N}(0, 0.3)$ (middle), $\mathcal{N}(0, 0.5)$ (right).

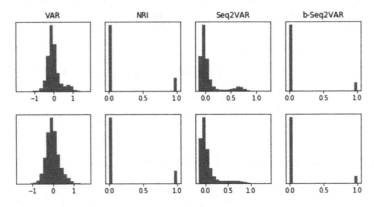

Fig. 3. Histogram of the distribution of the entries of inferred transition matrices over a test set, using VAR, NRI, Seq2VAR and binary Seq2VAR, compared to ground truth, depending on the level of observation noise: $\mathcal{N}(0, 0.1)$ (left), $\mathcal{N}(0, 0.5)$ (right).

In Fig. 4, we see the boxplot representations of the distribution of the L_1 distance between ground truth and inferred causality graph within the test set, for several levels of observation noise. We first see that all methods suffer from noise. When noise is low, both NRI, Seq2VAR and binary-Seq2VAR offers almost perfect graph discover. However, the outliers (red crosses) of NRI spread further than the one of Seq2VAR, which means that NRI fails to find the latent graph not by simply missing some entries but by finding a completely different graph that still fits the decoding requirements.

3.3   Assessing Seq2VAR in Physical Setting

We now propose to assess the capacity of Seq2VAR to find Granger causality graph hidden in physical data. We use 10-ball-springs system data, consisting of the simultaneous trajectories of 10 identical balls in a 2D space, each ball being connected to others by springs with probability 0.5. The connection network is called interaction graph. System dynamics follows Newton's law of motion, sampled with $\Delta t = 0.001$ and then subsampled at frequency $1/100$. The system

Table 1. Test classification accuracy (%) and causality discovery (F1-score). The standard deviations correspond to the variation in results between different generated datasets (train and test). B-Seq2VAR stands for binary Seq2VAR.

Dataset	Perm. $+ \mathcal{N}(0, 0.1)$		Perm. $+ \mathcal{N}(0, 0.3)$		Perm. $+ \mathcal{N}(0, 0.5)$	
Tasks	Supervised classification	Causality detection	Supervised classification	Causality detection	Supervised classification	Causality detection
VAR [21]	100 ± 0.0	72.2 ± 0.2	96.85 ± 3.8	61.8 ± 4.5	96.5 ± 1.6	52.6 ± 3.9
NRI [9]	100 ± 0.0	95.63 ± 3.1	97.6 ± 3.4	84.3 ± 4.9	97.0 ± 2.1	68.3 ± 3.7
Seq2VAR	100 ± 0.0	$\mathbf{97.3 \pm 0.3}$	97.0 ± 4.3	92.5 ± 2.1	$\mathbf{97.8 \pm 3.9}$	83.6 ± 2.3
B-Seq2VAR	100 ± 0.0	97.2 ± 0.1	$\mathbf{100 \pm 0.0}$	$\mathbf{94.6 \pm 2.7}$	97.0 ± 4.3	$\mathbf{90.1 \pm 2.9}$

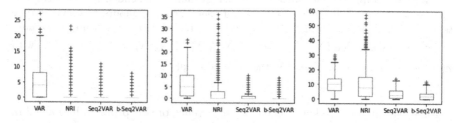

Fig. 4. Quartiles of the distribution of the L_1 distances between true and inferred causality graphs with VAR, NRI, Seq2VAR and binary Seq2VAR respectively with observation noise $\mathcal{N}(0, 0.1)$ (left), $\mathcal{N}(0, 0.3)$ (middle) and $\mathcal{N}(0, 0.5)$ (right). b-Seq2VAR stands for binary Seq2VAR.

can be represented as a Granger causality graph [2] (see Fig. 5). Each sample is 49 timesteps long. Note that this experiment is used in NRI paper [9].

For the experiments of this section, we sample 20 different balls-spring binary interaction graphs, 10 for the train set and 10 for the test set. Each of the 20 dynamical systems associated to the 20 graphs is built at random, with balls linked by a spring with probability 0.5. Each graph characterizes a class. We propose two different datasets: one with identical rigidity 1 for all springs (unweighted interaction graph) and one with variable rigidity (weighted interaction graph). For the later, the rigidity of each spring is uniformly sampled in [0.75, 1]. Each binary graph characterizes a class. We use 1000 samples per class. As for permutation MTS (see Sect. 3.2) we use different systems for the train set and the test set to challenge the generalization power of Seq2VAR.

We trained respectively a VAR, a Seq2VAR, a symmetric Seq2VAR and a sparse Seq2VAR. We chose $K = 2$ for all the experiments. For the later, we impose a slight regularization on the level of sparsity, i.e. on the number of null entries in the matrix. In Eq. 3 we use $\Omega(G_\phi(X^{(s)})) = \left| \frac{1}{100} \| G_\phi(X^{(s)}) \|_1 - 0.5 \right|$ and λ is set at $1e^{-3}$, 0.5 being the sparsity prior. Without this regularization, the sparse Seq2VAR generally converges naturally towards the right proportion of true zeros. The regularization is added for preventing an eventual trivial solution where the mask is a matrix of ones or local minima where only the

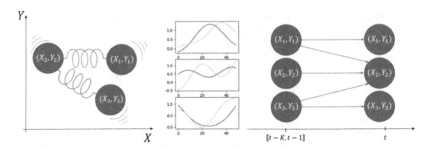

Fig. 5. Example of 3-ball-springs system (left) and its Granger causality graph (right). The causality graph represents the first-order dynamical dependencies between balls position at each time t and the positions of their direct neighbors at previous time steps $t-1\ldots t-K$. For all $t=K\ldots T$ and $i\in\{1,2,3\}$, arrows indicates a dynamical dependency between $(X_t^{(i)}, Y_t^{(i)})$ and $\left\{(X_{t-1}^{(j)}, Y_{t-1}^{(j)}), \ldots (X_{t-K}^{(j)}, Y_{t-K}^{(j)})\right\}_{j\in pa(i)}$, with $pa(i)$ the set of parents of node i in the directed graph.

diagonal parameters are kept. The only occurrence of this problem happened in the heterogeneous problem.

Table 2 gathers the results. We see that Seq2VAR scores better on both quality measures than the usual VAR approach learned on the test set. If NRI gives very good results of causality detection on homogeneous springs, its causality discovery performance drops when dealing with heterogeneous springs. On the contrary, Seq2VAR gives good results for both homogeneous and heterogeneous rigidity graph.

It is interesting to notice that using an expressive inference network that explicitly model dependencies between variables capitalize on the global information of the dataset and (1) generalize on new data and (2) overpass the statistical identifiability problem due to subsampling [4]. It is also interesting to notice that sparsity is not optimal in Seq2VAR as it is in NRI. As variable spring rigidity makes the distribution wider and makes the causality less identifiable in both linear (Seq2VAR) and nonlinear (NRI) decoding process, with respect to our experimental setup.

We find in Fig. 6 an illustration of the inference capacities of our model.

4 Discussions

This section proposes discussions around our Seq2VAR approach for MTS representation with VAR matrices and causality graph.

4.1 RINN vs. RNN as Seq2VAR Encoder

The main assumption when modeling time series data is the autoregressive structure of the observed signal. A generic and expressive autoregressive model is the

Table 2. Test classification accuracy (%) and causality discovery (F1-score). *Hyperparameters different than the one used for homogeneous springs case (from the original paper [9]) to obtain better results. See Appendix A for more details.

Dataset	Homogeneous springs		Heterogeneous springs	
Tasks	Supervised classification	Causality detection	Supervised classification	Causality detection
VAR [21]	17	55.7	14.2	54.0
NRI [9]	**100**	**96.1**	**100**	78.5*
Seq2VAR	**100**	89.4	**100**	84.5
Symmetric Seq2VAR	99.9	91.4	**100**	**90.4**
Sparse Seq2VAR	99.7	88.2	99.2	81.4

Fig. 6. Three examples of inferred transition matrices over a test set, using VAR, NRI, Seq2VAR, Symmetric Seq2VAR, Sparse Seq2VAR and Sparse Symmetric Seq2VAR, compared to ground truth.

recurrent neural network (RNN). Hence, in practice we could use RNN to take the MTS as input and do the inference of the tensor A.

Our different attempts with RNN encoder were not able to generalize over the notion of causal interactions, no matter the regularization technique used to avoid overfitting (reduction of network memory capacities, increasing of depth [17], dropout [24], batch-norm [16], L_1-norm and L_2-norm penalty on weights). We show in Fig. 7 an example of train and test performances evolution during training, respectively for permutation and ball-springs experiments with GRU encoder instead of RINN encoder. We can see that a Seq2VAR using RNN as encoder overfits.

We explain this by the fact that RINN explicitly takes as input all the pairs of univariate time series constituting the MTS and outputs a tensor whose entries represent an embedding of each pair. Therefore, this inductive bias incites the network to model one-to-one interactions. We remind that the causality graphs of the test set are different from the causality graphs of the train set. Hence we ask our inference network to generalize over a discontinuous manifold. RINN inference networks and its explicit one-to-one interactions modeling learns well to generalize. Conversely, RNNs implicitly learn the notion of interactions during training, with a vector output that needs to be folded into the right shape. The generalization is more difficult.

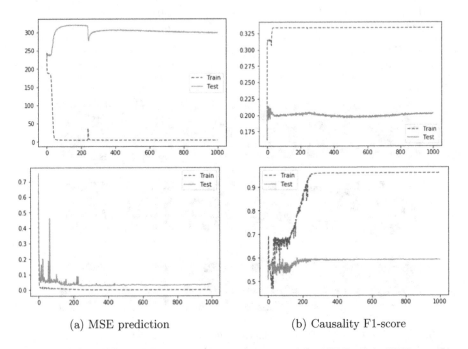

(a) MSE prediction   (b) Causality F1-score

Fig. 7. Train and test performances during training of Seq2VAR with GRU encoder instead of RINN encoder. Column (a): MSE of the 1-step VAR prediction. Column (b): F1-score of the inferred causality graph. Top row: permutation dataset. Bottom row: homogeneous 10-ball-springs dataset.

4.2   Relation with NRI

For the inference learning, the closer existing model is the Neural Relational Inference (NRI) [9], that uses a modified version of the interaction neural networks [18]. The NRI consists on a graph inference model, set as a VAE with binary latent space. The inferred graph is used as a variable selection procedure for a prediction model. This configuration specifically applies to physical interacting systems MTS (like ball-springs system). Three major differences appear between Seq2VAR and NRI.

First the form of the decoder. NRI decoding scheme is a non linear network that takes as input an embedding of the pairwise variable interactions at each time step and output the incremental change to predict next time step from current time step. On the contrary, we propose to leverage the simplicity of a linear autoregressive decoder that is potentially less expressive but do not require additional parameters.

Second, as a consequence of the form of the decoder: the latent representation. We can infer both binary and real latent representation to respectively represent existence and intensity of the causal interactions in the data. The real part is implicit in NRI. Experiment Sect. 3.3 shows that NRI does not disentangle existence and intensity of the interactions: when springs are not equally rigid, NRI is perturbed and finds a latent graph that does not correspond to physical reality. Our Seq2VAR, thanks to its continuous part, explicitly disentangles latent causal structure from other information and finds an acceptable causal graph.

Third difference, which is also as a consequence of the decoder: the minimal input information requirement. In fact, the notion of time lag is absent from NRI and lagged information needs to be furnished as input. For example, with the ball-springs systems data, Seq2VAR only needs measures of the location of each ball at each time step while NRI requires both location and velocity. Beyond the minimal input information requirement, the absence of lag in NRI modeling imposes that causality graph remains the same for all lags, like in physical structures.

Finally, these differences materialize with the results of the experiments presented in Sect. 3. Note that they also procure a significant advantage in term of complexity. We assess this complexity with the number of parameters and computing CPU time. These results are in Table 3.

Table 3. Memory and computing time. Absence of results means that model is not used.

Experiments	Permutations (batch size = 128)		Ball-springs (batch size = 64)	
	Number of parameters	CPU time per epoch (s)	Number of parameters	CPU time per epoch (s)
NRI [9]	65031	5.1	72966	38.8
Seq2VAR	47811	1.2	52550	4.7
Symmetric Seq2VAR	–	–	52550	4.7
Binary Seq2VAR	47811	1.4	–	–
Sparse Seq2VAR	–	–	61071	5.7

5   Conclusions and Future Works

In this paper, we propose the Seq2VAR model, which learns to represent multivariate time series as Granger causal graph. Seq2VAR a encoder-decoder model consists of a relational neural network for inference and a linear autoregressive for generation. By construction, our model is immune to information vanishing in neural autoregressive framework. It is also capable of generalizing over the notion of interaction and Granger causality, i.e. estimating good VAR representation for unseen samples. The chosen representation is robust to continuous structural changes in data, and can easily interpretated. We demonstrated these properties with experiments on two different cases, and compared to state-of-the-art methods.

In further work, we intend to generalize the model to non-linear settings, as well as extending the way sparsity is controlled and constrained.

Acknowledgments. This work is supported by the company Safran through the CIFRE convention 2017/1317.

A   Appendix: Hyperparameters

For our Seq2VAR, we used a succession of 2-layers perceptrons for our relational encoder, as in NRI [9]. The parameters to chose concern latent dimension for all layers and the temperature parameter τ for the relaxed binary sampling (see Sect. 2.3). They are presented in Table 4.

Table 4. Training parameters.

Experiments	Permutations		Homogeneous springs		Heterogeneous springs	
Parameters	Latent dimension	τ	Latent dimension	τ	Latent dimension	τ
NRI [9]	64	0.5	64	0.5	64	0.1
Seq2VAR	64	0.1	64	0.5	64	0.5
Symmetric Seq2VAR	64	0.1	64	0.5	64	0.5
Sparse Seq2VAR	64	0.1	64	0.5	64	0.5

For NRI, all other parameters are the one of the original paper for the homogeneous springs rigidity except for the dimensionality of the latent space which we set to 64 instead of 256, since in the experimental setup of the original paper, it gives the same results while diminishing computing time and memory needs. For the heterogeneous rigidity, the parameter *prediction_steps* is set to 5 instead of 10 and τ is set to 0.1. These parameters gave the best average results. In fact, due to the highly expressive form of its decoder, NRI was able to build good predictor with not the good graph. We played with parameters to get more stable and better results. For the experiments, we also tried to change the *skip first* parameter that is set to False or True in the original paper [9], depending on the dataset studied. It did not change the results of the experiments.

References

1. Davis, R.A., Zang, P., Zheng, T.: Sparse vector autoregressive modeling. J. Comput. Graph. Stat. **25**(4), 1077–1096 (2016)
2. Eichler, M., Didelez, V.: Causal reasoning in graphical time series models. arXiv preprint arXiv:1206.5246 (2012)
3. Esling, P., Agon, C.: Time-series data mining. ACM Comput. Surv. (CSUR) **45**(1), 12 (2012)
4. Gong, M., Zhang, K., Schoelkopf, B., Tao, D., Geiger, P.: Discovering temporal causal relations from subsampled data. In: International Conference on Machine Learning, pp. 1898–1906 (2015)
5. Haufe, S., Müller, K.-R., Nolte, G., Krämer, N., Sparse causal discovery in multivariate time series. In: Causality: Objectives and Assessment, pp. 97–106 (2010)
6. Jang, E., Gu, S., Poole, B.: Categorical reparameterization with gumbel-softmax. arXiv preprint arXiv:1611.01144 (2016)
7. Kaiser, L., Bengio, S.: Discrete autoencoders for sequence models. arXiv preprint arXiv:1801.09797 (2018)
8. Kingma, D.P., Welling, M.: Auto-encoding variational bayes. arXiv preprint arXiv:1312.6114 (2013)
9. Kipf, T., Fetaya, E., Wang, K.-C., Welling, M., Zemel, R.: Neural relational inference for interacting systems. arXiv preprint arXiv:1802.04687 (2018)
10. Larochelle, H., Murray, I.: The neural autoregressive distribution estimator. In: Proceedings of the Fourteenth International Conference on Artificial Intelligence and Statistics, pp. 29–37 (2011)
11. Li, Z., et al.: Towards binary-valued gates for robust LSTM training. arXiv preprint arXiv:1806.02988 (2018)
12. Locatello, F., Bauer, S., Lucic, M., Gelly, S., Schölkopf, B., Bachem, O.: Challenging common assumptions in the unsupervised learning of disentangled representations. arXiv preprint arXiv:1811.12359 (2018)
13. Louizos, C., Welling, M., Kingma, D.P.: Learning sparse neural networks through l_0 regularization. arXiv preprint arXiv:1712.01312 (2017)
14. Ma, X., Zhou, C., Hovy, E.: MAE: mutual posterior-divergence regularization for variational autoencoders. arXiv preprint arXiv:1901.01498 (2019)
15. Maddison, C.J., Mnih, A., Teh, Y.W.: The concrete distribution: a continuous relaxation of discrete random variables. arXiv preprint arXiv:1611.00712 (2016)
16. Merity, S., Keskar, N.S., Socher, R.: Regularizing and optimizing LSTM language models. arXiv preprint arXiv:1708.02182 (2017)
17. Sak, H., Senior, A., Beaufays, F.: Long short-term memory recurrent neural network architectures for large scale acoustic modeling. In: Fifteenth Annual Conference of the International Speech Communication Association (2014)
18. Santoro, A., et al.: A simple neural network module for relational reasoning. In: Advances in Neural Information Processing Systems, pp. 4967–4976 (2017)
19. Seabold, S., Perktold, J.: Statsmodels: econometric and statistical modeling with python. In: Proceedings of the 9th Python in Science Conference, vol. 57, p. 61. Scipy (2010)
20. Shen, X., Su, H., Niu, S., Demberg, V.: Improving variational encoder-decoders in dialogue generation. In: Thirty-Second AAAI Conference on Artificial Intelligence (2018)
21. Toda, H.Y., Phillips, P.C.B.: Vector autoregression and causality: a theoretical overview and simulation study. Econ. Rev. **13**(2), 259–285 (1994)

22. Tschannen, M., Bachem, O., Lucic, M.: Recent advances in autoencoder-based representation learning. arXiv preprint arXiv:1812.05069 (2018)
23. Yi, S., Pavlovic, V.: Sparse granger causality graphs for human action classification. In: Proceedings of the 21st International Conference on Pattern Recognition (ICPR 2012), pp. 3374–3377. IEEE (2012)
24. Zaremba, W., Sutskever, I., Vinyals, O.: Recurrent neural network regularization. arXiv preprint arXiv:1409.2329 (2014)

Modelling Patient Sequences for Rare Disease Detection with Semi-supervised Generative Adversarial Nets

Kezi Yu, Yunlong Wang$^{(\boxtimes)}$, and Yong Cai

IQVIA Inc., Plymouth Meeting, PA, USA
yunlong.wang@iqvia.com

Abstract. Rare diseases affect 350 million patients worldwide, but they are commonly delayed in diagnosis or misdiagnosed. The problem of detecting rare disease faces two main challenges: the first being extreme imbalance of data and the second being finding the appropriate features. In this paper, we propose to address the problems by using semi-supervised generative adversarial networks (GANs) to deal with the data imbalance issue and recurrent neural networks (RNNs) to directly model patient sequences. We experimented with detecting patients with a particular rare disease (exocrine pancreatic insufficiency, EPI). The dataset includes 1.8 million patients with 29,149 patients being positive, from a large longitudinal study using 7 years medical claims. Our model achieved 0.56 PR-AUC and outperformed benchmark models in terms of precision and recall.

Keywords: Rare Disease Detection · Sequence data modeling · Long Short Term Memory · Generative Adversarial Networks

1 Introduction

Rare diseases affect 350 million patients worldwide [17]. Collectively they are common but individually they are rare. Given rare diseases' low prevalence rate among population, the low disease awareness could lead to patients being misdiagnosed/undiagnosed and not getting the appropriate treatment. Patients with rare diseases often visit several physicians over the course of many years before they receive diagnoses for their conditions [2]. An effective detection method is crucial to help raise disease awareness and achieve early disease intervention [3]. On the other hand, interest in machine learning for healthcare has grown immensely during last several years [5]. Several machine learning methods, such as recurrent neural network [9], auto encoder [22], FHIR-formatted representation [26], etc. have been proposed to predict patient-level disease using electronic healthcare record (EHR) data. For more comprehensive overview of machine learning application on healthcare, we refer readers to [12,23,30].

Recently, deep learning based models, such as long short-term memory and attention models, have been widely applied for disease detection and made

© Springer Nature Switzerland AG 2020
V. Lemaire et al. (Eds.): AALTD 2019, LNAI 11986, pp. 141–150, 2020.
https://doi.org/10.1007/978-3-030-39098-3_11

improvements on prediction accuracy. In [7], the authors proposed an approach for converting the patient history into medical sequence and then train a long short term memory for sequence labeling task, based on which, an application was developed in [9]. To enhance the interpretability, there have been great efforts of trying to explain black-box deep models, including via attention mechanism [8], decay factor [1], mimic decisions of deep models with decision tree [4], etc.

Generative adversarial networks (GANs) [13] have drawn numerous attention for its potential to generate almost true samples from random noise inputs. Although the original idea was more focused on the generator, in [11,27], the authors proposed to use GANs in a semi-supervised learning (SSL) setting and demonstrated that GANs performed well by leveraging unlabeled data with novel training techniques. Meanwhile, the problem of rare disease detection falls perfectly under the setting of semi-supervised learning. Since the diagnosed patient population is extremely small, we have limited positive samples but a large number of patients who are under-diagnosed.

Instead of using hand-crafted features as input to a classifier [19], we directly worked with patient medical history sequences. This comes with multiple benefits, including the ability to capture more complex disease patterns, saving extensive efforts in feature engineering, and making the framework easily transferable to another disease. Since GANs were not intrinsically able to handle sequence data, we opted to use recurrent neural network (RNN)-based model for fix-length sequence embedding.

2   Method

The architecture of our framework is shown in Fig. 1.

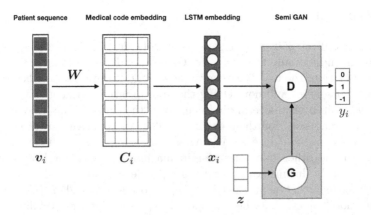

Fig. 1. Framework architecture illustrated. z is a random noise input to the generator of GAN.

Each patient is represented by a sequence $\boldsymbol{v}_i = \{v_{ij}, j = 1, \ldots, N\}$, of which v_{ij} is a medical code indicating a type of hospital visit (Dx) or prescription (Rx). A graphical illustration of such representation is shown in Fig. 2. The patient sequence is then transformed to its matrix representation $\boldsymbol{C}_i$ by embedding the medical codes, i.e. $\boldsymbol{c}_{ij} = \boldsymbol{W}h(v_{ij})$, where $\boldsymbol{W}$ is embedding matrix and $h(\cdot)$ denotes one-hot encoding. Then an LSTM network is used to encode the sequence to $\boldsymbol{x}_i$. The embedded medical sequence is fed into the discriminator D of a SSL GAN, where the prediction is either positive (1), negative (0) or generated sample by generator G (-1).

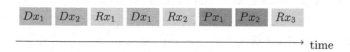

$$Dx_1 \quad Dx_2 \quad Rx_1 \quad Dx_1 \quad Rx_2 \quad Px_1 \quad Px_2 \quad Rx_3$$

$\longrightarrow$ time

Fig. 2. A toy example of a patient medical history sequence. Dx refers to diagnosis, Rx refers to prescription and Px refers to medical procedure. The subscripts denote different codes within each category.

2.1   Patient Record Embedding

Encode Medical Codes. In the patient medical history sequence, each medical code is essentially a categorical variable. The number of categories (different types of medical codes) depends on the level of specificity, i.e., the more specific the meaning of a code is, the more unique codes there would be. In our case, we end up with 5362 unique codes.

We are inspired by the concept of word embedding in natural language processing (NLP) community. Some notable examples include word2vec [21] and Glove [24]. In the original application, the vector representations retain semantic meanings, e.g., synonyms of a word tend to be closer to each other spatially. We will demonstrate a similar behavior of our medical code embedding in a later section.

We used skip-gram model with negative sampling to train the embedding network. The minimum count for valid code is 5, i.e., any codes that occur less than five times in all the sequences would be discarded for training the embedding model, and they were assigned a all-zero vector as their embedding. This left us with 5035, or 93% of all the unique codes. The dimension d_w of embedding vector was empirically chosen to be 300.

Embed Longitudinal Records. The most prominent model for processing time series or sequence data is recurrent neural network (RNN). Different variations of memory cells, including long short-term memory (LSTM) [15] and gated recurrent unit (GRU) [10], were proposed to handle the long-term dependencies over time, which significantly improved the performance of RNNs in various types of tasks, such as sequence classification, sequence tagging [16], and machine translation [6]. A commonly used technique in various tasks is to use the hidden state vector as a representation of the sequence.

We adopted the same idea for sequence embedding. Specifically, patient sequences were padded with a fixed length of N. Only labeled training patient sequences were used for training LSTM embedding model. A single-layer LSTM with dimension of the hidden state equal to d_S was used. The hidden state of each time stamp was retained, and then aggregated by max pooling operation over time, which resulted in a d_S-dimension vector. In our experiments, we empirically chose $N = 300$ and $d_S = 256$. After sequence embedding, we appended the patients' age and gender, and then scale all the features to the range between -1 and 1. The final feature vector has a dimension of 258.

2.2 Semi-supervised GAN

In the original framework of GANs [13], a GAN has a generator network G that takes random noise as input and produce samples that follow the real data distribution $p_{data}(x)$. The training of G is guided by the discriminator network D, which is trained to distinguish samples from the generator distribution $p_{model}(x)$ from real data. Suppose that the goal of D extends to finding the actual class assignment of real samples and K is the number of possible classes of labeled data, i.e., $p_D(y = K + 1|x)$ is the probability of a sample generated from G. Then the loss function for training D comes from three parts, labeled data $\mathcal{L}$, unlabeled data $\mathcal{U}$ and data from G:

$$
\begin{aligned}
L_{\mathcal{L}} &= -\mathbb{E}_{x,y\sim\mathcal{L}}\left[\log p_D(y|x, y < K + 1)\right], \\
L_{\mathcal{U}} &= -\mathbb{E}_{x\sim\mathcal{U}}\left[\log p_D(y \le K|x)\right], \\
L_{\mathcal{G}} &= -\mathbb{E}_{x\sim G}\left[\log p_D(y = K + 1|x)\right],
\end{aligned}
\tag{1}
$$

And the total discriminator loss becomes $L_D = L_{\mathcal{L}} + L_{\mathcal{U}} + L_{\mathcal{G}}$. The first term in Eq. 1 is the standard supervised cross-entropy loss, which minimizes the negative log probability of the label, given the data sample is labeled. The second term minimizes the negative log probability of an unlabeled sample coming from one of K possible classes. The third term minimizes the negative probability of a fake sample being recognized.

One thing to note is that the discriminator with $K + 1$ outputs is over-parameterized, since the outputs of a softmax function sum to one. Thus, we can set D with K outputs and the equivalent discriminator is given by $D(x) = \dfrac{Z(x)}{Z(x) + 1}$, where $Z(x) = \sum_{k=1}^{K} \exp[l_k(x)]$.

In our experiments, we set D and G to have the same architecture but mirroring each other, with five hidden layers. A tanh layer is added at the end of G that maps the output to the range between -1 and 1 (same as input features). We used weight normalization [28] and drop out [29] to accelerate training and prevent overfitting.

2.3   Training and Inference

Training GANs is notoriously difficult, particularly in a semi-supervised learning setting that requires jointly learning from labeled and unlabeled data. As noted in [27], using feature matching loss for G works well empirically for semi-supervised learning. The objective of feature matching is guiding the generator to generate samples that match the first order statistics of real data. Furthermore, instead of directly minimizing the distance between generated sample mean and real sample mean, the discriminator was used as a feature extractor and the intermediate layer output was used as the "feature" of data samples. The loss term of feature matching is expressed as

$$L_{FM} = ||\mathbb{E}_{x \sim G} f(x) - \mathbb{E}_{x \sim \mathcal{U}} f(x)||^2. \tag{2}$$

A more in-depth discussion of using GANs in semi-supervised learning setting can be found in [11]. It was suggested that the generator in SSL should generate samples that are complement to real samples. Intuitively, only if the generated sample distribution does not interfere the true sample distributions, it can help the discriminator to learn the manifolds of real samples from different classes. To achieve this, the paper proposed to increase the diversity of generated samples by increasing generator entropy, via introducing a new loss term pull-away term (PT) first proposed in [31]:

$$L_{PT} = \frac{1}{N(N-1)} \sum_{i=1}^{N} \sum_{j \neq i} \left(\frac{f(x_i)^T f(x_j)}{||f(x_i)|| ||f(x_j)||} \right)^2. \tag{3}$$

Additionally, in order for complement generator to work, the discriminator needs to have strong belief on fake-real on unlabeled data. This is achieved by adding a conditional entropy loss to discriminator:

$$L_{ent} = \mathbb{E}_{x \sim \mathcal{U}} \sum_{k=1}^{K} p_D(k|x) \log p_D(k|x). \tag{4}$$

Finally, the SSL GAN model has discriminator loss $L_D = L_{\mathcal{L}} + L_{\mathcal{U}} + L_{\mathcal{G}} + L_{ent}$ and generator loss $L_G = L_{FM} + L_{PT}$.

3   Experiment

3.1   Data

We leverage data from IQVIA longitudinal prescription (Rx) and medical claims (Dx) databases, which include hundreds of millions patients' clinical records. In our study, we focus on one type of rare disease, exocrine pancreatic insufficiency (EPI).

The detailed data preparation process is as follows. We pulled the diagnoses, procedures and prescriptions at transaction level from January 1, 2010 to July 31,

2017. We only kept a subset of patients by applying standard patient eligibility rules, which left us with a total number of 1,792,760 patients. Out of all the patients, 29,149 of them (1.6%) are found to be diagnosed with EPI, which are labeled as positive. 80% of the positive patients were used for training and validation and the rest were held for testing. It is important to note that the remaining patients are under-diagnosed, not essentially negative, so we cannot simply label them as is. Therefore, we applied business rules and identified 69,845 negative patients (three times as the number of positive training patients) for training and validation. The final numbers are shown in Table 1.

Table 1. Population distribution.

	Positive	Negative	Unlabeled
Total	29,149	506,450	1,257,161
Train/validation	23,395	69,845	1,257,161
Test	5,754	436,605	0

3.2 Baseline

For comparison, we chose logistic regression (LR), random forest (RF), XGBoost (XGB) and the discriminator (DNN) in the GAN architecture as baseline models. Note that the input to the benchmark classifiers is the output of LSTM embedding.

3.3 Evaluation Strategy

We used Adam optimizer [18] to train each model, with the default learning rate set to 0.001. The number of training epochs was 20. The model was implemented and tested in Tensorflow with GPU support on a system equipped with 128 GB RAM, 8 Intel Xeon E5-2683 at 2.10 GHz CPUs and one Tesla P100-PCIE GPU.

Because of the high imbalance of data, we used precision-recall (PR) curve and area of PR curve (PR AUC) as evaluation metrics. The PR AUC is computed by trapezoidal rule [25].

4   Result

In this section, we first present some descriptive results on medical code embedding, and then quantitative results of the model performance comparison.

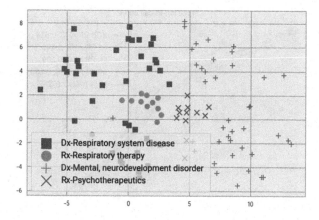

Fig. 3. The visualization result by t-SNE of medical codes. Blue and orange dots are respiratory diagnosis (Dx) and prescription (Rx) codes, respectively. The green and red are Dx and Rx codes for mental diseases. (Color figure online)

4.1   Embedding Visualization

As described in Sect. 2.1, each medical code was represented as a 300-dimension dense vector. In order to examine whether the embedding vectors retain meaningful medical information, we identified 67 diagnosis (Dx) codes within two therapeutic areas (TAs), respiratory disease and mental disorder, as well as corresponding prescription (Rx) codes. We used t-SNE [20] technique for visualization of the selected codes. The visualization result is shown in Fig. 3. We observe that two sets of Rx codes are centered, with each forming its own cluster. The corresponding Dx codes are clustered by their TAs, and aligned with Rx codes on either side.

4.2   Model Comparison

The PR-AUC by the SSL GAN was 0.56, and the deep neural network with the same architecture as the discriminator had a score of 0.52. We saw a relative increase of 6% over the best benchmark model. The precision-recall curves of all models are shown in Fig. 4.

5   Discussion

The problem of semi-supervised learning often comes with the issue of limited labeled data, and sometimes extreme class imbalance. In our problem of interest, we had both issues. In order to improve the classification performance, it is crucial to fully make use of unlabeled data. By comparing the PR curves, we may cautiously conclude that the performance gain over DNN was from the unlabeled data.

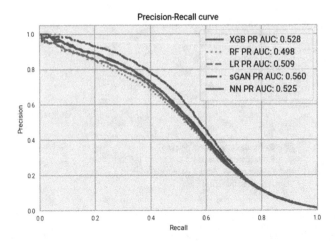

Fig. 4. Precision-recall curves of the SSL GAN and benchmark models, where sGAN refers to SSL GAN model.

Although the idea of generative adversarial nets is rather straightforward and intriguing, the training process is extremely cumbersome and difficult to reach convergence. According to [27], the training process equals to finding a Nash equilibrium of a non-convex game with continuous, high-dimensional parameters, which may fail to converge if using gradient descent based optimization algorithm [14]. Therefore, carefully designed loss functions are crucial to successfully using GAN-based model.

6   Conclusion

In this work, we present a novel framework which combines the merits of both recurrent neural networks and generative adversarial networks. We demonstrated that GANs used in a semi-supervised learning setting can benefit from the vast number of unlabeled data to improve prediction performance, even under an extreme data imbalance scenario. Furthermore, by utilizing RNN-based networks to directly work with patient medical sequences, we are free from extensive work of feature engineering. More importantly, our preliminary analysis of the medical code embedding shows some very interesting properties that are worth investigating in the future. Finally, this framework can be easily transferred to detecting another disease of interest.

References

1. Bai, T., Zhang, S., Egleston, B.L., Vucetic, S.: Interpretable representation learning for healthcare via capturing disease progression through time. In: Proceedings of the 24th ACM SIGKDD International Conference on Knowledge Discovery & Data Mining. pp. 43–51. ACM (2018)
2. Boat, T.F., Field, M.J., et al.: Rare Diseases and Orphan Products: Accelerating Research and Development. National Academies Press, Washington, DC (2011)

3. Cameron, M.J., Horst, M., Lawhorne, L.W., Lichtenberg, P.A.: Evaluation of academic detailing for primary care physician dementia education. Am. J. Alzheimer's Dis. Other Dement.® **25**(4), 333–339 (2010)
4. Che, Z., Purushotham, S., Khemani, R.G., Liu, Y.: Interpretable deep models for ICU outcome prediction. In: AMIA Annual Symposium Proceedings. AMIA Symposium, vol. 2016, pp. 371–380 (2016)
5. Ching, T., et al.: Opportunities and obstacles for deep learning in biology and medicine. J. R. Soc. Interface **15**(141), 20170387 (2018)
6. Cho, K., Van Merriënboer, B., Bahdanau, D., Bengio, Y.: On the properties of neural machine translation: encoder-decoder approaches. arXiv preprint arXiv:1409.1259 (2014)
7. Choi, E., Bahadori, M.T., Schuetz, A., Stewart, W.F., Sun, J.: Doctor AI: predicting clinical events via recurrent neural networks. In: Machine Learning for Healthcare Conference, pp. 301–318 (2016)
8. Choi, E., Bahadori, M.T., Sun, J., Kulas, J., Schuetz, A., Stewart, W.: Retain: an interpretable predictive model for healthcare using reverse time attention mechanism. In: Advances in Neural Information Processing Systems, pp. 3504–3512 (2016)
9. Choi, E., Schuetz, A., Stewart, W.F., Sun, J.: Using recurrent neural network models for early detection of heart failure onset. J. Am. Med. Inform. Assoc. **24**(2), 361–370 (2016)
10. Chung, J., Gulcehre, C., Cho, K., Bengio, Y.: Empirical evaluation of gated recurrent neural networks on sequence modeling. arXiv preprint arXiv:1412.3555 (2014)
11. Dai, Z., Yang, Z., Yang, F., Cohen, W.W., Salakhutdinov, R.R.: Good semi-supervised learning that requires a bad GAN. In: Advances in Neural Information Processing Systems, pp. 6510–6520 (2017)
12. Ghassemi, M., Naumann, T., Schulam, P., Beam, A.L., Ranganath, R.: Opportunities in machine learning for healthcare. arXiv preprint arXiv:1806.00388 (2018)
13. Goodfellow, I., et al.: Generative adversarial nets. In: Advances in Neural Information Processing Systems, pp. 2672–2680 (2014)
14. Goodfellow, I.J.: On distinguishability criteria for estimating generative models. arXiv preprint arXiv:1412.6515 (2014)
15. Hochreiter, S., Schmidhuber, J.: Long short-term memory. Neural Comput. **9**(8), 1735–1780 (1997)
16. Huang, Z., Xu, W., Yu, K.: Bidirectional LSTM-CRF models for sequence tagging. arXiv preprint arXiv:1508.01991 (2015)
17. Kaplan, W., Wirtz, V., Mantel, A., Béatrice, P.: Priority medicines for Europe and the world update 2013 report. Methodology **2**(7), 99–102 (2013)
18. Kingma, D.P., Ba, J.: Adam: a method for stochastic optimization. arXiv preprint arXiv:1412.6980 (2014)
19. Li, W., Wang, Y., Cai, Y., Arnold, C., Zhao, E., Yuan, Y.: Semi-supervised rare disease detection using generative adversarial network. arXiv preprint arXiv:1812.00547 (2018)
20. van der Maaten, L., Hinton, G.: Visualizing data using t-SNE. J. Mach. Learn. Res. **9**(Nov), 2579–2605 (2008)
21. Mikolov, T., Sutskever, I., Chen, K., Corrado, G.S., Dean, J.: Distributed representations of words and phrases and their compositionality. In: Advances in Neural Information Processing Systems, pp. 3111–3119 (2013)
22. Miotto, R., Li, L., Kidd, B.A., Dudley, J.T.: Deep patient: an unsupervised representation to predict the future of patients from the electronic health records. Sci. Rep. **6**, 26094 (2016)

23. Obermeyer, Z., Emanuel, E.J.: Predicting the future–big data, machine learning, and clinical medicine. New Engl. J. Med. **375**(13), 1216 (2016)

24. Pennington, J., Socher, R., Manning, C.: Glove: global vectors for word representation. In: Proceedings of the 2014 Conference on Empirical Methods in Natural Language Processing (EMNLP), pp. 1532–1543 (2014)

25. Purves, R.D.: Optimum numerical integration methods for estimation of area-under-the-curve (AUC) and area-under-the-moment-curve (AUMC). J. Pharmacokinet. Biopharm. **20**(3), 211–226 (1992)

26. Rajkomar, A., et al.: Scalable and accurate deep learning with electronic health records. NPJ Dig. Med. **1**(1), 18 (2018)

27. Salimans, T., Goodfellow, I., Zaremba, W., Cheung, V., Radford, A., Chen, X.: Improved techniques for training GANs. In: Advances in Neural Information Processing Systems, pp. 2234–2242 (2016)

28. Salimans, T., Kingma, D.P.: Weight normalization: a simple reparameterization to accelerate training of deep neural networks. In: Advances in Neural Information Processing Systems, pp. 901–909 (2016)

29. Srivastava, N., Hinton, G., Krizhevsky, A., Sutskever, I., Salakhutdinov, R.: Dropout: a simple way to prevent neural networks from overfitting. J. Mach. Learn. Res. **15**(1), 1929–1958 (2014)

30. Xiao, C., Choi, E., Sun, J.: Opportunities and challenges in developing deep learning models using electronic health records data: a systematic review. J. Am. Med. Inform. Assoc. **25**(10), 1419–1428 (2018)

31. Zhao, J., Mathieu, M., LeCun, Y.: Energy-based generative adversarial network. arXiv preprint arXiv:1609.03126 (2016)

Extended Kalman Filter for Large Scale Vessels Trajectory Tracking in Distributed Stream Processing Systems

Katarzyna Juraszek[1]([✉]), Nidhi Saini[2], Marcela Charfuelan[2], Holmer Hemsen[2], and Volker Markl[1,2]

[1] Technische Universität Berlin, Straße des 17. Juni 135, 1062 Berlin, Germany
kasia.juraszek@gmail.com
[2] DFKI GmbH, Alt-Moabit 91c, 10559 Berlin, Germany
https://www.tu-berlin.de, https://www.dfki.de

Abstract. The growing number of vessel data being constantly reported by a variety of remote sensors, such as the Automatic Identification System (AIS), requires new data analytics that can operate at high data rates and are highly scalable. Based on a real-world dataset from maritime transport, we propose a large scale vessel trajectory tracking application implemented in the distributed stream processing system Apache Flink. By implementing a state-space model (SSM) - the Extended Kalman Filter (EKF) - we firstly demonstrate that an implementation of SSMs is feasible in modern distributed data flow systems and secondly we show that we can reach a high performance by leveraging the inherent parallelization of the distributed system. In our experiments we show that the distributed tracking system is able to handle a throughput of several hundred vessels per ms. Moreover, we show that the latency to predict the position of a vessel is well below 500 ms on average, allowing for real-time applications.

Keywords: Time-series · State-space models · Extended Kalman filter · Stream processing · Spatio-temporal data · Remote sensing systems

1 Introduction

Analysing and understanding of maritime traffic is a topic of increasing interest, due to its direct implications on security and safety, as well as on environmental and socio-economic factors. Nowadays, there is a growing number of ship reporting technologies and remote sensing systems, such as the Automatic Identification System (AIS), Long Range Identification and Tracking (LRIT), radar tracking or Earth Observation. Each of these technologies provides spatio-temporal vessel positioning data that contributes to better monitoring of maritime transport. The AIS technology has become a standard in the industry, being mandatory for ships in international voyages, such as cargo vessels, fishing

© Springer Nature Switzerland AG 2020
V. Lemaire et al. (Eds.): AALTD 2019, LNAI 11986, pp. 151–166, 2020.
https://doi.org/10.1007/978-3-030-39098-3_12

vessels exceeding certain size as well as all passenger vessels, regardless of their size. The AIS information provided by vessels, as a stream of tuples, includes kinematic information such as latitude, longitude, speed and course, voyage information including destination port and estimated time of arrival, as well as static data such as size and type of a ship. The AIS technology, which was originally introduced for collision avoidance, is currently also used for vessel tracking, vessel behaviour identification and anomaly detection [3].

State-space models (SSMs) are popular methods used to model how different phenomena change over time [16]. The term *state-space* was originally coined by Kalman (1960) and applied to the field of control engineering. An SSM is a representation of some physical system, where input, output, and state variables are related by first-order differential equations. The state variables depend on input variables, while the output variables depend on the values of the state variables. SSMs have been successfully applied in various fields, including engineering, statistics, computer science and economics. The Kalman filter is well-known for being one of the most powerful techniques for state estimation. The purpose of the algorithm is to provide an estimation with minimum error variance. The nonlinear version of the algorithm, the so called Extended Kalman Filter (EKF) is widely used to estimate position in GPS receivers [13] or for robot tracking [17].

Academics using the EKF in practice usually focus on the motion of robots in constrained spaces. In contrast, applying state space models for vessel tracking imposes further challenges, such as infrequent or discontinued observations, arbitrary or noisy trajectories, and erratic movements.

Distributed computing helps in processing large amounts of raw data in real-time and in a timely manner by parallelising the computation, distributing the data and automatically handling failures [11]. In addition, distributed stream processing solutions are helping to overcome the main obstacles of real-time processing, which are achieving the consistency of states across the system as well as fault recovery, over long recovery times. Thanks to these features, new distributed processing engines, which provide users with the scalable execution of data analysis tasks are arising [12]. The main goal of current and popular engines, such as Hadoop [2], Apache Spark [7] or Apache Flink [6] is to enable developers to write distributed data analysis applications in an easy and efficient manner.

In this paper, we propose an implementation of the EKF in a distributed stream processing system for real-time trajectory tracking of many vessels in parallel. In our experiments, each vessel provides a stream of remote sensing AIS data, which is then used to create and continuously update its SSM. In this manner, we are then able to estimate in real-time a new position for each vessel. We show that in our use case, the distributed tracking system is able to handle a throughput of 200 vessels/ms and requires a latency below 500 ms on average to predict the next position of a vessel.

The paper is organised as follows. First, we summarize the selection of related work on processing streams, real-time data tracking and EKF. Section 3 includes the theory behind the EKF as well as the practical implementation of the algorithm in Apache Flink. Section 4 describes the technical setup behind the EKF in the distributed environment. In the subsequent part, Sect. 5, the data set characteristics, accuracy results of the experiments as well as performance evaluation is given, followed by the conclusion in the last section.

2 Related Work

As reported in the survey paper [24], AIS data is used nowadays in several works for mining relevant aspects of navigation, such as safety of seafaring, namely traffic anomaly detection, route estimation, collision prediction, and path planning.

In this survey several techniques are reported, including EKF as a learning-model-based method for route estimation.

EKF has been used for vessel tracking in many works. For example, in Perera and Soares [21], an EKF algorithm is proposed as a vessel state estimator due to its capabilities of fusing nonlinear system kinematics with a given set of noisy measurements. They use the EKF not only for state estimation (i.e., position, velocity and acceleration), but also for trajectory prediction. Their experiments were performed in MATLAB and only with simulated data.

SSMs and Kalman filters have been studied and implemented in various tools for a long time, but mainly applied to a single machine and relatively small sets of batch data. Several traditional tools are unable to process the large amounts of data that are generated daily or simply incapable of processing stream data. Therefore, some researchers have started to consider the possibility to use and implement these techniques in large-scale distributed dataflow systems. For example, Sheng et al. [23] implemented an extended Kalman filter (a recursive filter) using the MapReduce framework, to perform prediction in an industrial setting. Moussa [19] used Apache Spark Streaming to implement a scalable application for real-time prediction of vessels' future locations. The method used in this work for estimating a new position is based on a scalable computation of trip patterns, which are efficiently queried using a geo-hashing index. This work also uses the DEBS Challenge 2018 dataset, but unfortunately does not report thorough experiments on throughput or latency.

Another interesting work that already addresses the problem of processing streams of AIS data in real-time is reported by Brandt and Grawunder [9], where the whole trajectories of a vessel and its current neighbors are predicted in order to avoid critical situations, such as two vessels being too close to each other. In the setup of this work, the real-time arrival and processing of the data points is simulated by sampling the data and then estimating the trajectory of a vessel ten minutes into the future. In contrast to the approach presented in our paper, the authors calculate ten locations per predicted trajectory rather than the next location of the vessel. The authors admit that the simple linear extrapolation used in their work to predict the future trajectories of the moving objects leads to non-optimal predictions, especially when a vessel is turning. In addition, the authors perform the computation on a single machine and therefore the computationally demanding queries are far from delivering the results in near real-time. Dalsnes et al. [10] present a similar data-driven approach using cubic spline interpolation of trajectories sampled from an AIS historical database. They predict the position of a vessel between 5 and 15 min into the future also using the recent past trajectory of the vessel. This work relies heavily on the availability of historical data and there is no information regarding its use in a streaming fashion or real-time.

3   The Extended Kalman Filter

We apply distributed dataflow processing to analyse kinematic information, such as latitude, longitude, speed, and course from multiple vessels in parallel. While processing the data, we apply the extended Kalman filter to real-time stream data, to estimate the next position of a vessel. To the best of our knowledge, we present the first implementation of an extended Kalman filter on the distributed dataflow system Apache Flink.

3.1   EKF in Theory

As presented in Fig. 1, the EKF consists of two steps: a prediction step followed by a correction step. The prediction step starts with an approximation of the state ahead, the so-called a priori state $\hat{x}_t^-$. The $f(\hat{x}_{t-1}^+)$ function is a non-linear function relating the a posteriori state at the previous time $t - 1$ to the state at the current time t. The added w_{x_t} is a white Gaussian process noise with 0 mean and covariance Q_t. The second equation in the prediction step projects the error covariance P_t^-, called the a priori error covariance, where $F(\hat{x}_{t-1}^+)$ is the Jacobian matrix of partial derivatives of f with respect to x. The correction part of the algorithm starts now and the measurement equation z_t is introduced at this point.

$$z_t = h(x_t^-) + w_{z_t}, \tag{1}$$

where w_{z_t} is white Gaussian measurement noise with zero mean and R_t covariance. The $h(x_t^-)$ function in the measurement equation z_t is a nonlinear function relating the a priori state x_t^- to the actual measurement at time t.

    The correction part takes the a priori state and the a priori error covariance to compute three values. The first value calculated in the correction step is the *Kalman gain* K_t. It represents how a new measurement improves the predicted state vector, where $H(\hat{x}_t^-)$ is the Jacobian matrix of partial derivatives of h with respect to x. Next, the a posteriori state $\hat{x}_t^+$ is calculated by updating the a priori state with the actual measurement. In the end the a posteriori error covariance P_t^+ is computed using identity matrix, Kalman gain K_t, Jacobian matrix $H(\hat{x}_t^-)$ and a priori error covariance P_t^-. Now the algorithm loops by again starting the prediction part, using the calculated posteriori values as input in the prediction equations. The interested reader is referred to [20] and [25] for a detailed and practical description of SSM and EKF.

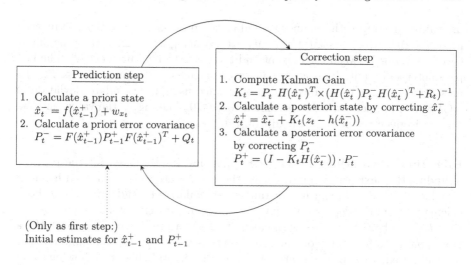

Fig. 1. Graphical representation of the extended Kalman filter operations (adapted from [25]).

3.2   EKF in Practice

One of the prerequisites for implementing EKF in practice is the a priori knowledge of the type of movement of an object. In case of tracking, such as vessels on waters, no a priori knowledge of the directions of the target is generally available, therefore in our case the behaviour of vessels is approximated by a constant velocity model. Since ocean vessels tend to follow a slow parabolic-type movement, where fast changing manoeuvres are not present, this assumption goes in line with other scholars' findings [22]. In order to use the coordinate data, the geodetic coordinates (WGS 84), which are not suitable for data processing are converted so that the next location of a vessel is not predicted with respect to longitude and latitude values, but rather as a latitude and longitude distance in meters from the point where the last position of a ship was reported.

EKF Parameters Initialization. In order to start the EKF for the first time, two parameters need to be initialized, a posteriori state and a posteriori error covariance. Since the starting point of the route is known, the a posteriori error covariance is set to a small value (0.01) on the main diagonal of the a posteriori error covariance matrix. The initial state estimate is set to zero, as the values will be replaced with the next run of the EKF. Two other parameters, being reused by the EKF on each run, are Q and R, which are the process noise covariance matrix and measurement noise covariance matrix. When using the EKF algorithm for tracking of moving objects, Q represents possible accelerations that allow the tracked object to deviate from constant velocity. Following the assumptions of the acceleration process noise, which can be assumed to be 8.8 m/s^2 and assuming 2 rad/s as maximum turn rate for the vehicle, the following values are set on the main diagonal of the process noise covariance matrix: $[(0.5 \cdot 8.8 \cdot \Delta t^2)^2, (0.5 \cdot 8.8 \cdot \Delta t^2)^2, (2 \cdot \Delta t)^2), (8.8 \cdot \Delta t)^2]$, where Δt is the time difference in seconds between the current and the previous measurement [8]. The last parameter to be initialised is the measurement noise covariance matrix R. The measurement noise covariance R can be defined using the standard deviation of a GPS measurement, which is assumed to be 6.0. The bigger the value, the less "trust" is given to the sensor readings [15].

EKF Implementation. In the EKF algorithm implemented for the purpose of finding the next position of a vessel, the belief state to be estimated has four variables: cumulative longitude distance x, cumulative latitude distance y (both calculated from the departure point), heading, and velocity of a vessel at a given time t. The algorithm starts with calculating the a priori state. To do so, the a posteriori state from previous measurements is used with the constant velocity model to predict the new a priori state. The a priori state has the following form:

$$\hat{x}_t^- = \begin{bmatrix} x_t^- \\ y_t^- \\ \psi_t^- \\ v_t^- \end{bmatrix} = \begin{bmatrix} x_{t-1}^+ + \Delta t \cdot v_{t-1}^+ \cdot \cos(\psi_{t-1}^+) \\ y_{t-1}^+ + \Delta t \cdot v_{t-1}^+ \cdot \sin(\psi_{t-1}^+) \\ (\psi_{t-1}^+) \bmod (2 \cdot \pi) - \pi \\ v_{t-1}^+ \end{bmatrix} \tag{2}$$

where $\hat{x}_t^-$ is the predicted a priori state, x_t^- and y_t^- are respectively the cumulative longitude and latitude distance in meters from the departure port, Δt is the time difference in seconds between the current and the previous measurement, ψ_{t-1}^+ is the heading of a vessel and v_{t-1}^+ is the velocity of a vessel in meters per second.

To calculate the a priori error covariance, the $F(\hat{x}_{t-1}^+)$, which is the Jacobian matrix of partial derivatives of $f(\hat{x}_{t-1}^+)$ with respect to x, needs to be calculated first.

$$F(\hat{x}_{t-1}^+) = \begin{bmatrix} 1 & 0 & -\Delta t \cdot v_{t-1}^+ \cdot \sin(\psi_{t-1}^+) & \Delta t \cdot \cos(\psi_{t-1}^+) \\ 0 & 1 & \Delta t \cdot v_{t-1}^+ \cdot \cos(\psi_{t-1}^+) & \Delta t \cdot \sin(\psi_{t-1}^+) \\ 0 & 0 & 1 & 0 \\ 0 & 0 & 0 & 1 \end{bmatrix} \tag{3}$$

The a priori error covariance is then predicted following the formula given for P_t^-. The input in the calculation of the a posteriori state is the actual measurement data z_t and the a priori state $\hat{x}_t^-$. In our EKF implementation, the actual measurement data is the actual longitude and latitude distance from the departure point, calculated as the cumulative sum of all the distances between the measurements until this point in time.

$$z_t = \begin{bmatrix} \text{measured cumulative longitudinal distance} \\ \text{measured cumulative latitude distance} \end{bmatrix} \tag{4}$$

The remaining parts of the algorithm are calculated following the equations from Fig. 1.

4 Distributed Pipeline

4.1 Technical Setup

The technical setup of the processing pipeline for this work is presented in Fig. 2. The real-time arrival of the time-series data is simulated using Apache Kafka and the distributed computing of the next location prediction given by the EKF is leveraged with the use of Apache Flink.

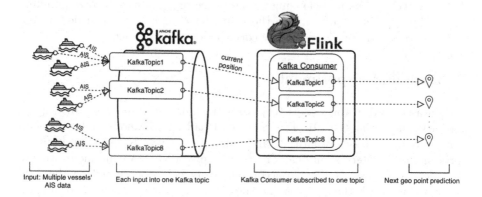

Fig. 2. Detailed Kafka Flink pipeline.

4.2 EKF in the Distributed Environment

Since every non-trivial streaming application is stateful, applying the EKF in a distributed environment using Flink requires working with the state abstraction. States are an important feature, but also have a serious performance impact on the processing in distributed dataflow systems, as they require synchronization across machines and need to be managed in a fault-tolerant way in case of machine failures. A stateful application remembers certain events or intermediate results, which can be accessed later, for instance when a new event is arriving [6]. Given the recursive nature of the EKF algorithm, where the a posteriori values calculated in the correction step are further used in the prediction step when a new event arrives, the use of *Keyed State* operators [4] is crucial for implementing this algorithm in a distributed system. We use four different states in our work:

- The first state `prevKalmanParams` is used to store a tuple consisting of a posteriori state and a posteriori error covariance calculated in the Correction step.
- The second state `prevTimestamp` stores the timestamp of the last arriving event so that the time difference (Δt) needed for the prediction of the a priori state can be calculated upon arrival of the next event.

- The third state prevGeoPoints remembers the last position reported in the last event, in order to calculate the distance travelled.
- The fourth state prevCumSum stores the cumulative sum of distance travelled from the reported departure port.

Each of these states is updated on every input tuple, whenever an event arrives. The state values from the previous run are fed to the current calculation. In the implementation of the EKF algorithm the *Managed Key State ValueState<T>* was used, which is a state scoped to the key of the current input element. It means that every keyed stream, belonging to one trajectory, will have a corresponding state. This type of state can keep the value, which can be then retrieved and updated per key. In our case one key corresponds to one vessel.

5   Data and Experiments

The dataset used in the vessels trajectory tracking use case, was provided by MarineTraffic during the 2018 DEBS Grand Challenge [1] and includes the geo-location data (in terms of latitude and longitude) of vessels departing from 25 ports in the Mediterranean Sea. The data is provided as a continuous stream of tuples. A ship sends a tuple according to its behaviour based on the AIS specifications. Each these tuples, includes also the name of the port of origin, unique ID of the vessel, timestamp, vessel course, heading and draught. The data include several types of vessels, corresponding to 503 trajectories obtained during a period of approximately three months in 2015 (10-03-15 13:13 to 19-05-15 7:32). Many of the vessels report their position every two minutes, but some have very irregular periods, including long periods of time (over several hours) with no report.

The experiments are conducted on a single server machine with 48 CPUs, 2.0 Ghz, 126 GB of RAM, running Ubuntu 16.04, Apache Kafka (v. 2.11) and Apache Flink (v. 1.8). Following the recommendations in the Flink documentation, we fixed the number of Flink task slots to 48. Thus, in our experiments the level of parallelism is given by the number of slots or CPUs used [5].

In the following we evaluate our system according to accuracy and large scale performance. In the first experiment, Sect. 5.1, we calculate the next position prediction error for every point of the 503 trajectories in the data. In the second experiment, Sect. 5.2, we evaluate the performance of the system in terms of event and processing time latency as well as ingestion rate.

5.1   Accuracy Evaluation

The result of the point prediction using the extended Kalman filter is a longitude and latitude pair of the next vessel's position. To evaluate accuracy, we use the RMSE, which is also used for example in [10] to analyse the proximity of the mean of predicted values to the true value. We apply RMSE to calculate the prediction error for latitude and longitude values, but also for distance, i.e., the distance between the predicted position point and the actual point. As it is done in [10,18], we define the distance RMSE for a vessel's trajectory, of L total number of reported AIS tuples, as:

$$RMSE_{dist} = \sqrt{\frac{\sum_{l=1}^{L} \Delta d(l)^2}{L}} \qquad (5)$$

where $\Delta d(l)$, for a particular position l, is the actual distance between the true position and the one predicted with EKF, both input as pair of longitude and latitude coordinates. The lower the RMSE, the better the prediction. In our case $\Delta d(l)$ is calculated using the *Haversine*[1] distance to calculate the great-circle distance between two points. The RMSE for longitude and latitude is calculated similarly, subtracting the true longitude (or latitude) from the predicted one.

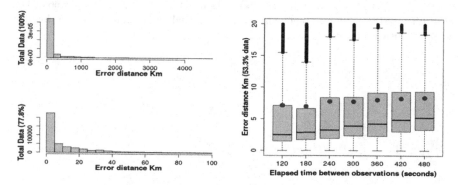

Fig. 3. Accuracy Evaluation: (left) Error distance distribution and (right) Impact of Elapsed Time (ET) between observations, round points corresponds to $RMSE_{dist}$.

After applying EKF to the 503 trajectories in the data, equivalent to 542,153 position points (AIS tuples), we analyse the overall distribution of distance errors. In Fig. 3 (left) we can observe in the histograms that most of the distance errors are below 20 km in around 78% of all the data and will therefore focus now on the data with distance error below 20 km. In a preliminary study we observed that the number of observations per kilometer has an impact on the RMSE for latitude and longitude, i.e., the more the number of positions are reported per kilometer of trajectory, the better the prediction. Thus, we analyse the error distance with respect to the elapsed time between observations. We can observe in the boxplot of Fig. 3 (right) that the more frequent the observations (120 s), the lower the distance error, in fact, for some trajectories the $RMSE_{dist}$ is well below 1 km (see below Fig. 4 and Tables 1 and 2). These levels of $RMSE_{dist}$ (below 1 km) are also obtained by Dalsnes et al. [10], in a batch setting where the approach is slightly different than ours and the results are given in *median* $RMSE_{dist}$ values calculated for partial trajectories.

---

[1] https://www.movable-type.co.uk/scripts/latlong.html.

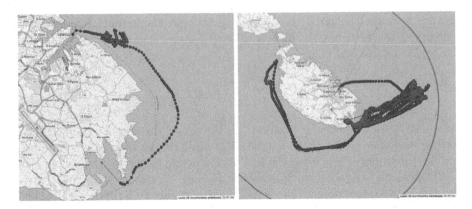

Fig. 4. Accuracy Evaluation: two trajectories corresponding to shipID-28 (left $RMSE_{dist} = 334.14$ m, mean ET $= 167.2$ s) and shipID-57 (right $RMSE_{dist} = 664.23$ m, mean ET $= 667.9$ s), round points correspond to actual values and crosses to the ones predicted with EKF.

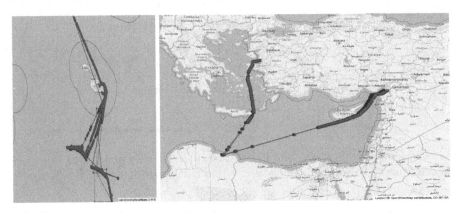

Fig. 5. Accuracy Evaluation: two trajectories corresponding to shipID-2 (left $RMSE_{dist} = 4755.24$ m, mean ET $= 1279.7$ s) and shipID-95 (right $RMSE_{dist} = 20279.30$ m, mean ET $= 1644.7$ s), round points correspond to actual values and crosses to the ones predicted with EKF.

As we will discuss later, there are various factors that impact the accuracy of the prediction, but first of all let us consider some examples of trajectories, in Figs. 4 and 5 and corresponding statistics in Tables 1 and 2. In cases where the tracking data is frequently reported per kilometer of distance traveled, the EKF algorithm has the chance to go through more iterations and therefore improve its prediction with each run. As shown in Fig. 4, the two vessels have a $RMSE_{dist}$ of 334 and 664 m respectively and in both cases the ET between observations is below 3 and 10 min in average.

In the case shown in Fig. 5, the infrequent observations lead to inaccurate route prediction. For shipID-2 (left) the ET is around 20 min on average and the

Table 1. Accuracy Evaluation: Distance error quantiles for selected ship trajectories.

Ship ID	Distance error quantiles					
	Min	1Q	Median	Mean	3Q	Max
28	40.0	133.4	233.5	271.5	361.4	1978.1
57	0.3	17.4	45.2	363.0	612.7	6442.5
2	1.0	331.1	580.1	1110.0	889.1	105040.3
95	601.9	2251.2	4844.1	9034.3	11213.3	477542.5

Table 2. Accuracy Evaluation: Distance RMSE for selected ship trajectories.

Ship ID	RMSE			No. of reported positions
	Distance error [m]	Longitude degrees	Latitude degrees	
28	334.1	0.00169	0.00127	193
57	664.2	0.00337	0.00174	2735
2	4755.2	0.02438	0.02725	3881
95	20279.3	0.15373	0.03960	1884

route is pretty complex, with several turns, however its $RMSE_{dist}$ is still below 5 km. For shipID-95 (right) the ET is around 27 min in average, including long periods of no reporting at all, which makes the prediction deviate a lot.

Factors Influencing Accuracy of the EKF Prediction. In the EKF algorithm, each new received event provides an adjustment to the model, improving the chances of correctly predicting the next state. The less events arrive, the smaller the chances that the estimated values will be accurate. In order to investigate if more data points indeed improve the prediction, the number of observation points per km of distance traveled was calculated for each trajectory. Figure 6 shows respectively longitude RMSE and latitude RMSE against the number of observations per km. The majority of analyzed vessels report less than two observations per km of distance traveled. In line with the expectations coming from the nature of the EKF algorithm, both diagrams in Fig. 6 confirm that the higher number of received observations per km results in more accurate predictions (smaller longitude and latitude RMSE). Another factor, which causes the results to be imprecise is the reported departure port. As the EKF algorithm requires initialization values to be input in the first step of the algorithm, the longitude and latitude of the departure port are used as the initial location coordinates. In some cases, the route was reported to start in the wrong position, which results in a significantly longer convergence time.

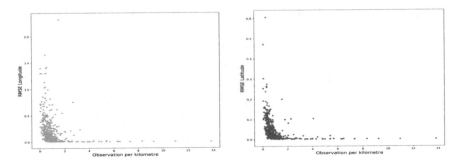

Fig. 6. Accuracy Evaluation: RMSE for Longitude and Latitude.

5.2 Performance Evaluation

In our large scale performance experiment we start simulating the streaming process by injecting the data into Kafka using several topics.

Each Kafka topic is then read as a stream data source by Apache Flink. Each tuple in the stream source is processed by Flink using its event time, i.e., the timestamp when the position is reported. In the data, on average 10 vessels report their position at the same time with peaks of up to 50 different vessels reporting their position simultaneously. This means that our processing system must be able to track in real-time many vessels simultaneously. In order to cover this situation and stress the system even more, we replicated four times the input data assigning different *ships_id*. In this manner, we simulate the processing of more than 2000 trajectories with peaks of maximum 200 vessels simultaneously reporting their position.

According to the benchmarking study of Karimov et al. [14], in modern distributed stream processing systems two notions of time are distinguished: event- and processing-time latencies. From this study, we use the following metrics:

- *event-time latency*, which measures the time that a given event has spent in a queue waiting to be processed. In our case, it is the time a tuple spends in the Kafka queue until the EKF operator is able to produce a new position prediction for this tuple.
- *processing-time latency*, which measures the time it took for an event to be processed by the streaming system, which in our case means the time it takes for the EKF operator to produce an output.
- *ingestion rate*, which is the throughput of a streaming system and in our case is measured as the number of tuples per millisecond processed by the EKF operator in Flink.

As pointed out by Karimov et al. [14], in practical scenarios, *event-time latency* is very important as it defines the time in which the user interacts with a given system and should be minimized. It should be noted that processing-time latency makes part of the event-time latency. Thus, our objective is to find the configuration that minimizes the processing-time in our system.

As shown in our Kafka-Flink pipeline (see Fig. 2) we use 8 Kafka topics and 8 corresponding Flink sources. The input source in each Kafka topic is the data replicated four times, which contains trajectories of more than 2000 vessels. Overall the system receives and processes 17.4 million AIS events.

We use the default configuration settings for Kafka, so the number of partitions per topic is 1. We change the level of parallelism from 1 to 48 and repeat each experiment five times, averaging the results afterwards. To be precise, parallelism 1 means using only one slot or CPU, which is the equivalent of executing the experiment on a single machine. The results are presented in Fig. 7. We use logarithmic scale on the y-axis to facilitate comparison.

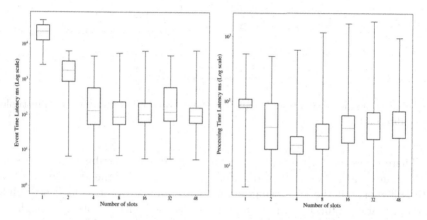

Fig. 7. Performance Evaluation: Boxplot of *event-time latency* and *processing-time latency* in server machine using 8 Kafka topics and 8 Flink sources.

For a single machine (in Fig. 7 number of slots equal to 1), we obtain on average the highest *processing-time latency* and *event-time latency*. For parallelism 2 we can observe that the *processing-time latency* decreases, but the *event-time latency* is also in the order of seconds, which is still too high for real-time processing. The *processing-time latency* decreases significantly when increasing the level of parallelism, with optimal latency values for this setting between parallelism 4 (mean 27.7 ms) and 8 (mean 37.1 ms). Using higher parallelism (parallelisation 8) also helps us to reduce the *event-time latency* to a mean minimum of 574.7 ms.

We can observe that for parallelism above 2 the *event-time latency* is below a second, which can be explained by an increase of the *ingestion rate*. Therefore, in the following, we further investigate the *ingestion rate* in our system.

As a comparison in Fig. 8 we show a boxplot of the *ingestion rate* in Flink in terms of tuples per millisecond. We can observe that without parallelism the ingestion rate on average is minimum with approx. 170 tuples/ms, when increasing the parallelism the ingestion rate is on average stable in approx. 200 tuples/ms, reaching maximum rates of approx. 500 tuples/ms.

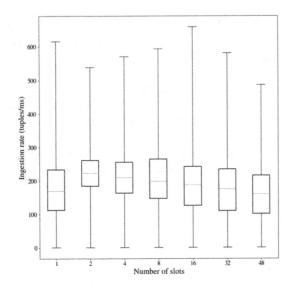

Fig. 8. Performance evaluation: Boxplot of the average Flink ingestion rate in tuples per millisecond.

There are several aspects that are interrelated and contribute to the overall performance of the system. For example, for parallelism 2 the average ingestion rate is higher, but the processing latency with only two processors is still high. The optimal configuration in our system is obtained with 8 slots. Although the ingestion rate is stable at approximate 200 tuples/ms, by adding more than 8 slots we do not gain any performance. Such behaviour could be explained by the fact that the overall input data (17.4 million AIS events) is not large enough, so we do not benefit from increasing parallelism, but instead we introduce distribution overhead.

6   Conclusion

In line with the expectations coming from recursive nature of the EKF, where predictions are corrected upon the arrival of a next data point, the frequency of events reception turned out to be an important factor influencing the accuracy of prediction produced. The results show that the complexity or stability of the routes are not the most important factor contributing to the accurate prediction of the vessels' routes. Irrespective of the trajectory complexity, the high frequency of the incoming sensor measurements as well as correct initialisation of the parameters can provide a precise estimation of even more complex routes.

Regarding large-scale performance, we showed that using a distributed stream processing system we can process on average 200 different vessels' positions per ms (200 tuples/ms), and our system, under this rate, requires below 500 ms to predict the next position of a vessel. In our setting, this optimal performance was obtained when using 8 Kafka topics and the corresponding 8 Flink sources. Beyond this optimal value, when we increase the number of Kafka topics and Flink sources, the system introduces some overhead that is reflected on the latencies.

As future work we will consider a more realistic scenario, where massive real data is used and experiments conducted on a compute cluster. In a cluster setting we should take into account the additional overhead due to the communication between nodes, thus we will study the optimal combination of parallelism, Kafka topics and ingestion rate, in particular when actual big sets in the order of GBs are used. Furthermore, we will address the issue of visualization in real-time, including a dashboard for indicating various conditions of the vessels, such as elapsed time since last report, distance traveled or big error predictions, which may correspond to possible anomalies.

Acknowledgements. This work was partly supported by the German Federal Ministry for Education and Research (BMBF) as Berlin Big Data Center (BBDC2) (grant no. 01IS18025A), the German Federal Ministry of Transport and Digital Infrastructure (BMVI) through the Daystream Project (grant no. 19F2031A).

References

1. DEBS 2018 Grand Challenge. http://www.cs.otago.ac.nz/debs2018/calls/gc.html. Accessed 27 Nov 2018
2. Hadoop. http://hadoop.apache.org/. Accessed 27 Nov 2018
3. Alessandrini, A., et al.: Mining vessel tracking data for maritime domain applications. In: 2016 IEEE 16th International Conference on Data Mining Workshops (ICDMW), pp. 361–367. IEEE (2016)
4. Apache Flink: Application Development, Working with State. https://ci.apache.org/projects/flink/flink-docs-stable/dev/stream/state/state.html. Accessed 10 June 2019
5. Apache Flink: Configuration. https://ci.apache.org/projects/flink/flink-docs-release-1.8/ops/config.html#configuring-taskmanager-processing-slots. Accessed 10 June 2019
6. Apache Flink: Fast and reliable large-scale data processing engine. http://flink.apache.org. Accessed 27 Nov 2018
7. Apache Spark. https://spark.apache.org/. Accessed 27 Nov 2018
8. Balzer, P.: Multidimensional Kalman-Filter (2017). https://github.com/balzer82/Kalman/. Accessed 27 Nov 2018
9. Brandt, T., Grawunder, M.: Moving object stream processing with short-time prediction. In: Proceedings of the 8th ACM SIGSPATIAL Workshop on GeoStreaming, pp. 49–56. ACM (2017)
10. Dalsnes, B.R., Hexeberg, S., Flåten, A.L., Eriksen, B.H., Brekke, E.F.: The neighbor course distribution method with Gaussian mixture models for AIS-based vessel trajectory prediction. In: 2018 21st International Conference on Information Fusion (FUSION), pp. 580–587, July 2018. https://doi.org/10.23919/ICIF.2018.8455607
11. Dean, J., Ghemawat, S.: MapReduce: simplified data processing on large clusters. Commun. ACM **51**(1), 107–113 (2008)
12. He, B., et al.: Comet: batched stream processing for data intensive distributed computing. In: Proceedings of the 1st ACM Symposium on Cloud Computing, pp. 63–74. ACM (2010)

13. Jwo, D.J., Wang, S.H.: Adaptive fuzzy strong tracking extended Kalman filtering for GPS navigation. IEEE Sens. J. **7**(5), 778–789 (2007)
14. Karimov, J., Rabl, T., Katsifodimos, A., Samarev, R., Heiskanen, H., Markl, V.: Benchmarking distributed stream data processing systems. In: 2018 IEEE 34th International Conference on Data Engineering (ICDE), pp. 1507–1518. IEEE (2018)
15. Kelly, A.: A 3D state space formulation of a navigation Kalman filter for autonomous vehicles. Technical report, Carnegie-Mellon University Pittsburgh PA Robotics Institute (1994)
16. Korn, U.: A simple method for modelling changes over time. Casualty Actuarial Society E-Forum (2018)
17. Lee, J.W., Kim, M.S., Kweon, I.S.: A Kalman filter based visual tracking algorithm for an object moving in 3D. In: Proceedings 1995 IEEE/RSJ International Conference on Intelligent Robots and Systems. Human Robot Interaction and Cooperative Robots, vol. 1, pp. 342–347. IEEE (1995)
18. Lipka, M., Sippel, E., Vossiek, M.: An extended Kalman filter for direct, real-time, phase-based high precision indoor localization. IEEE Access **7**, 25288–25297 (2019). https://doi.org/10.1109/ACCESS.2019.2900799
19. Moussa, R.: Scalable maritime traffic map inference and real-time prediction of vessels' future locations on apache spark. In: Proceedings of the 12th ACM International Conference on Distributed and Event-based Systems, pp. 213–216. ACM (2018)
20. Murphy, K.P.: Machine Learning: A Probabilistic Perspective. The MIT Press, Cambridge (2012)
21. Perera, L.P., Oliveira, P., Soares, C.G.: Maritime traffic monitoring based on vessel detection, tracking, state estimation, and trajectory prediction. IEEE Trans. Intell. Transp. Syst. **13**(3), 1188–1200 (2012)
22. Perera, S., Suhothayan, S.: Solution patterns for realtime streaming analytics. In: Proceedings of the 9th ACM International Conference on Distributed Event-Based Systems, DEBS 2015, pp. 247–255. ACM, New York (2015). https://doi.org/10.1145/2675743.2774214. http://doi.acm.org/10.1145/2675743.2774214
23. Sheng, C., Zhao, J., Leung, H., Wang, W.: Extended Kalman filter based echo state network for time series prediction using mapreduce framework. In: 2013 IEEE 9th International Conference on Mobile Ad-hoc and Sensor Networks, pp. 175–180. IEEE (2013)
24. Tu, E., Zhang, G., Rachmawati, L., Rajabally, E., Huang, G.B.: Exploiting AIS data for intelligent maritime navigation: a comprehensive survey from data to methodology. IEEE Trans. Intell. Transp. Syst. **19**(5), 1559–1582 (2017)
25. Welch, P., Bishop, G.: An Introduction to the Kalman Filter (coursePack) (2001). http://www.cs.unc.edu/~tracker/media/pdf/SIGGRAPH2001_CoursePack_08.pdf. Accessed 27 Nov 2018

Unsupervised Anomaly Detection in Multivariate Spatio-Temporal Datasets Using Deep Learning

Yildiz Karadayi[1,2]([✉])

[1] Kadir Has University, Istanbul, Turkey
yildiz.karadayi@stu.khas.edu.tr
[2] Innova, Istanbul, Turkey

Abstract. Techniques used for spatio-temporal anomaly detection in an unsupervised settings has attracted great attention in recent years. It has extensive use in a wide variety of applications such as: medical diagnosis, sensor events analysis, earth science, fraud detection systems, etc. Most of the real world time series datasets have spatial dimension as additional context such as geographic location. Although many temporal data are spatio-temporal in nature, existing techniques are limited to handle both contextual (spatial and temporal) attributes during anomaly detection process. Taking into account of spatial context in addition to temporal context would help uncovering complex anomaly types and unexpected and interesting knowledge about problem domain. In this paper, a new approach to the problem of unsupervised anomaly detection in a multivariate spatio-temporal dataset is proposed using a hybrid deep learning framework. The proposed approach is composed of a Long Short Term Memory (LSTM) Encoder and Deep Neural Network (DNN) based classifier to extract spatial and temporal contexts. Although the approach has been employed on crime dataset from San Francisco Police Department to detect spatio-temporal anomalies, it can be applied to any spatio-temporal datasets.

Keywords: Unsupervised anomaly detection · Multivariate · Spatio-temporal data · Deep learning

1 Introduction

By the advancement of the hardware technology for data collection, generation of contextually rich data has become part of many processes. Data from many applications of today's world are temporal in nature such as sensor data, financial data, sales transaction data, and system diagnostics data. In addition to time context, many temporal data have also another context called spatial. In such settings where a spatial attribute is also a contextual attribute, we face with a new type of anomalies: spatiotemporal anomalies. Anomalies and outliers are two terms used most commonly in the context of anomaly detection; sometimes interchangeably [1].

In spatial or temporal data domains, attributes are partitioned into contextual and behavioral attributes. In such cases, behavioral attribute values (e.g. temperature at

© Springer Nature Switzerland AG 2020
V. Lemaire et al. (Eds.): AALTD 2019, LNAI 11986, pp. 167–182, 2020.
https://doi.org/10.1007/978-3-030-39098-3_13

current time, money spent in a specific location) are treated as dependent variables [2]. Contextual attributes (e.g., location and time) are used to build neighborhoods in which the model of the normal data is built to predict the dependent variables or quantify the outlier scores of each data point within the neighborhood. In a credit card fraud detection scenario, dependent variable might be the total amount of many spent in a given time period, whereas independent variables might be customer demographics data, location, etc. In some datasets, it is possible for both spatial and temporal attributes to be contextual attributes. Such data can be referred to as spatiotemporal data. In spatiotemporal datasets, behavioral attributes like sea-surface temperatures, car speed, and transaction amount are often measured in the context of specific time or location. In these cases, both spatial and temporal continuity plays important role in identifying anomalies. A spatial-temporal outliers (ST-Outlier) are objects whose behavioral (non-spatial and non-temporal) attributes are different from other objects in their contextual neighborhoods [5].

Spatio-temporal data is extremely common in many problem settings where collecting data from various spatial locations for the nature of the problem are important. We need to emphasize that spatial and temporal continuity may not be equally important in all problem settings. For example, in an application where water temperature of an ocean is measured every minute by sensors located in many different locations, spatial continuity may be more important than temporal continuity. On the other hand, time context might play more significant role or might have at least equal significance along with spatial context in finding irregular spending patterns in a spatio-temporal financial dataset. For example, a customer cannot use his or her credit card in two different stores in 5 min if there is 100 km distance between two stores.

There have been many studies on finding anomalies in time-series data considering only temporal context, or finding anomalies in spatial data considering only spatial context. There are limited researches on finding spatio-temporal outliers (ST-Outlier) which considers both context at the same time. Most of the ST-Outlier detection techniques follow a similar approach: Find spatial outliers and then compare them with temporal neighbors to verify whether they are ST-Outlier or not. Spatiotemporal methods for outlier detection [4, 5] are significantly more challenging because of the additional challenge of modeling the temporal and spatial components jointly [2].

In the unsupervised scenarios, previous examples of interesting anomalies are not available. In such cases, modelling the normal behavior in the presence of noise and anomaly pose extra difficulty. Generally, unsupervised methods can be used for either noise removal or anomaly detection, and supervised methods are designed for application-specific anomaly detection. Unsupervised methods are often used in an exploratory setting, where the discovered outliers are provided to the analyst for further examination of their application-specific importance [2].

1.1 Related Work

Outlier analysis is an important research area in data mining and machine learning communities. Outliers are also referred to as abnormalities, deviants, or anomalies in the data mining and statistics literature. It has been studied extensively in the context of time series data analysis. Time-series outlier detection studies find outliers considering only temporal context [2, 3, 12, 13]. Whereas some other researches focus on finding outliers with respect to spatial context only [6–9].

Birant and Kut [11] propose a neighborhood-based ST-Outlier detection mechanism. They propose a three-step approach to identify the spatio-temporal outliers. First, they use a modified version of DBSCAN algorithm to identify the spatial neighborhoods within the dataset. They define spatial outliers based on these neighborhoods. Then, they check the temporal context of spatial-outlier objects by comparing them to temporal neighbor objects.

Cheng and Li [5] propose a four-step approach to identify spatio-temporal outliers: classification (clustering), aggregation, comparison and verification. Their aim is to address the semantic and dynamic properties of geographic phenomena for ST-outlier detection. At the clustering step, the prior knowledge of the data is used to form some regions that have significant semantic meanings. The aggregation is also called filtering since the outliers (noises) will be filtered by changing the spatial scale. The main idea here is that if there are spatial outliers, they usually disappear if the scale of processing is reduced, clustering results will be different with different scales. With a decrease in scale, the difference between the objects and their spatial neighbors will decrease and the small regions that contain outliers will be removed. At comparison step, the results obtained at two spatial scales are compared in order to detect the potential spatial outliers. At the verification step, the outliers detected in the previous step can be suspected as ST-outliers. Therefore, the verification step checks the temporal neighbors of the suspected ST-outliers detected in the previous step. If the attribute value of such a ST-outlier is not significantly different from its temporal neighbors, this is not a ST-outlier. Otherwise, it is confirmed as a ST-outlier.

Adam et al. [10] propose a spatio-temporal outlier detection approach methodology based on Voronoi Diagrams. Their methodology is based on building micro and macro neighborhoods using the spatial and semantic relationships among the objects. They first build Voronoi diagrams using spatial properties of each object to find micro neighborhood. By using spatial and semantic relationships between objects, they find the Macro Neighborhood, which is an extended neighborhood, of each object. Using these neighborhoods, they detect outliers based on distance (Euclidean distance) values among various points. A data object is said to be a spatio-temporal outlier if it differs sufficiently from other points in the macro neighborhood. Here the Macro neighborhood consists of all the micro neighborhood merged into it under the spatial and the semantic relationship restrictions.

Gupta et al. [14] introduce the notion of context-aware anomaly detection in distributed systems by integrating the information from system logs and time series measurement data. In addition to temporal context, they use system specific performance metrics such as number of tasks running, memory usage, and CPU usage to create additional contextual data. They propose a two-stage clustering methodology to extract context and metric patterns using a PCA-based method and a modified K-Means algorithm. They instantiate their framework for Apache Hadoop platform. They extract additional context variables using the job history logs. They first cluster instances based on non-temporal context variables to extract context patterns, then apply time context using time-series metrics variables to detect outliers.

Aforementioned methods explained above have something in common: They first apply spatial (or non-temporal) context to find spatial outliers using a distance based technique. Then, spatial outliers are compared with other spatial objects using temporal neighborhoods to detect if they are temporal outliers too. They all use either spatial clustering base outlier detection algorithms such as DBSCAN [19], or locality based outlier detection algorithms such as LOF [20] to find neighborhoods. They can only detect simple anomalies like extreme cases, cannot detect collective anomalies. Another problem about distance-based methods are that they are well known to be computationally expensive and not suitable for multivariate datasets [2].

2 Proposed Model

The main inductive bias in this proposed model is the assumption that the same physics apply to all input sequences irrespective of which spatial neighborhood it comes from. The same model can be applied to any sequences which come from different geographical locations to extract useful representations to help find irregularities.

The proposed hybrid model composed of two main components: LSTM Encoder to extract temporal context and deep neural network classifier to learn the spatial context and detect anomalies. To learn the temporal representation that extracts all that is needed to predict the future sequence and reconstruct the input sequence at the same time, the combined framework idea proposed by [18] was employed. Their research was focused to unsupervised learning of video representations to predict the future frames. In this study, combined LSTM models were used to build encoder which can extract useful temporal context so that it can be used to build spatial classifier to extract spatial context and detect spatio-temporal anomalies. When the classifier is not successful in assigning correct spatial context label (location information) for the given sequence, we may assume that the sequence was generated by a process that do not comply with temporal and spatial regularities of the given world.

2.1 LSTM Encoder

The first step in the proposed spatio-temporal anomaly detection framework is to extract temporal context. The component responsible of doing this is Long Short Term Memory (LSTM) Encoder. It is similar to composite model proposed in [18]. It contains a LSTM Autoencoder and LSTM Future Predictor which trained in parallel to extract temporal context from dataset. There is one encoder, but two decoder LSTMs: one that decodes the representation generated by encoder into the input sequence, and another that decodes the same representation to predict the future multivariate time series.

By combining the two tasks (reconstructing the input and predicting the future) to create a composite model as shown in Fig. 1, a powerful LSTM Encoder component can be trained to extract temporal context. Here the reconstruction part is LSTM Autoencoder Model and predictor part is LSTM Future Predictor Model. As explained in [3], composite model tries to overcome the shortcomings that each model suffers on its own.

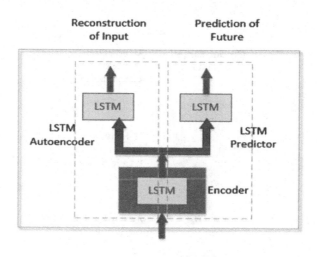

Fig. 1. Composite LSTM encoder-decoder model.

2.2 Deep Neural Network Classifier

The second component of proposed framework is deep neural network (DNN) based classifier which is responsible for extracting spatial context and doing classification of input data to identify anomalous input sequences within given data. DNN based classifier and overall architecture of proposed hybrid framework is given in Fig. 2. Input sequences to this component first fed into the LSTM Encoder component built at first step. The output of the LSTM Encoder is the latent representation of temporal data. The classifier receives this latent representation as input and extracts spatial context from it. To be able to extract useful spatial context, the classifier was trained with the goal of predicting correct spatial location. If the unsupervised learning model built at first step, which is a LSTM Encoder, comes up with useful temporal representations then the classifier should be able to perform better.

The unsupervised anomaly detection problem is formulated as multiclass classification problem by training the classifier to learn regions which each input sequence comes from. The better spatial context extracted from data the better classification results have been achieved. The aim of this step is to build a final classifier which is successful in assigning the correct location label to each input sequence and at the same time would be able to detect spatio-temporal anomalies which do not confirm with overall trend within each spatio-temporal neighborhoods.

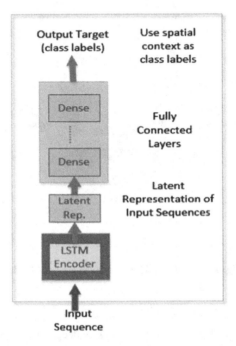

Fig. 2. Proposed hybrid framework with DNN classifier

3   Case Study

To verify the proposed deep-learning based spatio-temporal outlier detection framework, we performed a case study on a real spatio-temporal dataset. Our goals in this case study are:

- To detect spatio-temporal outliers and analyze and study the results.
- Examine the spatio-temporal outliers detected by proposed approach, with base LSTM models (LSTM Autoencoder and LSTM Future Predictor) and LOF [20] algorithm.

3.1 Dataset Description

The dataset used in this study is the historical San Francisco Police Department Incident Report, which covers from January 1, 2003 to May 15, 2018. It is open and can be accessed through [16]. A different version of this data was made available through a Kaggle competition [17] on crime classification and has been used as sample dataset for various crime prediction and classification researches. The dataset contains 2215023 incident records, each consisting of date, time of day, one of 39 crime categories, a short description of the incident, the day of week, one of 10 police districts in which the incident occurred, the resolution of the incident, the address, the longitude, and the latitude fields. For this study, latitude, longitude and address information is ignored and only police district information is used as spatial context variable.

3.2 Data Preprocessing

In order to convert incident report data more convenient for time series analysis, the data is aggregated on daily basis based on crime categories. As a result, a multivariate dataset has been constructed covering 5613 days of data for each 39 crime categories. See Fig. 3 for time series multivariate data example from one of the districts, for daily crime counts of 6 different crime categories taken from January 1, 2017 to December 31, 2017.

In this study, to decide the correct temporal window size for analysis, we looked at the weekly crime pattern for each district. See Fig. 4 for weekly crime pattern for each district. The weekly crime count analysis shows a clear pattern for each district that one week time frame can be used for anomaly analysis as it shows strong predictability.

Figure 5 shows weekly crime pattern for district Northern for 6 years, from the beginning of 2005 until the end of 2010. It shows that each year has its own weekly pattern. Figure 6 shows this weekly crime count broken-down to top 12 occurring crime categories. For each district we can observe this clear weekly pattern for each type of crimes.

Data in this dataset is divided into standard weeks, 7 day time frames, which begin on a Sunday and end on a Saturday. Dataset which starts on January 1, 2003 to May 15, 2018 was divided into a total of 801 weeks. Spatio-temporal anomaly detection analysis were conducted on weekly data windows for each district.

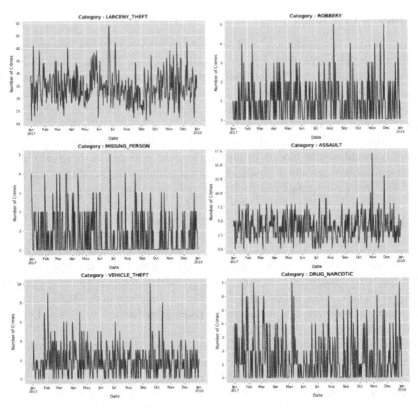

Fig. 3. Daily Crime counts for district Northern. 6 crime categories were shown as time series data example: Larceny/Theft, Robbery, Missing Person, Assault, Vehicle Theft, and Drug/Narcotic.

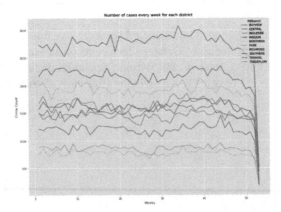

Fig. 4. Weekly crime pattern for each district from 2005 to 2011.

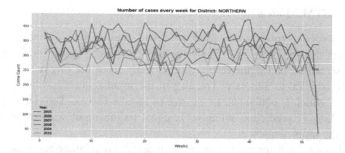

Fig. 5. Weekly crime pattern for district Northern from 2005 till by the end of 2010.

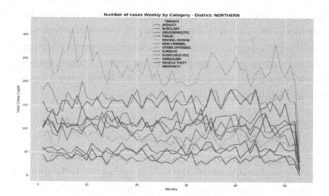

Fig. 6. Weekly crime pattern for district Northern broken down into the top 12 occurring crime categories.

4 Experimental Setup

Experiments were implemented in the Keras framework [21] using the Tensorflow [22] backend. All deep learning models were trained using backpropagation algorithm and Rectified Linear Unit (ReLU) activation function on all layers, except the output layer of the classifier which softmax function was used. ADAM optimizer algorithm was used to optimize the loss function, which was "mean squared error" for all LSTM based models and "categorical crossentropy" for multiclass classifier. For LSTM based future prediction model, two hidden layers with 200 and 100 hidden units each. For LSTM Autoencoder, one hidden layer with 100 hidden units gives the best result for this dataset. Deeper LSTMs did not improve results significantly. For all LSTM models 10 epochs with batch size of 64 were used. First 14 years (730 standard weeks starting from January 5th, 2003 till December 31st, 2016) of dataset were used for training of all models, rest of the data (71 standard weeks starting from January 1st, 2017 till May 12, 2018) were used as test set.

4.1   Base LSTM Models

LSTM Autoencoder models are used to detect multivariate anomalies based on reconstruction errors. They try to build the input sequence using small dimensional latent representation, and if the result varies greatly from the original input then the input can be labelled as anomaly. The size of the input sequence, which is the input window, is 7, which is equivalent to the size of standard week. The size of the output sequence, which is prediction window, is equal to the input window as it tries to reconstruct the input sequence.

LSTM Future Predictor models are used to detect multivariate anomalies based on prediction errors. They try to predict future sequence given the input sequence, and if the prediction varies greatly from the real data, then the input sequence can be labelled as anomaly. The size of prediction window and input window was kept same throughout the experiment as 7, which is equivalent the number of days in a standard week. LSTM Future Predictor model tries to predict the next week's number of crimes for each 7 days and for each 39 different crime categories for each district given the current week's data.

To quantitatively measure the prediction and reconstruction performance of base LSTM models, the root mean squared error (RMSE) is calculated for each 39 variable for 7 time-steps as follows:

$$RMSE = \sqrt{\frac{1}{N * T} \sum_{n,t} \left(y_{n,t} - \hat{y}_{n,t}\right)^2} \tag{1}$$

where N is the total number of features (crime categories), T is the number of time steps (size of input window) considered for this problem, $y_{n,t}$ ve $\hat{y}_{n,t}$ is the exact crime count and the predicted (or reconstructed based on the type of LSTM decoder used) crime for given time step and crime category. The RMSE for all input sequences (test weeks) were calculated and interquartile range for error values was defined to select threshold for anomaly detection. Test weeks whose errors fall outside of 1.5 times of the interquartile range above the 3rd quartile were flagged as anomaly. Table 1 shows number of anomalous weeks and their indexes detected by LSTM models.

Table 1. Anomalous weeks detected by base LSTM models.

Model name	District - # anomalous weeks	Anomalous week indexes
LSTM Future Predictor	Mission – 1	1
	Tenderloin – 1	13
	Northern – 1	5
	Richmond – 2	27, 37
	Bayview – 2	30, 55
	Central – 3	5, 15, 63
	Park – 1	1
	Taraval – 0	
	Southern – 0	
	Ingleside – 0	

(continued)

Table 1. (*continued*)

Model name	District - # anomalous weeks	Anomalous week indexes
LSTM Autoencoder	Mission – 0	
	Tenderloin – 0	
	Northern – 2	5, 40
	Richmond – 2	27, 37
	Bayview – 1	55
	Central – 2	5, 15
	Park – 2	1, 36
	Taraval – 2	9, 34
	Southern – 1	11
	Ingleside – 1	48

Out of 71 test weeks, LSTM Future Predictor model flags 11 weeks as anomalous, LSTM Autoencoder flags 13 weeks as anomalous. For some districts (Richmond, Bayview, Central and Park), weeks flagged as anomalous are matching.

4.2 Spatio-Temporal Classifier

The proposed deep learning based spatio-temporal anomaly detector is composed of a LSTM Encoder component and a fully connected deep neural network classifier as depicted in Fig. 2. LSTM Encoder component was trained in a composite framework where an LSTM Autoencoder and an LSTM Future Predictor were trained in parallel with a common encoder component. After the encoder has been trained, it was put in front of the DNN classifier as a temporal context extractor for the input data. The classifier is designed to predict the location label of each 7-day long multivariate input sequence in a supervised training settings. Each 10 different district constitutes 10 different labels, and the anomaly detection problem converts to multi-class classification problem. The number of inputs is equal to the dimension of LSTM Encoder. The first hidden layer has 200 neurons, and second hidden layer has 50 neurons. ReLU activation function was used for hidden layers. The final layer of the deep neural network classifier is the softmax classifier using "categorical crossentropy" as loss function with neuron numbers equals to number of spatial labels. Cross entropy loss function formula can be given as following:

$$MCCE = -\frac{1}{N} \sum_{i}^{N} \sum_{l}^{C} [y_{il} \log(\hat{y}_{il})] \tag{2}$$

where C is the number of class labels and N is the number of test sequences (test weeks for the given dataset).

Although the second component of the hybrid framework is a classifier, the ultimate purpose is to detect spatio-temporal anomalies. We train the classifier using district information of input sequences as labels to enforce the deep neural network classifier to learn spatial context. If the classifier can learn useful representation of spatial context, it gets higher accuracy on classification problem. The input sequences which are classified wrongly would be flagged as potential spatio-temporal anomalous sequences.

Metrics. Precision and recall were used to measure the accuracy of the classifier. Precision is the number of true positive results divided by the number of all positive results (true positives + false positives), whereas recall is the number of true positive results divided by the number of actual positive results (true positives + false negatives). Accuracy is the total number of true positive and true negative cases divided by all number of cases. The classifier gave the total accuracy of 77.18%. Table 2 shows the performance of the classifier for each class label.

Table 2. Precision and recall results for each class labels.

Class Labels	Precision	Recall
Taraval	76.36%	59.15%
Mission	77.90%	94.36%
Bayview	70.77%	64.79%
Ingleside	100%	66.20%
Central	64.77%	80.28%
Northern	75%	46.48%
Southern	64.42%	94.37%
Park	97%	91.55%
Tenderloin	63.86%	74.65%
Richmond	100%	100%

As a sample case, district Taraval was investigated for all 39 features. The week numbers 59 and 61 from test weeks (which are 71 in total) were misclassified by spatio-temporal classifier and not detected by LSTM models as anomaly. We would flag those weeks as spatio-temporal anomalies. The Fig. 7 shows crime counts for selected crime types occurred on week 59 and 61 for district Taraval. The crime values corresponding to weeks 59 and 61 were colored red.

Dimension reduction using LSTM Autoencoder was employed to input data to graphically visualize the detected spatio-temporal anomalies. Data from districts Central, Richmond, and Southern were projected into 3-dimensional space along with detected spatio-temporal anomalies. The Fig. 9 shows spatio-temporal anomalies detected by proposed framework visualized in 3D.

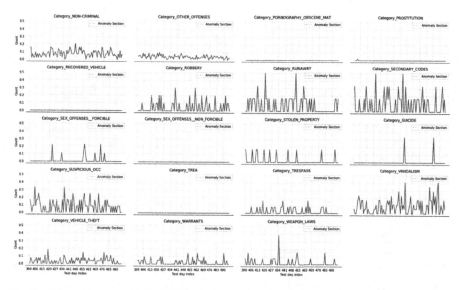

Fig. 7. Crime count analysis for different crime categories for test weeks 59 and 61 which were detected as spatio-temporal anomaly by the hybrid model for district Taraval. (Color figure online)

4.3 Comparison of Proposed Model and LOF

Local Outlier Factor (LOF) [20], is one of the most popular algorithms that quantifies the outlierness of an object. To evaluate the effectiveness of the proposed framework, detected anomalies by LOF and proposed framework were projected in lower dimensional space and visualized. Figure 8 shows the visualization of data and outliers. A more distinctive decision boundary for outliers can be seen compared to not so obvious boundary of LOF algorithm.

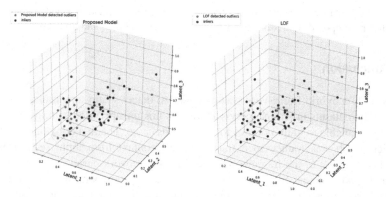

Fig. 8. 3D graphic visualization of multivariate time series data and detected spatio temporal anomalies by proposed framework for districts Central, Richmond, and Southern.

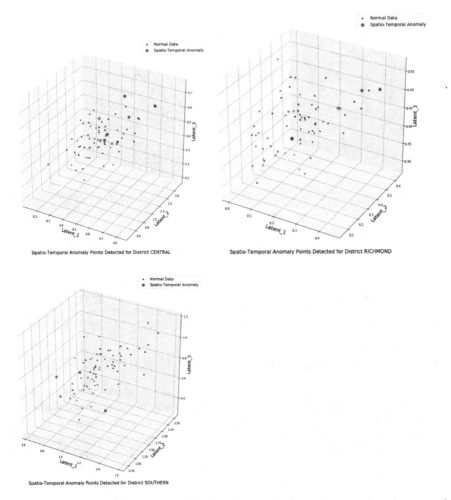

Fig. 9. 3D graphic visualization of multivariate time series data and detected spatio-temporal anomalies by proposed framework for districts Central, Richmond, and Southern.

5   Conclusion

In this study a hybrid framework was proposed to detect spatio-temporal anomalies of multivariate datasets in an unsupervised way. In this unsupervised settings, no labeled dataset is available to train modules for anomalous cases. The first component is LSTM Encoder which was trained to extract temporal context from input sequences. The second component of the framework is deep neural network based classifier to extract spatial context from encoded data. The framework learn temporal and spatial contexts separately and uses those representations to identify spatio-temporal anomalies. If the classifier classify the input sequence based on spatial labels, then the input can be considered as anomaly. The hybrid model was able to persistently detect spatio-temporal anomaly sequences well beyond the LSTM based prediction models and LOF algorithm. To further get improvements on spatial classifier, the model can be extended by applying convolutional neural network base spatial context extractor using finer grained neighborhood data.

References

1. Chandola, V., Banerjee, A., Kumar, V.: Anomaly detection: a survey. ACM Comput. Surv. **41**(3), Article 15 (2009)
2. Aggarwal, C.C.: Outlier Analysis. Springer, Heidelberg (2017)
3. Gupta, M., Gao, J., Aggarwal, C.C., Han, J.: Outlier detection for temporal data: a survey. IEEE Trans. Knowl. Data Eng. **26**(9), 2250–2267 (2014)
4. Cheng, T., Li, Z.: A hybrid approach to detect spatial-temporal outliers. In: International Conference on Geoinformatics (2004)
5. Cheng, T., Li, Z.: A multiscale approach for spatio-temporal outlier detection. Trans. GIS **10** (2), 253–263 (2006)
6. Shekhar, S., Lu, C.T., Zhang, P.: A unified approach to detecting spatial outliers. Geoinformatica **7**(2), 139–166 (2003)
7. Lu, C.-T., Chen, D., Kou, Y.: Algorithms for spatial outlier detection. In: ICDM Conference (2003)
8. Shekhar, S., Lu, C.T., Zhang, P.: Detecting graph-based spatial outliers: algorithms and applications. In: ACM KDD Conference (2001)
9. Kou, Y., Lu, C.T., Chen, D.: Spatial weighted outlier detection. In: SIAM Conference on Data Mining (2006)
10. Adam, N.R., Janeja, V.P., Atluri, V.: Neighborhood-based detection of anomalies in high-dimensional spatio-temporal sensor datasets. In: ACM SAC Conference (2004)
11. Birant, D., Kut, A.: Spatio-temporal outlier detection in large databases. In: 28th International Conference on Information Technology Interfaces, Cavtat/Dubrovnik (2006)
12. Yaminshi, K., Takeuchi, J.: A unifying framework for detecting outliers and change points from time series non-stationary data. In: ACM KDD Conference (2002)
13. Cheng, H., et al.: Detection and characterization of anomalies in multivariate time series. In: SDM (2009)
14. Gupta, M., Sharma, A.B., Chen, H., Jiang, G.: Context-aware time series anomaly detection for complex systems (2013)
15. Smets, K., Verdonk, B., Jordaan, E.M.: Discovering novelty in spatio/temporal data using one-class support vector machines. In: International Joint Conference on Neural Networks (2009)
16. Police Department Incident Reports: Historical 2003 to May 2018. https://data.sfgov.org/Public-Safety/Police-Department-Incident-Reports-Historical-2003/tmnf-yvry. Accessed 19 June 2019
17. San Francisco Crime Classification Data, Kaggle. https://www.kaggle.com/c/sf-crime/data
18. Srivastava, N., Mansimov, E., Salakhutdinov, R.: Unsupervised learning of video representations using LSTMs. In: International Conference on Machine Learning (ICML) (2015)

19. Ester, M., Kriegel, H.P., Sander, J., Xu, X.: A density-based algorithm for discovering clusters in large spatial databases with noise. In: Proceedings of the Second International Conference on Knowledge Discovery and Data Mining, KDD 1996, pp. 226–231 (1996)
20. Breunig, M.M., Kriegel, H.P., Ng, R.T., Sander, J.: LOF: identifying density-based local outliers. In: Proceedings of the 2000 ACM SIGMOD International Conference on Management of Data, pp. 93–104 (2000)
21. Keras. https://keras.io/
22. Tensorflow. https://www.tensorflow.org/

Learning Stochastic Dynamical Systems
via Bridge Sampling

Harish S. Bhat[✉] and Shagun Rawat

Applied Mathematics Unit, University of California, Merced, CA 95343, USA
hbhat@ucmerced.edu

Abstract. We develop algorithms to automate discovery of stochastic dynamical system models from noisy, vector-valued time series. By discovery, we mean learning both a nonlinear drift vector field and a diagonal diffusion matrix for an Itô stochastic differential equation in $\mathbb{R}^d$. We parameterize the vector field using tensor products of Hermite polynomials, enabling the model to capture highly nonlinear and/or coupled dynamics. We solve the resulting estimation problem using expectation maximization (EM). This involves two steps. We augment the data via diffusion bridge sampling, with the goal of producing time series observed at a higher frequency than the original data. With this augmented data, the resulting expected log likelihood maximization problem reduces to a least squares problem. We provide an open-source implementation of this algorithm. Through experiments on systems with dimensions one through eight, we show that this EM approach enables accurate estimation for multiple time series with possibly irregular observation times. We study how the EM method performs as a function of the amount of data augmentation, as well as the volume and noisiness of the data.

Keywords: Stochastic differential equations · Nonparametric estimation · Diffusion bridges · Expectation maximization

1 Introduction

Often, the goal of mathematical modeling in the sciences and engineering is the development of equations of motion that describe observed phenomena. Classically, these equations of motion took the form of deterministic systems of ordinary or partial differential equations (ODE or PDE, respectively). In systems of contemporary interest where intrinsic noise must be modeled (e.g., in biology and finance), we find stochastic differential equations (SDE) used in place of deterministic ones. Regardless, comparisons of model predictions against observed data typically occur only after the model has been built from first principles.

H. S. Bhat was partially supported by NSF award DMS-1723272. Both authors acknowledge use of the MERCED computational cluster, funded by NSF award ACI-1429783.

V. Lemaire et al. (Eds.): AALTD 2019, LNAI 11986, pp. 183–198, 2020.
https://doi.org/10.1007/978-3-030-39098-3_14

Recent years have seen a surge of interest in using data to automate discovery of ODE, PDE, and SDE models. Such machine learning approaches complement traditional modeling efforts, using available data to constrain the space of plausible models, and shortening the feedback loop linking model development to prediction and comparison to real observations. We posit two additional reasons to develop algorithms to learn SDE models. First, SDE models—including the models considered here—have the capacity to model highly nonlinear, coupled stochastic systems, including systems whose equilibria are non-Gaussian and/or multimodal. Second, SDE models often allow for interpretability. Especially if the terms on the right-hand side of the SDE are expressed in terms of commonly used functions (such as polynomials), we can obtain a qualitative understanding of how the system's variables influence, regulate, and/or mediate one other.

In this paper, we develop an algorithm to learn SDE models from high-dimensional time series. To our knowledge, this is the most general expectation maximization (EM) approach to learning an SDE with multidimensional drift vector field and diagonal diffusion matrix. Prior EM approaches were restricted to one-dimensional SDE [8], or used a Gaussian process approximation, linear drift approximation, and approximate maximization [25]. To develop our method, we use diffusion bridge sampling as in [12,13], which focused on Bayesian nonparametric methods for SDE in $\mathbb{R}^1$. After augmenting the data using bridge sampling, we are left with a least-squares problem, generalizing the work of [6] from the ODE to the SDE context.

In the literature, variational Bayesian methods are the only other SDE learning methods that have been tested on high-dimensional problems [34]. These methods use approximations consisting of linear SDE with time-varying coefficients [1], kernel density estimates [2], or Gaussian processes [3]. In contrast, we parameterize the drift vector field using tensor products of Hermite polynomials; as mentioned above, the resulting SDE has much higher capacity than linear and/or Gaussian process models. Many other techniques explored in the statistical literature focus on scalar SDE [4,14,15,33].

Differential equation discovery problems have attracted considerable recent interest. A variety of methods have been developed to learn ODE [6,7,18,27, 28,30,32] as well as PDE [19,20,24,26]. We do not describe these methods in detail here because, generally speaking, methods for learning deterministic models (such as ODE/PDE) do not readily generalize to SDE. Note, however, that prior work on ODE/PDE learning has led to developments in model selection, which we do not address here. If needed, the method we propose can be combined with model selection procedures developed in the ODE context [10,11].

2   Problem Setup

Let W_t denote Brownian motion in $\mathbb{R}^d$—informally, an increment dW_t of this process has a multivariate normal distribution with zero mean vector and covariance matrix $I dt$. Let X_t denote an $\mathbb{R}^d$-valued stochastic process that evolves according to the Itô SDE

$$dX_t = f(X_t)dt + \Gamma dW_t. \tag{1}$$

For rigorous definitions of Brownian motion and SDE, see [5,35]. The nonlinear vector field $f : \Omega \subset \mathbb{R}^d \to \mathbb{R}^d$ is the *drift* function, and the $d \times d$ matrix Γ is the *diffusion* matrix. To reduce the number of model parameters, we assume $\Gamma = \text{diag}\,\gamma$.

Our goal is to develop an algorithm that accurately estimates the functional form of f and the vector γ from time series data.

We parameterize f using Hermite polynomials. The n-th Hermite polynomial takes the form

$$H_n(x) = (\sqrt{2\pi}n!)^{-1/2}(-1)^n e^{x^2/2} \frac{d^n}{dx^n} e^{-x^2/2} \tag{2}$$

Now let $\alpha = (\alpha_1, \ldots, \alpha_d) \in \mathbb{Z}_+^d$ denote a multi-index. We use the notation $|\alpha| = \sum_j \alpha_j$ and $x^\alpha = \prod_j (x_j)^{\alpha_j}$ for $x = (x_1, \ldots, x_d) \in \mathbb{R}^d$. For $x \in \mathbb{R}^d$ and a multi-index α, we also define

$$H_\alpha(x) = \prod_{j=1}^{d} H_{\alpha_j}(x_j). \tag{3}$$

We write $f(x) = (f_1(x), \ldots f_d(x))$ and then parameterize each component

$$f_j(x) = \sum_{m=0}^{M} \sum_{|\alpha|=m} \beta_\alpha^j H_\alpha(x). \tag{4}$$

We see that the maximum degree of $H_\alpha(x)$ is $|\alpha|$. Hence we think of the double sum in (4) as first summing over degrees and then summing over all terms with a fixed maximum degree. We say maximum degree because, for instance, $H_2(z) = (z^2 - 1)/(\sqrt{2\pi}2)^{1/2}$ contains both degree 2 and degree 0 terms.

There are $\binom{m+d-1}{d-1}$ possibilities for a d-dimensional multi-index α such that $|\alpha| = m$. Summing this from $m = 0$ to M, there are $\widetilde{M} = \binom{M+d}{d}$ total multi-indices in the double sum in (4). Let (i) denote the i-th multi-index according to some ordering. Then we can write

$$f_j(x) = \sum_{i=1}^{\widetilde{M}} \beta_{(i)}^j H_{(i)}(x). \tag{5}$$

Essentially, we parameterize f using tensor products of Hermite polynomials. Let $\langle f, g \rangle_w = \int_{\mathbb{R}} f(x)g(x) \exp(-x^2/2)\, dx$ denote a weighted L^2 inner product. Then, $\langle H_i, H_j \rangle_w = \delta_{ij}$, i.e., the Hermite polynomials are orthonormal with respect to the weighted inner product. With respect to this inner product, the one-dimensional Hermite polynomials form an orthonormal basis of $L_w^2(\mathbb{R}) = \{f \langle f, f \rangle_w < \infty\}$. Consequently, by taking $\widetilde{M}$ sufficiently large, a vector field whose j-th component is given by (5) can approximate any continuous vector field. *Hence the above model has the capacity to learn many SDE that occur in physics, including all Langevin equations driven by standard Brownian motions.*

We consider our data $\mathbf{x} = \{x_j\}_{j=0}^L$ to be direct observations of X_t at discrete points in time $\mathbf{t} = \{t_j\}_{t=0}^L$. Note that these time points do not need to be equispaced. In the derivation that follows, we will consider the data $(\mathbf{t}, \mathbf{x})$ to be one time series. Later, we indicate how our methods generalize naturally to multiple time series, i.e., repeated observations of the same system.

To achieve our estimation goal, we apply expectation maximization (EM). We regard $\mathbf{x}$ as the incomplete data. Let $\Delta t = \max_j(t_j - t_{j-1})$ be the maximum interobservation spacing. We think of the missing data $\mathbf{z}$ as data collected at a time scale $h \ll \Delta t$ fine enough such that the transition density of (1) is approximately Gaussian. To see how this works, let $\mathcal{N}(\mu, \Sigma)$ denote a multivariate normal with mean vector μ and covariance matrix Σ. Now discretize (1) in time via the Euler-Maruyama method with time step $h > 0$; the result is

$$\widetilde{X}_{n+1} = \widetilde{X}_n + f(\widetilde{X}_n)h + h^{1/2}\Gamma Z_{n+1}, \tag{6}$$

where $Z_{n+1} \sim \mathcal{N}(0, I)$ is a standard multivariate normal, independent of X_n. This implies that

$$(\widetilde{X}_{n+1}|\widetilde{X}_n = v) \sim \mathcal{N}(v + f(v)h, h\Gamma^2). \tag{7}$$

As h decreases, $\widetilde{X}_{n+1}|\widetilde{X}_n = v$—a Gaussian approximation—will converge to the true transition density $X_{(n+1)h}|X_{nh} = v$, where X_t refers to the solution of (1).

To augment or complete the data, we employ diffusion bridge sampling, using a Markov chain Monte Carlo (MCMC) method with origins in the work of [17, 23]. Let us describe our version here. We suppose our current estimate of $\theta = (\beta, \gamma)$ is given. Define the diffusion bridge process to be (1) conditioned on both the initial value x_i at time t_i, and the final value x_{i+1} at time t_{i+1}. The goal is to generate sample paths of this diffusion bridge. By a sample path, we mean $F - 1$ new samples $\{z_{i,j}\}_{j=1}^{F-1}$ at times $t_i + jh$ with $h = (t_{i+1} - t_i)/F$.

To generate such a path, we start by drawing a sample from a Brownian bridge with the same diffusion as (1). That is, we sample from the SDE

$$d\widehat{X}_t = \Gamma dW_t \tag{8}$$

conditioned on $\widehat{X}_{t_i} = x_i$ and $\widehat{X}_{t_{i+1}} = x_{i+1}$. This Brownian bridge can be described explicitly:

$$\widehat{X}_t = \Gamma(W_t - W_{t_i}) + x_i - \frac{t - t_i}{t_{i+1} - t_i}(\Gamma(W_{t_{i+1}} - W_{t_i}) + x_i - x_{i+1}). \tag{9}$$

Here $W_0 = 0$ (almost surely), and $W_t - W_s \sim \mathcal{N}(0, (t - s)I)$ for $t > s \geq 0$.

Let $\mathbb{P}$ denote the law of the diffusion bridge process, and let $\mathbb{Q}$ denote the law of the Brownian bridge (9). Using Girsanov's theorem [16], we can show that

$$\frac{d\mathbb{P}}{d\mathbb{Q}} = C \exp\left(\int_{t_i}^{t_{i+1}} f(\widehat{X}_s)^T \Gamma^{-2} d\widehat{X}_s - \frac{1}{2}\int_{t_i}^{t_{i+1}} f(\widehat{X}_s)^T \Gamma^{-2} f(\widehat{X}_s) ds\right), \tag{10}$$

where the constant C depends only on x_i and x_{i+1}. The left-hand side is a Radon-Nikodym derivative, equivalent to a density or likelihood; the ratio of two such likelihoods is the accept/reject ratio in the Metropolis algorithm [31].

Putting the above pieces together yields the following Metropolis algorithm (steps M1-3 below) to generate diffusion bridge sample paths. Fix $F \geq 2$ and $i \in \{0, \ldots, L-1\}$. Assume we have stored the previous Metropolis step, i.e., a path $\mathbf{z}^{(\ell)} = \{z_{i,j}^{(\ell)}\}_{j=1}^{F-1}$. Then:

M1 Use (9) to generate samples of $\widehat{X}_t$ at times $t_i + jh$, for $j = 1, 2, \ldots, F-1$ and $h = (t_{i+1} - t_i)/F$. This is the proposal $\mathbf{z}^* = \{z_{i,j}^*\}_{j=1}^{F-1}$.

M2 Numerically approximate the integrals in (10) to compute the likelihood of the proposal. Specifically, we compute

$$p(\mathbf{z}^*)/C = \sum_{j=0}^{F-1} f(z_{i,j}^*)^T \Gamma^{-2}(z_{i,j+1}^* - z_{i,j}^*)$$

$$-\frac{h}{4} \sum_{j=0}^{F-1} \left[f(z_{i,j}^*)^T \Gamma^{-2} f(z_{i,j}^*) + f(z_{i,j+1}^*)^T \Gamma^{-2} f(z_{i,j+1}^*) \right].$$

We have discretized the stochastic $d\widehat{X}_s$ integral using Itô's definition, and we have discretized the ordinary ds integral using the trapezoidal rule.

M3 Accept the proposal with probability $p(\mathbf{z}^*)/p(\mathbf{z}^{(\ell)})$—note the factors of C cancel. If the proposal is accepted, then set $\mathbf{z}^{(\ell+1)} = \mathbf{z}^*$. Else set $\mathbf{z}^{(\ell+1)} = \mathbf{z}^{(\ell)}$.

We initialize this MCMC algorithm with a Brownian bridge path and use post-burn-in steps as the diffusion bridge samples we seek.

We now justify the intuition expressed above, that employing the diffusion bridge to augment the data on a fine scale will enable estimation. Let $\mathbf{z}^{(r)} = \{z_{i,j}^{(r)}\}_{j=1}^{F-1}$ be the r-th diffusion bridge sample path. We interleave this sampled data together with the observed data $\mathbf{x}$ to create the completed time series $\mathbf{y}^{(r)} = \{y_j^{(r)}\}_{j=1}^N$, where $N = LF + 1$. By interleaving, we mean that $y_{1+iF}^{(r)} = x_i$ for $i = 0, 1, \ldots, L$, and that $y_{1+j+iF}^{(r)} = z_{i,j}$ for $j = 1, 2, \ldots, F-1$ and $i = 0, 1, \ldots, L-1$. With this notation, we can more easily express the EM algorithm.

Assume that we currently have access to $\boldsymbol{\theta}^{(k)}$, our estimate of the parameters after k iterations. If $k = 0$, we set $\boldsymbol{\theta}^{(0)}$ equal to an initial guess. Then we follow two steps:

E-step: For the expectation (E) step, we first generate an ensemble of R diffusion bridge sample paths. Interleaving as above, this yields R completed time series $\mathbf{y}^{(r)}$ for $r = 1, \ldots, R$. Define the Q function, or complete data expected log likelihood:

$$Q(\boldsymbol{\theta}, \boldsymbol{\theta}^{(k)}) = \mathbb{E}_{\mathbf{z}|\mathbf{x}, \boldsymbol{\theta}^{(k)}}[\log p(\mathbf{x}, \mathbf{z} \mid \boldsymbol{\theta})]. \tag{11}$$

In what follows, we will use an empirical average over diffusion bridge paths to approximate the expected value on the right-hand side of the Q function. Let h_j denote the elapsed time between observations y_j and y_{j+1}. Using the completed data, the temporal discretization (6) of the SDE, the Markov property, and property (7), we have:

$$Q(\boldsymbol{\theta}, \boldsymbol{\theta}^{(k)}) \approx \frac{1}{R} \sum_{r=1}^{R} \log p(\mathbf{y}^{(r)} \mid \boldsymbol{\theta}) = \frac{1}{R} \sum_{r=1}^{R} \sum_{n=1}^{N-1} \log p(y_{n+1}^{(r)} \mid y_n^{(r)}, \boldsymbol{\theta})$$

$$= -\frac{1}{R} \sum_{r=1}^{R} \sum_{n=1}^{N-1} \left[\sum_{j=1}^{d} \frac{1}{2} \log(2\pi h_n \gamma_j^2) \right.$$

$$\left. + \frac{1}{2h_n} \left\| \Gamma^{-1} \left(y_{n+1}^{(r)} - y_n^{(r)} - h_n \sum_{\ell=1}^{\widetilde{M}} \beta_{(\ell)} H_{(\ell)}(y_n^{(r)}) \right) \right\|_2^2 \right]. \quad (12)$$

M-step: For the maximization (M) step, we have

$$\boldsymbol{\theta}^{(k+1)} = \arg \max_{\boldsymbol{\theta}} Q(\boldsymbol{\theta}, \boldsymbol{\theta}^{(k)}).$$

Starting from the approximation of Q developed in (12), we maximize over $\boldsymbol{\theta}$ analytically. In what follows, note that $y_j^{(r)} \in \mathbb{R}^d$—we denote the i-th component by $y_j^{(r),i}$. The maximization over β yields a least squares problem—we omit the derivation here. The upshot is that to find $\beta^{(k+1)}$ we solve $\mathcal{M}\beta = \rho$ where $\mathcal{M}$ is the $\widetilde{M} \times \widetilde{M}$ matrix

$$\mathcal{M}_{k,\ell} = \frac{1}{R} \sum_{r=1}^{R} \sum_{n=1}^{N-1} h_n H_{(k)}(y_n^{(r)}) H_{(\ell)}(y_n^{(r)}), \quad (13)$$

and ρ is the $\widetilde{M} \times d$ matrix

$$\rho_{k,i} = \frac{1}{R} \sum_{r=1}^{R} \sum_{n=1}^{N-1} H_{(k)}(y_n^{(r)})(y_{n+1}^{(r),i} - y_n^{(r),i}). \quad (14)$$

We return to (12) and maximize over γ. This yields a formula for $\gamma^{(k+1)}$:

$$\gamma_i^2 = \frac{1}{R(N-1)} \sum_{r=1}^{R} \sum_{n=1}^{N-1} h_n^{-1}(y_{n+1}^{(r),i} - y_n^{(r),i} - h_n \sum_{\ell=1}^{\widetilde{M}} \beta_{(\ell)}^i H_{(\ell)}(y_n^{(r)}))^2, \quad (15)$$

where $\beta_{(\ell)}^i$ denotes the ℓ-th row and i-th column of the $\beta^{(k+1)}$ matrix. We then set $\boldsymbol{\theta}^{(k+1)} = (\beta^{(k+1)}, \gamma^{(k+1)})$.

We iterate EM steps until $\|\boldsymbol{\theta}^{(k+1)} - \boldsymbol{\theta}^{(k)}\|/\|\boldsymbol{\theta}^{(k)}\| < \delta$ for some tolerance $\delta > 0$.

When the data consists of multiple time series $\{\mathbf{t}^{(i)}, \mathbf{x}^{(i)}\}_{i=1}^{S}$, everything scales accordingly. For instance, we create an ensemble of R diffusion bridge samples for each of the S time series. If we index the resulting completed time series appropriately, we simply replace R by RS in (13), (14), and (15) and keep everything else the same.

There are three sources of error in the above algorithm. The first relates to replacing the expectation by a sample average; the induced error should, by the law of large numbers, decrease as $R^{-1/2}$. The second stems from the approximate nature of the computed diffusion bridge samples—as indicated above, we use numerical integration to approximate the Girsanov likelihood. The third source of error is in using the Gaussian transition density to approximate the true transition density of the SDE. Both the second and third sources of error vanish in the $F \to \infty$ limit [9].

3   Experiments

We present a series of experiments with synthetic data. We have made available all source code required to reproduce our results and/or run further tests: https://github.com/hbhat4000/pathsamp/. For further details regarding simulations, experiments, and results, see [21].

To generate synthetic data, we start with a known stochastic dynamical system of the form (1). Using Euler-Maruyama time stepping from a randomly chosen initial condition, we march forward in time from $t = 0$ to a final time $t = 10$. In all examples, we step forward internally at a time step of $h = 0.0001$, but for the purposes of estimation, we only use data sampled every 0.1 units of time, discarding 99.9% of the simulated trajectory. We use a fine internal time step to reduce, to the extent possible, numerical error in the simulated data. We save the data on a coarse time scale to test the proposed EM algorithm.

To study how the EM method performs as a function of data augmentation, data volume, and noise strength, we perform four sets of experiments. In all experiments, we treat all noise strengths γ_j as known and estimate β only. When we run EM, we randomly generate the initial guess $\beta^{(0)} \sim \mathcal{N}(\mu = 0, \sigma^2 = 0.5)$. We set the EM tolerance parameter $\delta = 0.01$. The only regularization we include is to threshold β—values less than ν are set to zero. In the figures presented below, we refer to this value of ν as the threshold. Finally, in the MCMC diffusion bridge sampler, we use 10 burn-in steps and then create an ensemble of size $R = 100$.

To quantify the error between the estimated $\widetilde{\beta}$ and the true β, we use the Frobenius norm

$$\varepsilon = \sqrt{\sum_i \sum_\ell \left(\beta^i_{(\ell)} - \widetilde{\beta}^i_{(\ell)} \right)^2} \tag{16}$$

The $\widetilde{\beta}$ coefficients are the Hermite coefficients of the estimated drift vector field f. For each example system, we compute the true Hermite coefficients β by multiplying the true ordinary polynomial coefficients by a change-of-basis matrix that is easily computed.

We test the method using stochastic systems in dimensions $d = 1, 2, 3, 4, 8$. In 1D, we use

$$dX_t = (1 + X_t - X_t^2)dt + \gamma dW_t.$$

Table 1. Results for average compute time (in seconds) per EM iteration for varying amount of data augmentation. As the Brownian bridge is created explicitly using the discretized version of (9), increasing the amount of data augmentation does significantly increase in the compute time. The time required to compute each EM iteration increases with the dimensionality of the system.

$\frac{F}{\text{System}}$	1	2	3	4	5	6	7	8	9	10
1D	0.59	0.54	0.54	0.54	1.00	0.57	0.58	0.57	0.85	0.55
2D	0.65	0.57	0.58	0.57	0.57	0.57	0.57	0.62	0.56	0.57
3D	6.51	9.58	6.29	6.55	6.46	6.82	6.47	6.36	6.69	6.59
4D	24.08	24.34	23.94	23.98	24.93	25.65	23.99	23.17	25.64	24.54

In 2D, we use a stochastic Duffing oscillator with no damping or driving:

$$dX_{0,t} = X_{1,t}dt + \gamma_0 dW_{0,t} \qquad dX_{1,t} = (-X_{0,t} - X_{0,t}^3)dt + \gamma_1 dW_{1,t}$$

For the 3D case, we consider the stochastic, damped, driven Duffing oscillator:

$$dX_{0,t} = X_{1,t}dt + \gamma_0 dW_{0,t}$$
$$dX_{1,t} = (X_{0,t} - X_{0,t}^3 - 0.3X_{1,t} + 0.5\cos(X_{2,t}))dt + \gamma_1 dW_{1,t}$$
$$dX_{2,t} = 1.2dt + \gamma_2 dW_{2,t}$$

Next, we consider linear, stochastic, coupled oscillator systems with $d = 2d'$. Assume we have a mass vector $m \in \mathbb{R}^{d'}$ and a spring constant vector $k \in \mathbb{R}^{d'+1}$. The network then consists of the following equations, for $j = 0, 1, 2, \ldots, d' - 1$, with the convention that $X_{i,t} \equiv 0$ if $i < 0$ or $i \geq d$:

$$dX_{2j,t} = X_{2j+1,t}dt + \gamma_{2j}dW_{2j,t}$$
$$dX_{2j+1,t} = [-k_j/m_j(X_{2j,t} - X_{2j-2,t}) - k_{j+1}/m_j(X_{2j,t} - X_{2j+2,t})]dt$$
$$+ g_{2j+1}dW_{2j+1,t}$$

We consider this system for both $d = 4$ and $d = 8$. In $d = 4$, we set $k = [1, 0.7, 0.6]$ and $m = [0.2, 0.3]$. In $d = 8$, we set $k = [1, 0.7, 0.6, 1.2, 0.9]$ and $m = [0.2, 0.3, 0.5, 1.1]$.

3.1 Experiment 1: Varying Data Augmentation

We start with $S = 10$ time series with $L + 1 = 51$ points each. Here we vary the number of interleaved diffusion bridge samples: $F = 1, \ldots, 10$. For $F = 1$, no diffusion bridge is created; the likelihood is computed by applying the Gaussian transition density directly to the observed data. The results, plotted in Figs. 1 and 2, show that increased data augmentation dramatically improves the quality

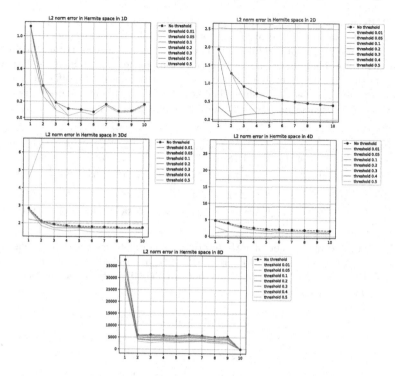

Fig. 1. As we increase the length F of the diffusion bridge interleaving observed data points, the quality of estimated drifts improves considerably. From left to right, top to bottom, we have plotted Frobenius errors (16) between true and estimated coefficients, for systems in $d = 1, 2, 3, 4, 8$.

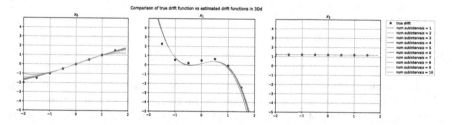

Fig. 2. Though Fig. 1 shows the Frobenius norm error for the 3D system is greater than ≈ 2.6 at all noise levels, when plotted, the estimated drift functions lie close to the true drift function. The three components of the vector field are plotted as in the third row of Fig. 3.

of estimated drifts for systems with $d = 1, 2, 3, 4, 8$. Though the Frobenius error for the 3D system exceeds 2.6, Fig. 2 shows that EM's estimates are still accurate.

We have not plotted results for the scarce data regime where we have $S = 10$ time series with $L = 11$ points each. In this regime, data augmentation enables

Table 2. Results for average acceptance rate for Metropolis-Hastings sampler for varying amount of data augmentation, F. For $F = 1$, no diffusion bridge has been created and thus the acceptance probability is 1. The algorithm in this case reduces to solving a least squares problem using only the observed time series. As we increase data augmentation, the acceptance probability decreases as it becomes more difficult to create a bridge between the observed values. The acceptance probability also decreases with an increase in the dimensionality and complexity of the system.

$\dfrac{F}{\text{System}}$	1	2	3	4	5	6	7	8	9	10
1D	100	75.04	67.08	61.78	61.23	58.71	55.22	53.57	52.58	49.52
2D	100	13.17	9.04	6.54	4.75	4.35	4.11	4.94	2.87	4.02
3D	100	6.07	3.20	2.82	2.74	2.54	2.48	2.27	2.51	2.41
4D	100	25.69	19.22	13.69	11.63	7.81	6.88	5.83	4.10	4.04

Table 3. Results for number of EM iterations required to converge. We consider a threshold of 0.01, 0.05, 0.1 and 0.1 for the 1D, 2D, 3D and 4D systems respectively. Note that the number of iterations does not vary significantly as a function of the amount of data augmentation F.

$\dfrac{F}{\text{System}}$	1	2	3	4	5	6	7	8	9	10
1D	2	3	3	3	3	3	3	3	3	3
2D	2	8	5	7	6	8	8	4	9	6
3D	2	3	3	3	3	3	9	3	3	3
4D	2	2	2	2	2	2	2	2	2	2

highly accurate estimation for the 2D and 3D systems. For the 1D system, the observations do not explore phase space properly, leading to poor estimation of the drift.

In Tables 1, 2, and 3, we report the average compute time (in seconds), the average MCMC acceptance rate, and the average number of iterations (for convergence), all as a function of F, the amount of data augmentation performed. Broadly speaking, none of these metrics show dependence on F. Instead, they depend primarily on d, the dimension of the problem under consideration.

The main point of EM, generally speaking, is to augment data. These experiments thus show that even with a basic diffusion bridge sampler, there is merit to the EM approach for estimating drift functions in diffusion processes. In ongoing/future work, we seek to explore using more sophisticated diffusion bridge samplers, e.g., those that use the drift function to guide the proposal, rather than only incorporating the drift into the accept/reject ratio. Such approaches may help to reduce the d-dependence of the metrics we have plotted/tabulated.

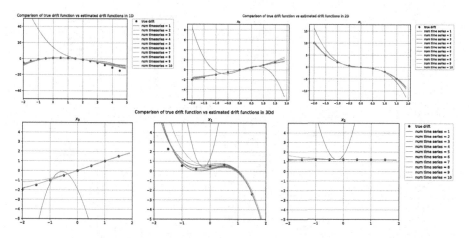

Fig. 3. As we increase the number S of time series used to learn the drift, the estimated drift more closely approximates the ground truth. From top to bottom, left to right, we have plotted estimated and true drifts for the 1D, 2D, and 3D systems. For the 1D and 2D systems, the true drifts depend on only one variable. For the $dX_{1,t}$ component of the 3D system, we have plotted the dependence of the drifts on X_0 only, keeping X_1 and X_2 fixed at 0.

3.2   Experiment 2: Varying Number of Time Series

Here we vary data volume by stepping the number S of time series from $S = 1$ to $S = 10$. Each time series has length $L + 1 = 101$. The results, as plotted in Figs. 3 and 4, show that increasing S leads to improved estimates of β, as expected. As a rule of thumb, the results indicate that at least $S \geq 4$ time series are needed for accurate estimation.

3.3   Experiment 3: Varying Length of Time Series

Here we vary data volume by stepping the length $L + 1$ of the time series from $L + 1 = 11$ to $L + 1 = 101$, keeping the number of time series fixed at $S = 10$. Also note that in this experiment, observation times strictly between the initial and final times are chosen randomly. In Fig. 5, we have plotted the estimated and true drifts for only the 3D system; in Fig. 6, we have plotted the error (16) for all three systems. Comparing with Experiment 1, we see that randomization of the observation times improves estimation. That is, even with $L+1 = 11$ data points per time series, we obtain accurate estimates.

3.4   Experiment 4: Varying Noise Strength

Here we vary the noise strength γ, stepping from 0.5 to 0.0001 while keeping other parameters constant. Specifically, we take $S = 10$ time series each of length $L + 1 = 101$. In Fig. 7, we have plotted Frobenius errors for all three systems.

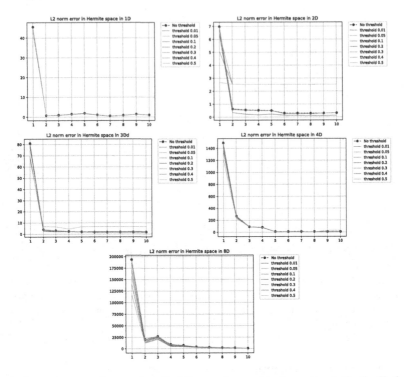

Fig. 4. As we increase the number S of time series used to learn the drift, the Frobenius norm error between estimated and true drifts—see (16)—decreases significantly. From left to right, top to bottom, we have plotted results for systems with $d = 1, 2, 3, 4, 8$.

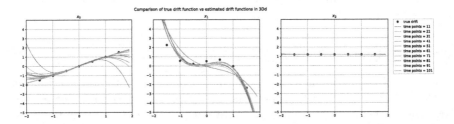

Fig. 5. We plot true and estimated drifts for the 3D system as a function of increasing time series length L. The three components of the vector field are plotted as in the third row of Fig. 3. The results show that randomization of observation times compensates for a small value of L, enabling accurate estimation.

Though the error in the estimated coefficients for the 3D system may seem large, the estimated and true drift functions are close—see Fig. 8. Even when the algorithm does not recover ground truth parameter values, it yields a drift function that reproduces qualitative features of the ground truth drift.

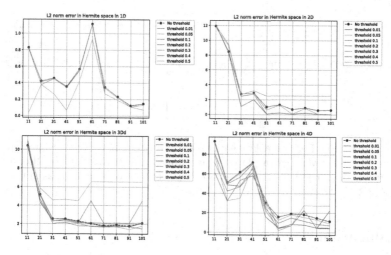

Fig. 6. As we increase the length L of each time series used for learning, the Frobenius norm error between estimated and true drifts—see (16)—decreases significantly. From left to right, we have plotted results for the 1D, 2D, 3D, and 4D systems.

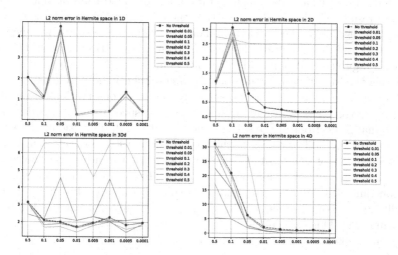

Fig. 7. Varying the strength of the noise in the simulated data alters the quality of estimated drift coefficients, quantified using the Frobenius error (16). We proceed from left to right. For the 1D and 2D systems, the maximum noise strength of 0.5 remains below the magnitude of the drift field coefficients. For these systems, as the noise strength decreases, the error drops close to zero. For the 3D system, the maximum noise strength of 0.5 is greater than or equal to two of the drift field coefficients, leading to apparently decreased performance—however, see Fig. 8.

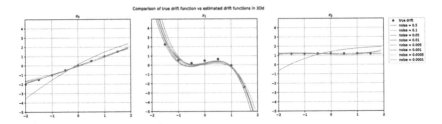

Fig. 8. Though Fig. 7 shows a Frobenius norm error for the 3D system greater than ≈ 1.8 at all noise levels, when plotted, the estimated drift functions lie close to the true drift function. The three components of the vector field are plotted as in the third row of Fig. 3.

4   Conclusion

We have developed an EM algorithm for estimation of drift functions and diffusion matrices for SDE. We have demonstrated the conditions under which the algorithm succeeds in estimating SDE. Specifically, our tests show that with enough data volume and data augmentation, the EM algorithm produces highly accurate results. Our tests also show that there is room for improvement, especially with regards to the basic Brownian bridge sampler incorporated here. In future work, we plan to study the effect of replacing the Brownian bridge sampler with a guided diffusion bridge sampler [29], especially with an eye towards increasing the MCMC acceptance rate for high-dimensional problems.

Here we have assumed direct access to discrete-time observations of the state $\mathbf{X}_t$ of the system. Such an assumption will be satisfied if we take as data low-dimensional projections of the solution process of a high-dimensional system; in this case, the method proposed in this paper can be used to derive SDE models for the evolution of the low-dimensional system. In future work, we also seek to further test our method on high-dimensional, nonlinear problems, problems with non-constant diffusion matrices, and real experimental data. In the latter case, we will explore coupling our EM method with a highly efficient batch filtering algorithm [22]. This will enable us to deal with observations of $\mathbf{Y}_t = \mathbf{X}_t + \varepsilon_t$, rather than observations of $\mathbf{X}_t$ itself.

References

1. Archambeau, C., Opper, M., Shen, Y., Cornford, D., Shawe-Taylor, J.S.: Variational inference for diffusion processes. In: Advances in Neural Information Processing Systems, pp. 17–24 (2008)
2. Batz, P., Ruttor, A., Opper, M.: Variational estimation of the drift for stochastic differential equations from the empirical density. J. Stat. Mech: Theory Exp. **2016**(8), 083404 (2016)
3. Batz, P., Ruttor, A., Opper, M.: Approximate Bayes learning of stochastic differential equations. Phys. Rev. E **98**, 022109 (2018)

4. Bhat, H.S., Madushani, R.W.M.A.: Nonparametric adjoint-based inference for stochastic differential equations. In: 2016 IEEE International Conference on Data Science and Advanced Analytics (DSAA), pp. 798–807 (2016)
5. Bhattacharya, R.N., Waymire, E.C.: Stochastic Processes with Applications. SIAM (2009)
6. Brunton, S.L., Proctor, J.L., Kutz, J.N.: Discovering governing equations from data by sparse identification of nonlinear dynamical systems. Proc. Nat. Acad. Sci. **113**(15), 3932–3937 (2016)
7. Chen, S., Shojaie, A., Witten, D.M.: Network reconstruction from high-dimensional ordinary differential equations. J. Am. Stat. Assoc. **112**(520), 1697–1707 (2017)
8. Ghahramani, Z., Roweis, S.T.: Learning nonlinear dynamical systems using an EM algorithm. In: Advances in Neural Information Processing Systems (NIPS), pp. 431–437 (1999)
9. Kloeden, P.E., Platen, E.: Numerical Solution of Stochastic Differential Equations. Springer, Heidelberg (2011). https://doi.org/10.1007/978-3-662-12616-5
10. Mangan, N.M., Brunton, S.L., Proctor, J.L., Kutz, J.N.: Inferring biological networks by sparse identification of nonlinear dynamics. IEEE Trans. Mol. Biol. Multi-Scale Commun. **2**(1), 52–63 (2016)
11. Mangan, N.M., Kutz, J.N., Brunton, S.L., Proctor, J.L.: Model selection for dynamical systems via sparse regression and information criteria. Proc. R. Soc. A **473**(2204), 20170009 (2017)
12. van der Meulen, F., Schauer, M., van Waaij, J.: Adaptive nonparametric drift estimation for diffusion processes using Faber-Schauder expansions. Statistical Inference for Stochastic Processes, pp. 1–26 (2017)
13. van der Meulen, F., Schauer, M., van Zanten, H.: Reversible jump MCMC for nonparametric drift estimation for diffusion processes. Comput. Stat. Data Anal. **71**, 615–632 (2014)
14. Müller, H.G., Yao, F., et al.: Empirical dynamics for longitudinal data. Ann. Stat. **38**(6), 3458–3486 (2010)
15. Nicolau, J.: Nonparametric estimation of second-order stochastic differential equations. Econ. Theory **23**(05), 880 (2007)
16. Papaspiliopoulos, O., Roberts, G.O.: Importance sampling techniques for estimation of diffusion models. Stat. Methods Stoch. Differ. Equ. **124**, 311–340 (2012)
17. Papaspiliopoulos, O., Roberts, G.O., Stramer, O.: Data augmentation for diffusions. J. Comput. Graph. Stat. **22**(3), 665–688 (2013)
18. Quade, M., Abel, M., Kutz, J.N., Brunton, S.L.: Sparse identification of nonlinear dynamics for rapid model recovery. Chaos **28**(6), 063116 (2018)
19. Raissi, M., Karniadakis, G.E.: Hidden physics models: machine learning of nonlinear partial differential equations. J. Comput. Phys. **357**, 125–141 (2018)
20. Raissi, M., Perdikaris, P., Karniadakis, G.E.: Machine learning of linear differential equations using Gaussian processes. J. Comput. Phys. **348**, 683–693 (2017)
21. Rawat, S.: Learning governing equations for stochastic dynamical systems. Ph.D. thesis, University of California, Merced (2018). Advisor: H.S. Bhat
22. Raziperchikolaei, R., Bhat, H.: A block coordinate descent proximal method for simultaneous filtering and parameter estimation. In: Chaudhuri, K., Salakhutdinov, R. (eds.) Proceedings of the 36th International Conference on Machine Learning. Proceedings of Machine Learning Research, Long Beach, California, USA, 09–15 June 2019, vol. 97, pp. 5380–5388. PMLR (2019)
23. Roberts, G.O., Stramer, O.: On inference for partially observed nonlinear diffusion models using the Metropolis-Hastings algorithm. Biometrika **88**(3), 603–621 (2001)

24. Rudy, S.H., Brunton, S.L., Proctor, J.L., Kutz, J.N.: Data-driven discovery of partial differential equations. Sci. Adv. **3**(4), e1602614 (2017)

25. Ruttor, A., Batz, P., Opper, M.: Approximate Gaussian process inference for the drift function in stochastic differential equations. In: Advances in Neural Information Processing Systems, pp. 2040–2048 (2013)

26. Schaeffer, H., Caflisch, R., Hauck, C.D., Osher, S.: Sparse dynamics for partial differential equations. Proc. Nat. Acad. Sci. **110**(17), 6634–6639 (2013)

27. Schaeffer, H.: Learning partial differential equations via data discovery and sparse optimization. Proc. R. Soc. A: Math., Phys. Eng. Sci. **473**(2197), 20160446 (2017)

28. Schaeffer, H., Tran, G., Ward, R.: Extracting sparse high-dimensional dynamics from limited data. SIAM J. Appl. Math. **78**(6), 3279–3295 (2018)

29. Schauer, M., van der Meulen, F., van Zanten, H.: Guided proposals for simulating multi-dimensional diffusion bridges. Bernoulli **23**(4A), 2917–2950 (2017)

30. Schön, T.B., Svensson, A., Murray, L., Lindsten, F.: Probabilistic learning of nonlinear dynamical systems using sequential Monte Carlo. Mech. Syst. Signal Process. **104**, 866–883 (2018)

31. Stuart, A.M.: Inverse problems: a Bayesian perspective. Acta Numerica **19**, 451–559 (2010)

32. Tran, G., Ward, R.: Exact recovery of chaotic systems from highly corrupted data. Multiscale Model. Simul. **15**(3), 1108–1129 (2017)

33. Verzelen, N., Tao, W., Müller, H.G.: others: Inferring stochastic dynamics from functional data. Biometrika **99**(3), 533–550 (2012)

34. Vrettas, M.D., Opper, M., Cornford, D.: Variational mean-field algorithm for efficient inference in large systems of stochastic differential equations. Phys. Rev. E **91**(1), 012148 (2015)

35. Øksendal, B.: Stochastic Differential Equations: An Introduction with Applications. Universitext, 6th edn. Springer, Heidelberg (2003). https://doi.org/10.1007/978-3-642-14394-6

Quantifying Quality of Actions Using Wearable Sensor

Mohammad Al-Naser[1,2(✉)], Takehiro Niikura[3], Sheraz Ahmed[1],
Hiroki Ohashi[4], Takuto Sato[4], Mitsuhiro Okada[4], Katsuyuki Nakamura[4],
and Andreas Dengel[1,2]

[1] German Research Center for Artificial Intelligence (DFKI),
Kaiserslautern, Germany
{mohammad.al_naser,sheraz.ahmed,andreas.dengel}@dfki.de
[2] TU Kaiserslautern, Kaiserslautern, Germany
[3] Hitachi Europe, Kaiserslautern, Germany
takehiro.niikura@hitachi-eu.com
[4] Hitachi Ltd., Tokyo, Japan
{hiroki.ohashi.uo,takuto.sato.hn,mitsuhiro.okada.uf,
katsuyuki.nakamura.xv}@hitachi.de

Abstract. This paper introduces a novel approach to quantify the quality of human actions. The presented approach uses expert action data to define the space in order to gauge the performance of any user to identify expertise level. The proposed approach uses pose estimation model to identify different body attributes (legs, shoulders, head ...) status (left, right, bend, curl ...), which is further passed to autoencoder to have a latent representation encoding all the relevant information. This encoded representation is further passed to OneClass SVM to estimate the boundaries based on latent representation of expert data. These learned boundaries are used to gauge the quality of any questioned user with respect to the selected expert. The proposed approach enables identifying any critical situations in real work environment to avoid risky positions.

Keywords: Autoencoder · OneClass SVM · Actions evaluation · Wearable sensor

1 Introduction

Human-activity recognition (HAR) is one of the important research topics for the systems involving human-machine system [9,13]. It has a wide variety of applications such as health care, rehabilitation, education, sport, and worker assistance [15,17,19,20,25]. Especially, if the system can assess the quality of action and gives moderate feedback to the users about how they can improve. Forevermore, it can be used for training as well as to avoid any critical situations.

With the recent progress in deep neural networks (DNN), the performance of HAR system has been significantly improved both in terms of accuracy and the number of actions [7,10,22,24]. While state-of-the-art HAR [7,22] research

© Springer Nature Switzerland AG 2020
V. Lemaire et al. (Eds.): AALTD 2019, LNAI 11986, pp. 199–212, 2020.
https://doi.org/10.1007/978-3-030-39098-3_15

accomplished promising performance for many action recognition tasks, most of the researches mainly focused on recognizing "which" action is being performed [6,10,22]. Though these researches are meaningful and can be utilized for an application to recognize whether the sequence of action executed or not, they do not focus on identifying the quality of recognized action. We found only limited number of research on how to assess the quality of action [7,8,15] and most of them based on video sequence analysis.

In this paper, we propose a novel approach to quantify the quality of action using wearable sensor, in which we use autoencoder and OneClass SVM. In contrast to the existing approaches [7,18] which work only with video data; the proposed approach deals with sensors data that obtained from wearable sensors (namely perception neuron [2]) to assess the quality of various actions. Sensors in the wearable device directly measure the movements of more than 30 body parts, and collected data is used to create attributes of the body joints, the attributes passed to the autoencoder to create the latent space. Then the model learns to estimate the boundaries based on latent representation of expert data. These learned boundaries are used to assess the quality of any questioned user with respect to the correspondent expert. The proposed approach provide both coarse as well as fine grained information about quality of an action. This means, it firstly provides an overall information about how good a particular action is. Then for fine details, it highlights part of the action which can be improved to increase overall quality of that particular action.

Our main contributions are as follows:

- We propose a novel method to assess the quality of various actions sensed by wearable sensor.
- We provided a new human action dataset using wearable sensors to be used for actions assessment.

The experimental results showed that our model achieved high accuracy for most of the actions.

2   Related Work

Only a limited number of research tackled the problem of action quality assessment [18,20,23]. Lv et al. proposed a system [14] which assesses the quality of driving behaviors based on radio signals. They used hand-crafted features for quality assessment, and the system can be used for differentiating a triple body status and for identifying among 15 drivers with high accuracy. An efficient system to detect and classify several swing motions in various kinds of sports has been developed by Anand et al. [3], by utilizing IMU sensor on users' wrist. Regarding the movement assessment for sport, there are some other studies [12,15], for example, Bacic [4] used vision-based motion capture system to analyze the swing motion of tennis whether the swing is good or bad. Although some of the research above aimed to develop a general system to assess the movements of users, their systems rely on some features and methods which are specific to their target movement, implicitly or explicitly.

Velloso et al. [21] also presented a system which assesses the performance of users in real time and provides feedback on how to improve their performance. Their system is also designed to their specific target action. However, they gave some important indications in their paper. They said, "This evidences that specifying a movement by natural language and estimating precise angles by observation is difficult", and therefore they adopted Programming by Demonstration (PbD) approach. PbD aims to make it possible to program systems by having a user demonstrate to them how they should behave, instead of hardcoding a system's behavior. This is a very important indication for us, because it is often the case that experts can't explain the key point of their skill by natural language. In other words, they have muscle memories about how they should execute, but it is very difficult for them to verbalize their skill. In this sense, PbD approach seems promising for our purpose.

In the domain of image processing research, deep-ranking approach has recently achieved a great success in skill assessment. Doughty et al. [7] presented a general method for assessing skill from video. The authors collected egocentric videos from both experts and novices, and defined which video has better skill level than the other. With this information, the model learned how to assess skill, like surgery, drawing, and rolling pizza dough, and so on. One advantage of their approach is that their model can deal with many kinds of activities, since the model is designed independently from task specific information. This is important because it can assess many kinds of actions with such generalization capability. Also, Doughty et al. [8] presented a temporal attention modules to determine relative skill from long videos, they use a rank-aware loss function to train a temporal attention model. The model learns to attend task-relevant video parts. Also they proposed a joint loss trains two attention modules to separately attend to video parts, which are indicative of higher (pros) and lower (cons) skill. Although the models show a very good results in skill determination, but such settings is difficult to use in the working environment, because of the privacy issues and the occlusions that usually happens for the video.

3 Target Actions and Data

3.1 Target Actions

Since most of the existing methods are based on video analysis, there is no publicly available dataset for evaluating the quality of action, we need to construct a dataset by ourselves.

Supposing that actions are in a real scenario, the key point of skills can exist at any part of the body. For example, if a user is using screw driver, the movement of arms and/or hands might be important, however if the user needs to use it in a narrow space, the movement of legs and waist are also important. Therefore, we designed our experiments where target actions are defined based on the following criteria.

– As a whole, target actions contain movements of whole body.
– To confirm the validity of our system after the development, both good action
  and bad action need to be definable by an existing metric.

Table 1. Target actions definition

Action	Pick up	Hold	Move
Good	Bend knees Put body closer to Object	Stretch elbows Keep object closer to Body	Use legs Don't twist waist
Bad	Don't bend knees Bend waist Keep body distant from object	 Bend elbows Keep object distant from body	 Twist waist

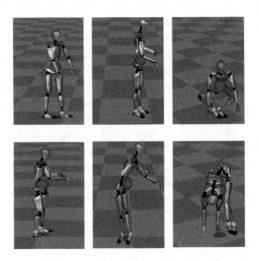

Fig. 1. Target actions. The top images are the good actions (expert) and the lower
ones are the bad actions (novice). Where the left column is 'hold' action, the middle
is 'move' action, and the right is 'pick up' action.

Based on these requirements, we chose three actions, which are 'pick up',
'hold', and 'move' an object 1. These three actions compose an activity of "carrying an object", and to carry an object the worker needs to use his/her whole body.
Also, it's important that these actions are basic and common in any real scenario. Additionally, there's a global metric for estimating workload with respect
to workers' posture, named as OWAS (The Ovako Working posture Assessment
System). By using this metric, we can define both good action and bad action.

In this paper we call the good action (expert) and bad action (novice), where we think the good skills lead to less workload. Figure 1 shows images of good and bad manner for each action, and Table 1 shows the definition of good and bad manner for each action. In 'pick up' action, a user picks up and puts down a printer from/on the floor. The key point of this action is the movement of waist and knees, and a worker may hurt his/her back in bad action. In 'hold' action, a worker keeps holding a projector, and he can walk around freely while holding it, and the key point for this action is the usage of elbows and upper arms. The bad manner of this action easily causes fatigue on upper arms. In 'move' action, a worker moves a projector from front to left/right side. In this case, if the worker twists his/her waist while 'move' action, it may damage his/her waist.

3.2 Wearable Sensor

Our goal is to quantify the quality of full-body action. Thus, a very dense sensor set across full-body is required. Perception Neuron from Noitom Ltd [2] as shown in Fig. 2 is one of the best commercial products that satisfies this requirement and it is available in the market. It has 31 IMU sensors across full body; 1 on head, 2 on shoulders, 2 on upper arms, 2 on lower arms, 2 on hands, 14 on fingers, 1 on spine, 1 on hip, 2 on upper legs, 2 on lower legs, 2 on feet. Each IMU is composed of a 3-axis accelerometer, 3-axis gyroscope and 3-axis magnetometer.

Fig. 2. The perception neuron sensor.

3.3 Dataset

We collected data of three actions in the laboratory. Table 2 gives the conditions when we collected the data. As we mentioned before, the target actions are 'pick up', 'hold', and 'move'. 11 participants joined the data collection. We collected data 3 times for both good action and bad action respectively, and 1 trial of data collection lasted for 1 min. During 1 trial, participants were asked to perform the

Table 2. Conditions of collecting action data

Number of actions	3 (Pick up, Hold, Move)
Number of participants	11
Number of trials for each action	Total: 6 (3 for good action, 3 for bad action)
Duration time for 1 trial	1 min

same action repeatedly. The definition of one repetition for 'pick up' is to pick up a printer and to put it down on the floor, and for 'move' is to move a projector from front to right, turn to the printer, and move it to the original position again. We collected data from 29 IMU sensors, all sensors without on feet, across full body. Since the magnetometer provides the position of the sensor in quaternion, each IMU provides 10 types of data at 60 fps.

4   Proposed Method

Our model is inspired by anomaly detection methods [5,11] which have a very good performance in outlier detection. These methods use the reconstruction loss of the autoencoder to detect the anomaly data, where the normal data have lower reconstruction loss than the outlier data as shown in Fig. 4. The model use only good actions (expert) data to define the expert space, to compare the performance of any user in order to identify the action level.

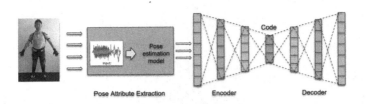

Fig. 3. Overview of the initial model.

In our model we employed a zero-shot pose estimation model [16]. The sensors raw data passed to the model to estimate the status of 14 major human-body joints, which we call attributes. The attributes represent various body poses, Where multi-class classification or regression are used for the joints depending on their characteristics, see Table 3. Note that each joint has left part and right part except head and waist. In the next step, we passed the attributes to the autoencoder to create the latent space of the good skills. The autoencoder which we use is deep autoencoder consists of three fully connected layers, and the reconstruction loss is mean square error. The overview of deep autoencoder is

Table 3. Pose estimation attributes which are used as an input for the autoencoder. It's to be noted that some of them are binary attributes, while others have continues values

Joint	Type	Value
Head	Classification	Up, down, left, right, front
Shoulder	Classification	Up, down, left, right, front
Elbow	Regression	0 (straight)-1 (bend)
Wrist	Regression	0 (reverse curl)-1 (curl)
Hand	Classification	Normal, grasp, pointing
Waist	Classification	Straight, bend, twist-L, twist-R
Hip joint	Regression	0 (straight)-1 (bend)
Knee	Regression	0 (straight)-1 (bend)

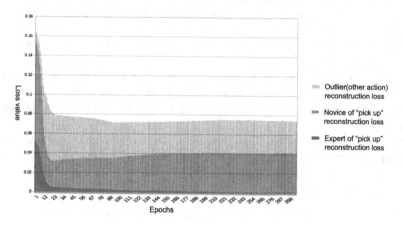

Fig. 4. Reconstruction loss values for 'pick up' action.

shown in Fig. 3. After testing the model with good actions (expert) and bad actions (novice), we found the reconstruction loss of the expert less than the novice reconstruction loss, as shown in Fig. 4, which means the autoencoder succeeded in learning the differences between the good and bad actions.

Then, we developed the model to score the actions. We substituted the decoder part in the autoencoder by OneClass SVM model, as shown in Fig. 5. For OneClass SVM, we used RBF(radial basis function) kernel since we are dealing with non-linear problem. The OneClass SVM learns the latent space of the experts' skills, so that it can output the decision scores on the test data.

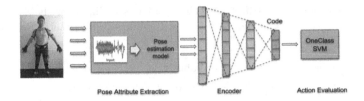

Fig. 5. Overview of encoder and OneClass SVM.

5   Training and Evaluation

5.1   Training

For training, evaluation, and testing, we manually separated the recorded data of 1 trial into several splits, which contains one repetition of action. We created 6 splits for 'Pick up' and 5 splits for "Move". As we recorded 'hold' action continuously, we don't have clear cut to create splits. For this experiment we divided the whole action data into 6 same duration splits. Table 4 shows the number of splits for each action.

Then, we separated the data into training, validation and test data. Since there is a lot of individual variations in data, we separated data in terms of person so that our model will be tested with completely new data in validation and test phase.

We train our model by feeding the sensors data to the pose estimation model, the model use 0.5 s time window to estimate the attributes of the body (joints status), where the number of the estimated attributes is 33 for each window.

Table 4. Number of splits for each action

Action	Number of splits from 1 trial	Number of splits in total
"Pick up"	6	396 (Expert: 198, Novice: 198)
"Hold"	6	396 (Expert: 198, Novice: 198)
"Move"	5	330 (Expert: 165, Novice: 165)

Then we concatenate 5 window attributes together to train the autoencoder as shown in Fig. 6. While training we save the latent space for each batch until the epoch is finished. Then we train the OneClass SVM by the saved latent space. We tried to train the OneClass SVM by latent space of each batch separately, but the results was worse than the training by the latent space for the whole data. Next step is to validate the OneClass SVM model using expert and novice data, and we keep doing this to the last epoch.

Also, we want to check how the increase of the training data affects the results, So we gradually increased the number of people for training data from

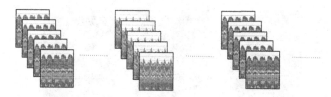

Fig. 6. Each 5 window attributes concatenated together then trained on the autoencoder

2 to 5, one by one. Practically, we always regarded one specific person as a test data. At the beginning of experiment, we used only the data from 2 participants as training data, and did the rest as validation data. After each experiment, we took 1 participant from validation data and added it in training data.

5.2 Evaluation

Finally, after training our model, we evaluated the model with accuracy, which is calculated with the following equation.

$$accuracy = \frac{L_{correct}}{L_{total}} \tag{1}$$

Where, L_{total} is the number of splits for test data. And $L_{correct}$ is the number of splits in which the score for expert was higher than 0, and the score is less than 0 for the novice.

6   Results

As described in the training section, we trained the model with 2 participants then increased the training data one by one to 5, we stopped at 5 participants because we didn't find improvement in performance with the increase of the training data. Where the model has already showed a very good performance with 2 training participant, as shown in Table 5. So all the presented results are for the model trained by 2 participants. And note that the avatar in Figs. 7 and 8 is for the participant during the experiment, it's created by the AXIS Neuron the perception neuron software [1]. We can see example of the scores for the target activities in Fig. 7, we can notice that the model has a very good performance in evaluating these actions. Note that the decision scores of OneClass SVM becomes positive when the data is recognized as an expert, and goes negative when recognized as a novice.

Also, to validate our results and to know which epoch model is the best to use, we tested in each epoch one expert data and one novice data and plotted the results as it appears in Fig. 10. This figure shows the average score of experts and novices over the epochs. It is clear that the model was able to learn and score the actions after a few epochs. We can notice from the results as shown

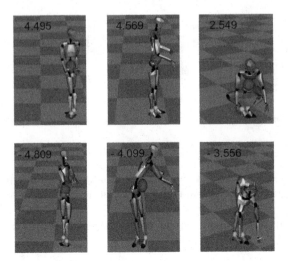

Fig. 7. Example of results for all actions. Top images for good actions, bottom images bad actions, where left is 'hold', middle 'move', and right 'pick up' action.

Table 5. The accuracy of the model for each action

	Pick up	Hold	Move
Expert	98%	99%	76.4%
Novice	99%	99%	76%

in Table 5 that the most challenging action for the model is 'move'. We assume it's because of the waist, which is the key attribute to identify novice and expert for this action, the waist has no clear joint movement as the other joints in the body. Still the model proved that it can evaluate the skills of the participants comparing to the expert action. Figures 8 and 9 show examples of results for experiment participants of 'move' and 'pick up' actions. We can see that when the performed action is closer to the good action (expert), the score becomes higher (4.56), and it gets gradually lower when the performance get closer to the bad action (novice).

7   Discussion

A quantification of action model has been developed to assess actions in real scenarios. Our initial model consists of body pose estimation model followed by autoencoder. Then we developed this model to score the action level. As shown in the results section, the recognition accuracies of quality evaluation is around 99% for 'pick up' and 'hold' action, and 76% for the 'move' action.

Figure 10 shows average scores of experts and novices over epochs. We notice that the model can learn the differences between expert and novice in all three

Fig. 8. Three examples of the 'move' action. We can see that with more twist in the waist the more negative the score. From left the novice to the right the expert.

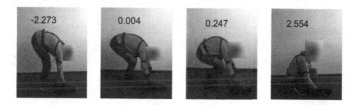

Fig. 9. Four examples of the 'pick up' action. We can notice that with more bend in the knees and less bend in the back the more positive the score is. Left the most novice to the right the most expert

actions, still the difference in the score value for the 'move' action is close between expert and novice, also we can see this in Fig. 11. To analyze further we checked the autoencoder reconstruction loss for this action, see Fig. 12. It's clear that the novice reconstruction values are close to the expert values, and its getting closer over epochs, which is not the case for the other actions, see Fig. 4.

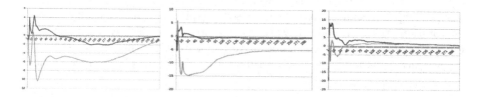

Fig. 10. Average score of experts (blue) and novices (red) over epochs. Where the left is 'Hold' action, middle for 'Pick up', and right for 'move' action. Where x-axis is the epochs and y-axis is the score (Color figure online)

Then, why our model have difficulties only for 'move' action? We assume mainly 2 reasons to this problem. The first reason is that 'move' action has only small differences between expert and novice action, compared to other 2 actions. The second reason is that the sensor we used may not provide enough data to

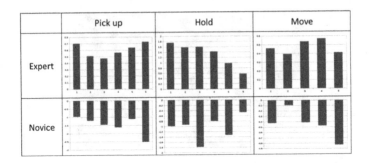

Fig. 11. OneClass SVM scores (each column represents one split)

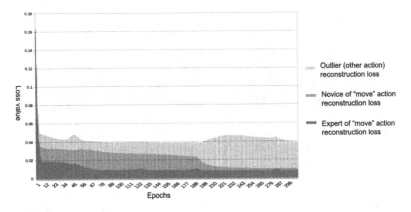

Fig. 12. Reconstruction loss for 'move' action. The values of the novice (bad) movement are close to the expert (good) values.

recognize twisting waist. Twisting waist can be explained as "the direction of upper body rotates to left or right while the direction of lower body remains as it is". Perception Neuron has 1 IMU sensor on spine, and it can work to detect the rotation of upper body, however it has no IMU sensor which is suitable to detect the direction of lower body. We think by improving the waist status representation the model will perform better as the 'pick up' and 'hold' action.

8   Conclusion

We presented a novel action quality quantifying model uses only the expert data to learn the good skills. The base of our architecture is pose estimation model followed by autoencoder, then on top of it a OneClass SVM model. The model learn to estimate the boundaries based on latent representation of expert data. These learned boundaries are used to assess the quality of any questioned user with respect to the selected expert. The model showed that it can asses the actions quality in high performance, where it achieved accuracy of 99% for 'hold' and 'pick up' actions, and 76% for 'move' action.

References

1. AXIS Neuron. https://neuronmocap.com/content/axis-neuron-software
2. Perception Neuron. https://www.noitom.com/solutions/perception-neuron
3. Anand, A., Sharma, M., Srivastava, R., Kaligounder, L., Prakash, D.: Wearable motion sensor based analysis of swing sports. In: 2017 16th IEEE International Conference on Machine Learning and Applications (ICMLA), pp. 261–267, December 2017. https://doi.org/10.1109/ICMLA.2017.0-149
4. Bačić, B.: Towards the next generation of exergames: flexible and personalised assessment-based identification of tennis swings (2018)
5. Borghesi, A., Bartolini, A., Lombardi, M., Milano, M., Benini, L.: Anomaly detection using autoencoders in high performance computing systems. CoRR abs/1811.05269 (2018)
6. Carreira, J., Zisserman, A.: Quo Vadis, action recognition? A new model and the kinetics dataset. In: 2017 IEEE Conference on Computer Vision and Pattern Recognition (CVPR), pp. 4724–4733 (2017)
7. Doughty, H., Damen, D., Mayol-Cuevas, W.W.: Who's better? Who's best? Pairwise deep ranking for skill determination. In: 2018 IEEE/CVF Conference on Computer Vision and Pattern Recognition, pp. 6057–6066 (2018)
8. Doughty, H., Mayol-Cuevas, W.W., Damen, D.: The pros and cons: rank-aware temporal attention for skill determination in long videos. CoRR abs/1812.05538 (2018)
9. Gaglio, S., Re, G.L., Morana, M.: Human activity recognition process using 3-D posture data. IEEE Trans. Hum.-Mach. Syst. 45(5), 586–597 (2015)
10. Jordao, A., Nazare Jr., A.C., de Souza, J.S., Schwartz, W.R.: Human activity recognition based on wearable sensor data: a standardization of the state-of-the-art. CoRR abs/1806.05226 (2018). http://arxiv.org/abs/1806.05226
11. Kiran, B.R., Thomas, D.M., Parakkal, R.: An overview of deep learning based methods for unsupervised and semi-supervised anomaly detection in videos. J. Imaging 4, 36 (2018)
12. Ladha, C., Hammerla, N.Y., Olivier, P., Plötz, T.: ClimbAX: skill assessment for climbing enthusiasts. In: UbiComp (2013)
13. Li, M., Wei, J., Zheng, X., Bolton, M.L.: A formal machine-learning approach to generating human-machine interfaces from task models. IEEE Trans. Hum.-Mach. Syst. 47(6), 822–833 (2017). https://doi.org/10.1109/THMS.2017.2700630
14. Lv, S., Lu, Y., Dong, M., Wang, X., Dou, Y., Zhuang, W.: Qualitative action recognition by wireless radio signals in human-machine systems. IEEE Trans. Hum.-Mach. Syst. 47(6), 789–800 (2017). https://doi.org/10.1109/THMS.2017.2693242
15. Müller, A., et al.: GymSkill: a personal trainer for physical exercises. In: 2012 IEEE International Conference on Pervasive Computing and Communications, pp. 213–220, March 2012. https://doi.org/10.1109/PerCom.2012.6199869
16. Ohashi, H., Al-Naser, M., Ahmed, S., Nakamura, K., Sato, T., Dengel, A.: Attributes' importance for zero-shot pose-classification based on wearable sensors. Sensors 18(8) (2018). Article no. 2485. https://doi.org/10.3390/s18082485
17. Parisi, G.I., Magg, S., Wermter, S.: Human motion assessment in real time using recurrent self-organization. In: 2016 25th IEEE International Symposium on Robot and Human Interactive Communication (RO-MAN), pp. 71–76 (2016)

18. Parmar, P., Morris, B.T.: Learning to score Olympic events (2017). https://doi.org/10.1109/CVPRW.2017.16

19. Parmar, P., Morris, B.T.: Learning to score Olympic events. CoRR abs/1611.05125 (2016). http://arxiv.org/abs/1611.05125

20. Pirsiavash, H., Vondrick, C., Torralba, A.: Assessing the quality of actions. In: Fleet, D., Pajdla, T., Schiele, B., Tuytelaars, T. (eds.) ECCV 2014. LNCS, vol. 8694, pp. 556–571. Springer, Cham (2014). https://doi.org/10.1007/978-3-319-10599-4_36

21. Velloso, E., Bulling, A., Gellersen, H.: MotionMA: motion modelling and analysis by demonstration. In: Proceedings of the SIGCHI Conference on Human Factors in Computing Systems. CHI 2013, pp. 1309–1318. ACM, New York (2013). https://doi.org/10.1145/2470654.2466171

22. Wang, J., Chen, Y., Hao, S., Peng, X., Hu, L.: Deep learning for sensor-based activity recognition: a survey. Pattern Recogn. Lett. **119**, 3–11 (2018)

23. Wnuk, K., Soatto, S.: Analyzing diving: a dataset for judging action quality. In: Koch, R., Huang, F. (eds.) ACCV 2010. LNCS, vol. 6468, pp. 266–276. Springer, Heidelberg (2011). https://doi.org/10.1007/978-3-642-22822-3_27

24. Zhang, W., Qin, L., Zhong, W., Guo, X., Wang, G.: Framework of sequence chunking for human activity recognition using wearables. In: Proceedings of the 2019 International Conference on Image, Video and Signal Processing. IVSP 2019, pp. 93–98. ACM, New York (2019). https://doi.org/10.1145/3317640.3317647

25. Zia, A., Sharma, Y., Bettadapura, V., Sarin, E.L., Clements, M.A., Essa, I.: Automated assessment of surgical skills using frequency analysis. In: Navab, N., Hornegger, J., Wells, W.M., Frangi, A.F. (eds.) MICCAI 2015. LNCS, vol. 9349, pp. 430–438. Springer, Cham (2015). https://doi.org/10.1007/978-3-319-24553-9_53

An Initial Study on Adapting DTW at Individual Query for Electrocardiogram Analysis

Daniel Shen[1]([✉]) and Min Chi[2]

[1] Enloe Magnet High School, Raleigh, NC 27610, USA
danielsongshen@gmail.com
[2] Computer Science Department, North Carolina State University,
Raleigh, NC 27695, USA
mchi@ncsu.edu

Abstract. This paper describes an initial investigation on adapting windowed Dynamic Time Warping (DTW) for enhancing the reliability of fast DTW for Electrocardiogram analysis in Cardiology, a domain where risks are especially important to avoid. The key question it explores is whether it is worthwhile to adapt the window size of DTW for *every query* temporal sequence, a factor critically determining the speed-accuracy tradeoff of DTW. It in addition extends the adaptation to cover also the order of sequences for lower bound calculations. Experiments on ECG temporal sequences show that the techniques help significantly reduce risks that windowed DTW algorithms are subject to and at the same time keeping a high speed.

Keywords: DTW · Time series analytics · Algorithm optimizations · Electrocardiogram

1 Introduction

As a way to record temporal electrical signals in heart, Electrocardiogram (ECG) plays an essential role in Cardiology. ECG data analysis is essential for helping identify heart conditions and diagnose heart diseases. As one of the commonly used methods for calculating the distances between two temporal sequences, Dynamic Time Warping (DTW) [7] is fundamental to ECG analysis. Compared to alternative machine learning methods (e.g., Deep Neural Networks), DTW-based clustering or classification is more agile with much fewer parameters, and gives competitive and, importantly, interpretable results. It remains the mostly adopted approach in Cardiology data analysis [21].

The basic DTW algorithm has a quadratic computational complexity. A large number of studies (e.g., [1, 7, 12, 13, 15, 16, 18, 19]) have proposed various methods to improve its speed. These improvements often introduce approximations and hence incur accuracy loss.

Despite the many studies, modern applications in Cardiology call for a deeper look at the tradeoff for ECG analysis. It is particularly driven by the recent trend towards

© Springer Nature Switzerland AG 2020
V. Lemaire et al. (Eds.): AALTD 2019, LNAI 11986, pp. 213–228, 2020.
https://doi.org/10.1007/978-3-030-39098-3_16

continuous real-time health monitoring. In this envisioned paradigm, people with heart malfunction risks (or other time-critical diseases, e.g., Sepsis Shock [2–5]) wear sensing devices in their everyday life. The sensors keep tracking the health conditions and send the ECG data to automatic diagnosis systems, where the time series data are processed on the fly to enable *real-time* diagnosis for the patent to receive timely alarms and/or treatment.

The application poses high requirements on both speed and accuracy. Accuracy loss could potentially lead to many false alarms, or more seriously, cause the system to miss the critical moments for patient treatment. Speed or computing efficiency, on the other hand, is also very important for such a system. They determine how timely the diagnosis could be; moreover, if the diagnosis runs on mobile devices (e.g., smart-phones) carried by the patent, the computing efficiency of the repeated DTW executions may greatly affect the energy usage of the battery-powered devices, which, in turn, could affect the availability of the health monitoring service for the patent.

Therefore, the better the speed-accuracy can be, the more reliable a *continuous real-time health monitoring* is, and the fewer risks the patients may be subject to.

In our research on ECG analysis in Cardiology, we observe that a large room still exists for improvement over existing treatments to the speed-accuracy tradeoff in DTW. A factor particular important for *windowed DTW*, for instance, is the size of the window used to constraint the DTW distance calculations (explained in Sect. 2). The smaller the window is, the faster the DTW can run, but at the same time, a larger probability is there for DTW to miss the best mapping between the two time series and hence subject to larger DTW distances than the accurate distances. Although its importance for accuracy-speed tradeoff has been well perceived, the state-of-the-art treatment is yet preliminary: A single window size is used for an entire dataset. The size is either a value from experience (e.g., 10% of sequence length), or from training (e.g., leave-one-out validation) [12].

Our observation is that the best window size varies substantially across sequences in a given Cardiology dataset. The bars in Fig. 1, for instance, show the best window sizes for each of the over 60 pairs of ECG temporal sequences in a broadly used ECG dataset, CinCECGTorso [22] (detailed in Sect. 4). Here, the best window size is a window size with which the computed DTW distance is subject to no more than 5% errors from the accurate DTW distance. The large variations of the window sizes indicate the different needs from different pairs of sequences. In contrast, if only one single window size can be used for all the pairs of sequences, the size has to be at least 350 to ensure the average DTW distance error is within 5%, as the horizontal line illustrates in Fig. 1. That size is unnecessarily large on many of the sequence pairs, and hence causes longer runtimes than actually necessary.

Motivated by the observation, in this work, we initiate the first exploration on individualizing windowed DTW on each query. The central idea and also the key novelty of this work is to customize DTW based on the properties of *every sequence* (rather than an entire dataset as prior work does [12]) to strike an improved speed-accuracy tradeoff. This idea is fundamental and may help temporal analysis in many domains, but as the first step, this study focuses on ECG analysis in Cardiology, for the

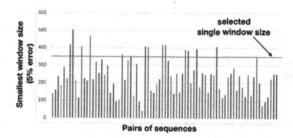

Fig. 1. The bars show the optimal window sizes of a number of pairs of sequences. Their differences motivate the per-query adaptation. The horizontal line segment indicates the selected single window size to meet the 5% average error requirement.

importance of the tradeoff in its applications. (Sect. 5 will discuss the plans for future extensions).

Specifically, we focus on adapting windowed DTW on two aspects: the window size and the lower bound calculations. The former adapts the window size in finding the best mapping between two sequences, and the latter adapts the ordering of sequences in lower bound calculations. A key challenge for the adaptive solution at this fine-grained level is how to make beneficial adaptations without introducing too much runtime overhead—as the adaptation has to happen at runtime for each sequence. We conduct a series of investigations in the cost-benefit tradeoffs of various designs. We observe promising results of *regression tree* as a method for determining the proper window size in *adaptive window sizing,* and *lightweight sampling* as an effective approach to finding the proper order of sequences in *adaptive ordering.* We call the resulting DTW algorithm *adaptive DTW.* On a Cardiology dataset with 1420 sequences, *adaptive DTW* speeds up windowed DTW by 16% while reducing DTW errors by 10-30X and hence reducing the risk of misuses of window-based DTW.

The rest of the paper is organized as follows. Section 2 gives the background of DTW and some related work, Sect. 3 describes *adaptive DTW,* Sect. 4 reports the experimental results, Sect. 5 discusses the limit of this study and the future work, Sect. 6 concludes the paper with a short summary.

2   Background

In this section, we review DTW and the most relevant work on accelerating DTW. DTW is an algorithm to find a non-linear mapping between two time series and calculate the similarity (or distance) between them. Consider two sequences Q and C of lengths of n and m respectively:

$$Q = q_1, q_2, \ldots, q_i, \ldots, q_n$$

$$C = c_1, c_2, \ldots, c_j, \ldots, c_m$$

To align these two sequences, DTW constructs an n-by-m difference matrix where the (i^{th}, j^{th}) element of the matrix corresponds to the squared distance, $d(q_i, c_j) = (q_i - c_j)^2$, which corresponds to the alignment between points q_i and c_j. The best match between these two sequences is a path through the matrix that minimizes the total cumulative distance.

DTW finds the path through dynamic programming. The basic algorithm has computational complexity O(NM). Many prior studies have tried to improve the speed of DTW. They fall mainly into three categories.

1. Adding constraints. These methods limit the number of cells in the difference matrix to be evaluated. One of the commonly used constraints is Sakoe-Chuba Band [10], which evaluates only the cells surrounding the diagonal of the difference matrix as illustrated in Fig. 2(A). There are other constraints such as the Itakura Parallelogram [23] and so on. DTW using such constraints are also called windowed DTW. It assumes that the best path does not deviate too much from the diagonal; by limiting the range of search, it reduces the amount of computations.
2. Using lower bounds. These methods use lower bounding functions to reduce the number of times that DTW must be run during time series classification or clustering. An example is the Keogh lower bounds [7]. The lower bound technique uses the warping window to create a bounding envelope above and below the query sequence. Then the lower bound is calculated as the squared sum of the distances from every part of the candidate sequence outside the bounding envelope to the nearest orthogonal edge of the bounding. The technique is illustrated in Fig. 2(B).
3. Using reduced data representations. These methods apply DTW on a reduced representation of the time series, such as the series at a reduced resolution [24, 25]. A particularly effective method in this category is FastDTW [26]. For a given time series, FastDTW derives multiple versions of it at a spectrum of resolutions. It starts by running DTW on the version of the lowest resolution, then gradually refines the path as moving from a low resolution to a high resolution. The refinement leverages the mapping from the low-resolution case to limit the range of mappings to compute for each data point at the high resolution. It is worth noting that this method has a parameter *radius*, which defines the range of mappings to consider in a refinement step. Like the window size in windowed DTW, the choice of *radius* affects the speed-accuracy tradeoff of the result.

This current study is distinctive in adaptation at individual query level. It is complementary to the prior methods. In principle, the proposed idea can be applied to improve the effectiveness of the methods in all three categories. For FastFTW, for instance, the adaptation may adjust the value of radius for each query sequence. In this study, we concentrate our explorations on the first two categories by adapting the window size and the ordering of the sequences in computing the distance lower bounds.

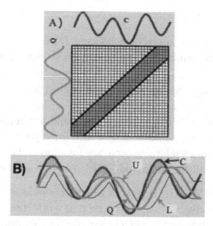

Fig. 2. (A) The difference matrix between two sequences Q and C, and the Sakoe-Chuba Band. (B) The warping envelope of sequence Q is used for computing the Keogh lower bounds (summation of the shaded area) of the DTW distance between Q and C.

3 Proposed Solution: Adaptive DTW

This section describes how the proposed adaptive DTW adapts the window size of DTW and the lower bound computing for each individual query sequence. The focused data domain is ECG temporal sequences, as Fig. 3 illustrates.

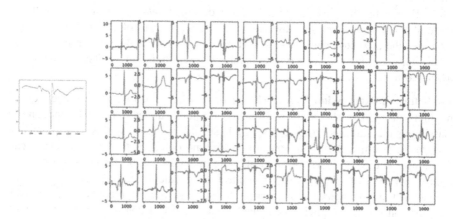

Fig. 3. Illustration of a number of ECG temporal sequences.

3.1   Adaptive Window Sizing

As the previous section has mentioned, windowed DTW faces an efficiency-accuracy dilemma. The smaller the window is, the faster DTW runs, but the accuracy of the DTW becomes lower. How to identify the sweet point (i.e., the smallest window size that still meets the accuracy requirement) is challenging because the best window size changes from one query sequence to another.

Our idea behind *adaptive window sizing* is to build a predictor that can accurately and efficiently predict the best window size to use for a given pair of sequences. The best size is the one that causes tolerable accuracy loss and at the same time achieves the maximal speedups. We call the improved DTW *selective windowed DTW*.

Selective Windowed DTW. The design of selective windowed DTW is based on an observation we made in our investigations on real-world time series in Cardiology, particularly, the Electrocardiogram (ECG) samples. ECG time series show myriad variations; some are amenable for the use of a small window for DTW, others would be subject to large errors if a small window is used. Figure 4 shows some empirical measurements. Each curve in Fig. 4 shows the average errors that windowed DTW causes to the calculation of the minimal DTW distance between a query sequence and a collection of reference sequences (ECG samples in dataset CinCECGTorso [13, 22]). It is intuitive that a larger window causes smaller errors: The set of mapping paths when a smaller window is used is a subset of the set when a larger window is used. The errors in the first nine cases in Fig. 4 become marginal when the window size becomes larger than 200, while the errors in the other graphs remain substantial for most part of the window size spectrum. Experiments on other time series datasets exhibit similar phenomena.

... Driven by the observations, we have designed *selective windowed DTW*. Its basic idea is to run a best window size predictor on the pair of query sequences, and then uses the predicted window to do DTW. To help reduce the risks from imprecise predictions, we take a conservative strategy when building up the predictors as described next.

Predictors on Regression Trees. The best window predictor needs to meet several requirements. (1) It should be reasonably accurate—at least, accurate enough for classifying the safe and risky cases. (2) It should run fast. Because the prediction happens at runtime, the prediction time adds time overhead to the entire DTW cal-culations. (3) Finally, it would be ideal if the predictor can be easily interpreted; the domain experts (e.g., doctors) can then check the predictor for verifications.

The method we select is *regression trees*. As a simple predictive model with questions on features explicitly contained in each non-leaf tree node, regress trees are fast to run and easy to interpret. We also experimented with polynomial regression; the results are similar to regression trees.

There are many off-the-shelf implementations of Regression Trees available to public. In our implementation, we used Scikit Learn package. We collect the following list of features based on our examinations of 40 training sequences from CinCECG-Torso [13], as Table 1 shows.

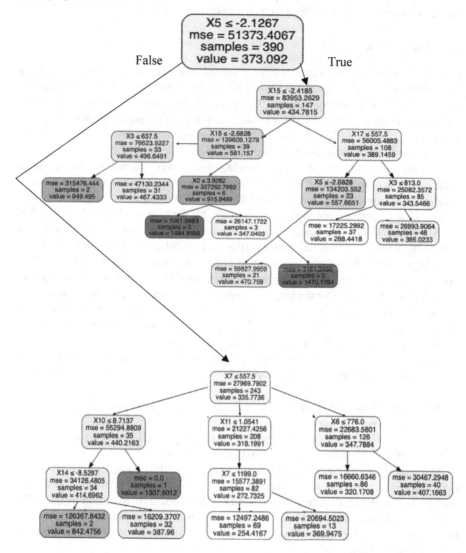

During the feature collection, when locating the peaks and valleys, we use local filtering (3-point wide at minimum) to alleviate the effects of noise. In addition to the features of sequences, we have collected the best window size for each pair of training sequences at a spectrum of allowed DTW distance errors (2%, 5%).

In training the regression models for a given tolerance level of the DTW distance error, we use the concatenation of the features of the two sequences in interest as the input features and use the best window size at the error level as the label. We have totally 390 training pairs. The left figure on the previous page shows the Regression

Tree we built when the target average DTW distance error is 2%. During the construction process, we control the depth of the tree to avoid overfitting; through cross-validation, we settle on a depth of four as shown in the graph.

3.2 Adaptive Ordering

In addition to the window size, we have explored adaptation of sequence ordering in the calculation of DTW distance lower bounds. We call this optimization adaptive ordering. As Sect. 2 mentions, Keogh lower bounds are useful for avoiding the computation of the exact DTW distances between a query series and an unpromising time series. The tightness of Keogh lower bounds is essential: The tighter it is, the more unnecessary distance calculations it can help avoid.

Adaptive ordering is based on the following observation. For two time series, A and B, the tightness of their Keogh lower bounds depends on their order in the lower bound calculation. In another word, even though the exact DTW distance is symmetric, Keogh bound is not. Mathematically, even though DTW(A, B) = DTW(B, A), often LB_Keogh(A, B) $\neq$ LB_Keogh(B, A). Figure 5 shows two example temporal sequences, in red and green respectively. (For easy visibility, we here use knee motion sensor signal sequences which give a more clear illustration of the bounds than ECG sequences do). For them, LB_Keogh(red, green) is only 17.96, while LB_Keogh(green, red) is 83.48. The reason for the large difference is that when computing LB_Keogh(A, B), the algorithm sums up the part of A sequence that resides outside the envelope of B series. For the sequences in Fig. 5, the envelope of the green sequence is quite large, leaving very small part of the red sequence outside, hence the small value of LB_Keogh (red, green). But the envelope of the red sequence is much narrower, leaving most part of the green sequence outside the envelope, hence the large value of LB_Keogh(green, red).

As a result of the asymmetricity of the lower bound calculations, what order to use for computing Keogh lower bounds can significantly affect the tightness of the bounds and hence the effectiveness of the bounds for speeding up DTW. Obviously, the best order depends on the time series involved in the calculation.

The goal of adaptive ordering is to quickly figure out the best order for a given pair of time series and use that order to compute the lower bound. The method to do that must be fast as the process happens at run time and adds time overhead to the DTW calculations. A previous study [12] simply computes the lower bounds in both orders and selects the smaller to use. The drawback is the time overhead of the two times of lower bound calculations.

In this work, we investigate lightweight sampling as a more efficient way to select the order for a given query.

Specifically, for a given pair of time series A and B, the sampling method first randomly picks a small number (e.g., k) of short segments from each of the two time series (such as SA1, SA2, ..., SAk, SB1, SB2, ..., SBk). It then computes $\sum$LB_Keogh(Ai, Bi) and $\sum$LB_Keogh(Bi, Ai) (i = 1, 2, ..., k). Based on the results, it picks the order that gives the largest lower bound value and uses it for the computation of the full time series.

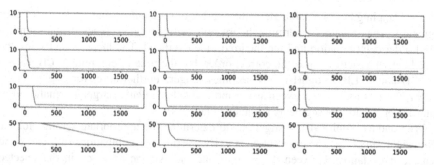

Fig. 4. Errors of windowed DTW vary with window size. Each graph corresponds to one query sequence, showing the average errors that windowed DTW causes to the calculation of the minimal DTW distance between a query sequence and a collection of reference sequences (ECG samples in dataset CinCECGTorso [13]). X-axis is the window size, Y-axis is the error in distance).

Table 1. Features of a ECG sequence

Feature	Value domain
Primary peak value	Numerical
2nd peak value	Numerical
Primary peak location	Time or event number
2nd peak location	Time or event number
Primary valley value	Numerical
2nd valley value	Numerical
Primary valley location	Time or event number
2nd valley location	Time or event number
Does 2nd peak appear earlier than the main peak?	Yes or no
Does 2nd valley appear earlier than the main peak?	Yes or no

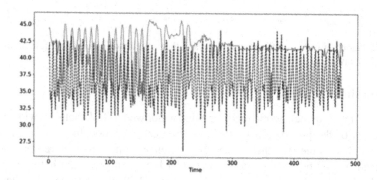

Fig. 5. Two example temporal sequences in AReM dataset [14] and their Keogh lower bounds. (Color figure online)

The sampling has two parameters, the number of segments k, and the length of each segment s. They together determine the tradeoff between the accuracy of the samples-based order determination and the incurred time overhead. The larger k and s are, the more likely the method finds the correct order, but the time to compute $\sum$LB_Keogh (Ai, Bi) and $\sum$LB_Keogh(Bi, Ai) becomes longer. Furthermore, for a given time budget, there is a choice between using more small segments (larger k, smaller s) or using fewer but longer segments (smaller k, larger s).

We conduct empirical investigations to determine the appropriate settings for the lightweight sampling. The exploration is to try a series of combinations of k and s and measure the relations between the settings and the average accuracy in the selected order. Figure 6 shows the measurements on training dataset from CinCECGTorso. The number of segments varies from 1 to 10, and the length of a segment varies from 1% to 10% of the full sequence length. The combination covers the sampling rates from 1% to 100% of the sequence. Note that the calculations of the lower bounds (on either the sampled segments or the full sequences) use the same window size as the DTW does. To achieve a comprehensive understanding, we further vary the window size from 2 to 42. From Fig. 6 we can see that there are some variations among the curves on different window sizes, but the trends are very much similar. Considering the overhead and the accuracy together, we find the setting (k = 1, s = 5%) a reasonable choice for all window sizes. It is hence selected as the setting for our lightweight sampling for adaptive ordering.

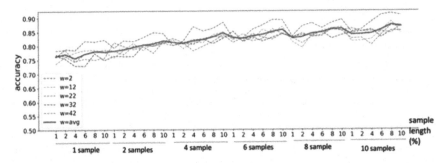

Fig. 6. Relation between sampling parameters and the accuracy of order determination for lower bound calculations.

3.3   Working Together

The two adaptations can work together with windowed DTW, helping with the different stages of the process. In DTW-based Nearest Neighbor, for instance, adaptive ordering applies to the step that prunes the reference sequences that are impossible to be the nearest neighbor of the query; the tighter bounds it gives can help prune more effectively. For the remained references sequences, DTW needs to be calculated from each of them to the query sequence; adaptive window sizing can apply to this step to prevent the risks that a small window may create and at the same time keep the speed benefits of the use of windows for DTW.

To use adaptive DTW, there is a training process, which builds a classifier for safe and risky classes and determines the window size good for each class. It is worth noting that adding a training stage is not a new burden added by this work. Prior DTW proposals have already required training to determine the appropriate window size [12]; the differences are mainly on what the training process produces: A single window size for an entire dataset in the prior work, but a predictive model in our work.

4 Evaluation

This section reports our observations on the benefits that the query-level adaption brings to temporal data analysis in ECG analysis. We use CinCECGTorso dataset for our experiments. This dataset is derived from one of the Computers in Cardiology challenges, an annual competition that runs with the conference series of the same name and is hosted on physionet[1]. Data is taken from ECG data for multiple torso-surface sites. There are 4 classes (4 different people). It consists of 1420 ECG temporal sequences with each containing 1639 events.

We center the discussion around the following two questions:

1. How accurately can the adaptive window sizing help strike a good tradeoff between accuracy and speed?
2. How much speedups can adaptive ordering help DTW achieve? How window size affects the speedups? What is the time overhead of adaptive ordering?

Methodology. All of our experiments happen on a desktop computer equipped with Intel(R) Xeon(R) CPU E5-1607 v2 clocked at 3 GHz, running Linux 4.4.0. Our implementation is in Python 3.5 with Scikit Learn 0.20.2 package. For time measurements, we repeat the measurements five times and report the average when there are marginal variations.

For assessment, we focus on the speed of DTW as well as the quality of the DTW result. For the quality, we use DTW distance error as the metric—that is, the difference between the DTW distance from the windowed DTW and the precise DTW distance when no window is used. An alternative is to use the result of an ultimate usage (e.g., classification accuracy) of DTW as the metric. We choose DTW distance because of its direct characterization of the quality. The results of usage are affected by many other factors; for different usage, the influence of DTW distances vary. DTW distance, on the other hand, is independent from the usage and hence offers a more objective metric.

Results on Adaptive Window Sizing. Recall that the core of our designed adaptive window sizing is a regression tree-based predictor of the best window size for a query sequence. To build the predictor, it is necessary to first build a collection of training data with the best window size labeled with each training time series. The previous section has already showed the regression tree when the expected error of DTW distances is 2%. Figure 7 reports the average running time and the average distance error when the

---

[1] https://physionet.org/.

predicted window sizes are used in DTW. For comparison, it also reports the data of five other configurations of DTW. We explain all the six versions as follows:

- *(1) "win = 100"*: the window size is set to 100 (the default size in the report in previous UCRiverside results [27]);
- *(2) "win = %10*len(seq)"*: the length of the window size is set to 0.1 of the entire sequence length (a suggested size in previous work [12]);
- *(3) "opt"*: the optimal choice of window size for each pair of sequences. We obtained the data by first running DTW on the testing sequence pairs many times with a spectrum of window sizes, measured the errors in each case, and then use linear interpolation to figure out the "optimal" window size for a given level of error tolerance;
- *(4) "pred"*: DTW with our predicted window size;
- *(5) "single"*: using a single window size for all sequences such that the average error level can be met. It can be regarded as the ideal version of prior training-based window size selection work [12], which selects the best single window size for an entire dataset through training. In our implementation, we identify it directly on the testing data to avoid the training errors.
- (6) "single (no err)": using a single window size for all sequences such that no distance errors are on any of the sequence pairs.

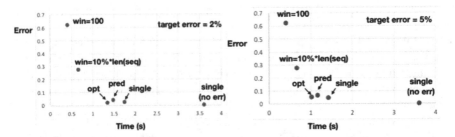

Fig. 7. The DTW time of one pair of sequence and the corresponding DTW distance error, computed by the various methods. Left: 2% is the target DTW distance error; Right: 5% is the target DTW distance error.

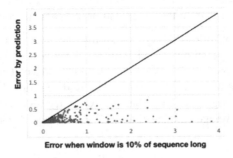

Fig. 8. Error scatter graph

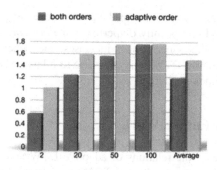

Fig. 9. Speedups over default

Figure 7 shows the results of the six ways to run DTW when the tolerable error is 2% or 5%. The patterns in the two graphs are similar. Compared to the traditional experience-based window sizes (100, and 10% sequence length), adaptive window size reduces the distance error from 0.67 and 0.28 to about 0.02, a 10–30X error reduction, while the running time increases by only 2–3X. Compared to the idealized training-based selection of one single window size ("single"), it gets 1.15X speedup with slight sacrifice of accuracy. Figure 8 provides the scatter graph of the errors from the use of 10% sequence length and the adaptive method. It shows that on all the tested sequence pairs, the errors become smaller (often much smaller) when the adaptive method is used. The prediction time overhead is negligible: As a fast inference algorithm, regression trees take virtually no time compared to the time DTW takes.

Results on Adaptive Ordering. The benefits of adaptive ordering are sensitive to datasets and window size. Our comparison baseline includes a prior method which computes lower bounds in both orders and picks the larger one. That method (named *both orders* in this paper) obviously can get 100% order accuracy, but doubles the lower bound computing time.

Our experiments the ECG dataset show that the adaptive ordering does not give obvious benefits over the *both order method*, for the large window its DTW uses.

We applied the technique on another dataset, AReM dataset, which is a motion sensor dataset representing a real-life benchmark in the area of Activity Recognition applications [14]. For each activity 15 temporal sequences of input RSS data are present. The dataset contains 480 sequences, for a total number of 42240 instances.

Our empirical study on its training datasets indicate that (k = 1, s = 5%) is a good configuration for the lightweight sampling. The sampling time is marginal, only 5% of the lower bound calculation time, but at the same time, the average order prediction accuracy is as much as 77%. Figure 9 reports the speedups the method achieves compared to windowed DTW that uses the default order. When the window size is very small (2), the DTW distance computation takes a similar time as the lower bound calculations. The benefits of using lower bounds are hence not significant. The *both orders* method, as it doubles the lower bound calculations, causes significant slow-downs, an issue our method is not subject to for its lightweight sampling. As the window size increases, the benefits of using lower bounds become more obvious: The relatively fast lower bounds calculations help skip some expensive DTW distance calculations. Our method consistently outperforms the *both orders* method for its low time overhead. But as the window size increases, the benefits from the adaptive ordering diminishes, because DTW time increases to a level where the time for lower bound calculation becomes negligible.

5   Discussion and Future Work

In this section, we discuss the relations of adaptive DTW and other DTW optimizations, and the generalization of adaptive DTW to a broader range of aspects and domains.

Adaptive DTW should not be viewed as a competitor but a complement to existing DTW optimization methods. Query-level adaptation essentially offers a more detailed treatment to DTW configurations. As Sect. 2 mentions, prior DTW optimizations mainly take one of the three angles to enhance DTW speed: adding constraints, using lower bounds, and leveraging reduced data representations. This paper has shown that query-level adaptation can benefit the methods in the first two categories. It is expected to be beneficial to the third category as well, by, for instance, selecting the best radius in FastDTW for each query. Empirical validation is left for the future.

As an initial study in equipping DTW with query-level adaptations, this work has a focused scope, ECG analysis. But the principle potentially applies to other time-critical domains (e.g., sepsis shocks [6–11, 17]). The sampling-based method for adapting lower bound calculations can be directly applied to data in other domains, although the sample length and number of samples may need to be selected in the training stage for each domain. The adaptation of window size is based on the predictive model. We built the model on the properties of ECG data. So, another domain may need a different sets of data features and new predictive models. A question worth exploring is whether a genetic set of time series features and a kind of predictive models could cover many domains. A positive answer would ease the adoption of query-level adaptations for new domains. These questions are left for future to explore.

6   Conclusion

This paper gives a focused study on query-level adaptation for DTW, its potential, challenges, and solutions. It shows that a regression-tree—based predictive model can help select a good window size for each query sequence in windowed DTW, which leads to improvement of the speed-accuracy tradeoff in ECG analysis. In addition, it investigates the benefits of a simple sampling-based method for adapting the ordering of sequences in lower bound calculations. Experiments demonstrate that adaptive window sizing can reduce distance calculation errors and/or improve the speed. Adaptive ordering does not show visible effects on ECG analysis, but has the potential to benefit other time series analysis where small windowed DTW is suitable.

References

1. Ratanamahatana, C.A., Keogh, E.: Three myths about dynamic time warping. In: Proceedings of SIAM International Conference on Data Mining (SDM 2005), Newport Beach, CA, 21–23 April 2005, pp. 506–510 (2005)
2. Coba, V., Whitmill, M., et al.: Resuscitation bundle compliance in severe sepsis and septic shock: improves survival, is better late than never. J. Intensive Care Med. **26**, 304–313 (2011)
3. Dellinger, R.P., Levy, M.M., et al.: Surviving Sepsis Campaign: international guidelines for management of severe sepsis and septic shock: 2008. Intensive Care Med. **34**, 17–60 (2008)
4. Elixhauser, A., Friedman, B., Stranges, E.: Septicemia in U.S. Hospitals, 2009. HCUP Statistical Brief #122. Agency for Healthcare Research and Quality, Rockville, MD, October 2011. http://www.hcup-us.ahrq.gov/reports/statbriefs/sb122.pdf
5. Henry, K.E., et al.: A targeted real-time early warning score (TREWScore) for septic shock. Sci. Transl. Med. **7**(299), 299ra122 (2015)
6. U.S. Department of Health and Human Service: Health, United States, 2016: With Chartbook on Long-term Trends in Health (2017)
7. Keogh, E.: Exact indexing of dynamic time warping. In: 28th International Conference on Very Large Data Base, Hong Kong, pp. 406–417 (2002)
8. Kumar, A., et al.: Duration of hypotension before initiation of effective antimicrobial therapy is the critical determinant of survival in human septic shock. Crit. Care Med. **34**, 1589–1596 (2006)
9. Martin, G.S., et al.: The epidemiology of sepsis in the United States from 1979 through 2000. N. Engl. J. Med. **348**, 1546–1554 (2003)
10. Sakoe, H., Chiba, S.: Dynamic programming algorithm optimization for spoken word recognition. Trans. Acoust. Speech Signal Process. **ASSP-26**, 43–49 (1978)
11. Torio, C., Andrews, R.: National inpatient hospital costs: the most expensive conditions by payer, 2013. Agency for Healthcare Research and Quality, Rockville, MD (2013)
12. Mueen, A., Keogh, E.J.: Extracting optimal performance from dynamic time warping. In: KDD 2016, pp. 2129–2130 (2016)
13. Bagnall, A., Lines, J., Bostrom, A., Large, J., Keogh, E.: The great time series classification bake off: a review and experimental evaluation of recent algorithmic advances. J. Data Min. Knowl. Discov. **31**(3), 606–660 (2017)
14. Palumbo, F., Gallicchio, C., Pucci, R., Micheli, A.: Human activity recognition using multisensor data fusion based on reservoir computing. J. Ambient Intell. Smart Environ. **8**(2), 87–107 (2016)
15. Shokoohi-Yekta, M., Wang, J., Keogh, E.: On the non-trivial generalization of dynamic time warping to the multi-dimensional case. In: Proceedings of the 2015 SIAM International Conference on Data Mining, pp. 289–297 (2015)
16. Froese, V., Jain, B.: Fast exact dynamic time warping on run-length encoded time series. arXiv (2019)
17. Moor, M., Horn, M., Rieck, B., Roqueiro, D., Borgwardt, K.: Temporal convolutional networks and dynamic time warping can drastically improve the early prediction of sepsis. arXiv (2019)
18. Tan, C.W., Petitjean, F., Webb, G.I.: Elastic bands across the path: a new framework and method to lower bound DTW. In: SIAM International Conference on Data Mining (2019)
19. Silva, D.F., Batista, G.E.A.P.A.: Speeding up all-pairwise dynamic time warping matrix calculation. In: SIAM International Conference on Data Mining (2016)

20. Al-Naymat, G., Chawla, S., Taheri, J.: SparseDTW: a novel approach to speed up dynamic time warping. In: Proceedings of the Eighth Australasian Data Mining Conference. AusDM 2009 (2009)

21. Caiani, E., et al.: Warped-average template technique to track on a cycle-by-cycle basis the cardiac filling phases on left ventricular volume. In: Computers in Cardiology, vol. 5, pp. 73–76 (1998)

22. CinCECGtorso dataset. http://www.timeseriesclassification.com/description.php?Dataset=CinCECGtorso

23. Itakura, F.: Minimum prediction residual principle applied to speech recognition. IEEE Trans. Acoust. Speech Signal Process. **ASSP-23**, 52–72 (1975)

24. Chu, S., Keogh, E., Hart, D., Pazzani, M.: Iterative deepening dynamic time warping for time series. In: Proceedings of the Second SIAM International Conference on Data Mining, Arlington, Virginia (2002)

25. Keogh, E., Pazzani, M.: Scaling up dynamic time warping for datamining applications. In: Proceedings of the Sixth ACM SIGKDD International Conference on Knowledge Discovery and Data Mining, Boston, Massachusetts, pp. 285–289 (2000)

26. Salvador, S., Chan, P.: Toward accurate dynamic time warping in linear time and space. Intell. Data Anal. **11**(5), 561–580 (2007)

27. UCRiverside Time Series. https://www.cs.ucr.edu/~eamonn/time_series_data_2018/

Author Index

Printed in the United States
By Bookmasters